THE CONCISE DICTIONARY OF
PASTORAL CARE AND COUNSELING

The Concise Dictionary of Pastoral Care and Counseling

Edited by
Glenn H. Asquith Jr.

Abingdon Press
Nashville

THE CONCISE DICTIONARY OF
PASTORAL CARE AND COUNSELING

Library of Congress Cataloging-in-Publication Data

The concise dictionary of pastoral care and counseling / edited by Glenn H. Asquith, Jr.
    p.   cm.
    ISBN 978-1-4267-0231-0 (trade pbk. : alk. paper)
1. Pastoral care—Dictionaries.   2. Pastoral counseling—Dictionaries.   I. Asquith, Glenn H., 1946-
BV4005.5.C66 2010
    253.5—dc22

2010006878

10 11 12 13 14 15 16 17 18 19—10 9 8 7 6 5 4 3 2 1

MANUFACTURED IN THE UNITED STATES OF AMERICA

To all of my former students in pastoral theology at Moravian Theological Seminary, who dutifully bought (and mostly read) the original and expanded editions of the *DPCC* for my classes. You inspired me and you gave me great suggestions for improving this work. May this *Concise* version inspire the next generation of students with the legacy that you are continuing.

CONTENTS

INTRODUCTION

Early in June 1988, after having been invited by Dr. Rodney J. Hunter and Abingdon Press to serve as principal editorial consultant for the original *Dictionary of Pastoral Care and Counseling (DPCC)*, I stood in Rod's office at Candler School of Theology, about to turn a major corner in my professional and academic career. Rod gestured toward an entire wall of shelves in his office, containing 5,200 pages of paper manuscript, and said, "This is what we have to read and edit in the next six months!" The *Mission Impossible* theme started playing in my head and continued on and off through days of monastic existence in a cubicle at Woodruff Library and several sometimes painful editorial meetings with Abingdon Press, where our progress and even the feasibility of the project were questioned. I celebrated with my colleagues in the spring of 1990 when the final product appeared on the market, the culmination of a decade of hard and inspired work by a team of leaders in our field, led by Rod Hunter. The original *DPCC* was the first-ever major reference work in the field, designed to help further define the parameters, theological framework, and methodology of pastoral care and counseling at that point in time.

Almost exactly twenty years after my first encounter with the *DPCC*, Dr. Kathy Armistead, editor at Abingdon Press, offered me another "mission impossible," the result of which is presented herewith. Abingdon was conceiving a *Concise Dictionary of Pastoral Care and Counseling*. My job, should I choose to accept it, was to take the "classic, timeless articles" from the original *DPCC* (not including the supplemental articles in the 2005 expanded edition) that still address the history, critical issues, and methodology of pastoral care and counseling and combine them in topical chapters that would be useful to students and practitioners. In this process, some of the original articles have been shortened and updated, and seven new articles have been added that address important topics in contemporary pastoral care and counseling.

I have written a short introduction to each of the topical chapters that follow, summarizing the contents, frame of reference, and rationale for the articles in that group. In this combined presentation of classic and contemporary articles, consideration is given to the "long history" of the religious and theological traditions that inform pastoral care and counseling and the "short history" of the behavioral and social science insights that shape the methods of pastoral care and counseling. Good pastoral theological method (and good pastoral theology) weaves both of these histories together to address the whole person in the contemporary world who is seeking to faithfully live his or her life in the context of eternal spiritual and theological truths.

This last statement constitutes our "working philosophy" in the selection of articles to include in this volume. The definitions presented in chapter 1 involve the perspectives of history, theology, and contemporary practice that inform the field. Some are about counseling methodologies, some are about clinical and pastoral terms, and some are about theological concepts that inform practice.

The important history presented in chapter 2 should never be lost to current and future practitioners in the field. It outlines the people, the movements, the biblical understandings, the theological perspectives, and the church history that made pastoral care and counseling *pastoral*, as distinct from other forms of care. In my admittedly biased view, this chapter alone should be carefully studied by all theological and clinical pastoral education students so that they will enter the field with a working knowledge of their "roots" as well as the postmodern, postcolonial challenges to pastoral care and counseling.

Chapter 3 addresses an important concern in the contemporary practice of pastoral care and counseling that was named and discussed by Nancy J. Ramsay and Christie Cozad Neuger in the 2005 expanded edition of the *DPCC: Issues of Power and Difference*. Ten years into the twenty-first century, pastoral theology, care, and counseling are faced with the large challenge of transforming and redefining the Western, patriarchal, and liberal Protestant theological norms that provided the primary context for the original *DPCC*. In the postmodern, post-9/11 world, these previously dominant norms will no longer work for the church, pastoral counseling centers, or health care providers. This chapter reminds us that good, effective theology is contextual to persons engaged in particular struggles of life and faith. It reminds us that Native Americans and various other ethnic and global groups, persons in the GLBT community, and people in economic poverty all struggle for their legitimate voice and self-empowerment in a world that has systematically denied them both power and voice. This is a compelling *pastoral* issue that is addressed not just by a concern for individuals but also by concern for the structures, social movements, and values that oppress individuals.

Chapter 4 speaks to the reality that pastoral care and counseling in the postmodern world is unavoidably interfaith in its practice. Faith and culture are inextricably linked; to understand and appreciate one's faith also usually leads to understanding and appreciation of one's culture. The original *DPCC* recognized that and thus sought to provide discussions of care and counseling in various faith traditions as well as in the context of various traditional religious practices in order to intentionally "expand the horizons" of pastoral theology, care, and counseling in the latter twentieth century. In correspondence to me on October 8, 2009, Rod Hunter, in response to my question to him about these articles in light of the aforementioned context of the original *DPCC*, made the following statement: "It seems pertinent and helpful today to lift out and publish the relatively small number of important, ground-breaking interfaith articles in the *DPCC* [that] are historically significant, pioneering works in their own right." Those articles are assembled in this chapter.

Chapter 5 includes articles on what I believe are the basic clinical issues faced by everyone who engages in pastoral care and counseling. These include alcohol and drug addiction; HIV and AIDS; crisis intervention; marriage, family, and family systems issues, including family violence; and grief. Fundamental to clinical method in all pastoral care and counseling is "use of the self"; Pamela Cooper-White provides a contemporary commentary on intersubjectivity in this work.

Finally, chapter 6 addresses pastoral theological method. In 1985, the Society for Pastoral Theology was founded with commitments to "collaborative reflection that revises, refines and extends the conceptual base and methodological resources of pastoral theology," "a critical engagement of behavioral and social sciences with theological and biblical resources" and "intellectual rigor within a praxis orientation" ("Our Mission Statement, Identity and Purpose," Society for Pastoral Theology website, http://www.societyforpastoraltheology.com/aboutspt.html [accessed March 4, 2010]). Those of us who are charter members of that group recognized that pastoral care and counseling was always going to need an academically oriented, intellectual discourse that would theologically ground and inform pastoral practice. We are standing in the heritage of Anton Boisen, Charles Gerkin, Seward Hiltner, James Lapsley, Liston Mills, Thomas Pugh, Peggy Way, and many other early leaders in the field who continually provided this corrective, methodological voice. Chapter 6 includes theological, methodological, and liturgical commentary on issues of pastoral practice.

Obviously, no project like this is done in isolation. I express heartfelt thanks to Kathy Armistead at Abingdon Press for the invitation and faithful direction that she provided in helping me complete this project. I am very grateful to several of my colleagues from the Society for Pastoral Theology: Pamela Cooper-White, Carrie Doehring, Martha Jacobi, and Christie Cozad Neuger for their excellent contributions to this current volume. I also wish to acknowledge all of the authors in this volume, who made excellent contributions to the original *DPCC*. Please forgive the changes that were made to some of your work (including my own article in chapter 6) in order to meet space limitations or add contemporary understandings of a topic.

I express special gratitude also to two of my former students who provided wonderful and beautifully meaningful articles for this book. The Reverend Tuntufye A. Mwenisongole is a professor in pastoral theology at the Moravian-sponsored theological school in Mbeya, Tanzania. The Reverend Susan E. Vollmer has served very faithfully and effectively as a hospice chaplain in the Lehigh Valley (Pennsylvania) area. Having just retired from thirty-one years of teaching pastoral theology at Moravian Theological Seminary, I have dedicated this book to *all* of my former students there, who challenged and inspired me as true co-learners. One of them even suggested that I add an entry for "Living Human Document" (which appears in chapter 1), perhaps because of my endless commentary on the value of narrative for pastoral theology.

Finally, I acknowledge my wife, Connie, a United Methodist pastor, who literally, operationally, and patiently "watched my back" as I toiled to put this volume together, providing encouragement and pastoral advice along the way. Thank you!

Glenn H. Asquith Jr.
Editor

ABBREVIATIONS

Old Testament

Genesis	Gen.
Exodus	Exod.
Leviticus	Lev.
Numbers	Num.
Deuteronomy	Deut.
Joshua	Josh.
Judges	Judg.
Ruth	Ruth
1 Samuel	1 Sam.
2 Samuel	2 Sam.
1 Kings	1 Kings
2 Kings	2 Kings
1 Chronicles	1 Chron.
2 Chronicles	2 Chron.
Ezra	Ezra
Nehemiah	Neh.
Esther	Esther
Job	Job
Psalm, Psalms	Ps., Pss.
Proverbs	Prov.
Ecclesiastes	Eccles.
Song of Solomon	Song of Sol.
Isaiah	Isa.
Jeremiah	Jer.
Lamentations	Lam.
Ezekiel	Ezek.

Daniel	Dan.
Hosea	Hos.
Obadiah	Obad.
Jonah	Jon.
Micah	Mic.
Nahum	Nah.
Habakkuk	Hab.
Zephaniah	Zeph.
Haggai	Hag.
Zechariah	Zech.
Malachi	Mal.

New Testament

Matthew	Mt.
Mark	Mk.
Luke	Lk.
John	Jn.
Acts of the Apostles	Acts
Romans	Rom.
1 Corinthians	1 Cor.
2 Corinthians	2 Cor.
Galatians	Gal.
Ephesians	Eph.
Philippians	Phil.
Colossians	Col.
1 Timothy	1 Tim.
2 Timothy	2 Tim.
Titus	Titus
Philemon	Philem.
Hebrews	Heb.
James	Jas.
1 Peter	1 Pet.
2 Peter	2 Pet.
1 John	1 Jn.
2 John	2 Jn.
3 John	3 Jn.
Revelation	Rev.

Other References

CPE	Clinical Pastoral Education
KJV	King James Version (Bible)
LXX	Septuagint
NAB	New American Bible
NAS	New American Standard (Bible)
NEB	New English Bible
NT	New Testament
OT	Old Testament
TET	Today's English Translation

CONTRIBUTORS

LeRoy Aden, PhD
Glenn H. Asquith Jr., PhD
Joyce A. Babb, LCSW
Walter Becket, PhD
Gary Brainerd, PhD
J. Russell Burck, PhD
Nancy Evans Bush, MS
Howard Clinebell, PhD (Deceased)
David G. Congo, PhD
Pamela Cooper-White, PhD
Pamela Couture, PhD
Carrie Doehring, PhD
Constance Doran, PhD
Charlotte Ellen, MSW, PhD
Gabriel Fackre, PhD
Patrick Daniel Gaffney, CSC, PhD
Charles V. Gerkin, BD (Deceased)
Larry Kent Graham, PhD
Earl A. Grollman, DD
B. John Hagedorn, PhD
Norbert F. Hahn, PhD
Howard L. Harrod, PhD (Deceased)
Paul Hiebert, PhD
E. Brooks Holifield, PhD
Rodney J. Hunter, PhD
Martha S. Jacobi, MDiv, MSSW, LCSW
Theodore W. Jennings Jr., PhD
Stephen D. King, PhD

Charles H. Kraft, PhD
Jon W. Magnuson, MDiv
David E. Massey, PhD
Albert L. Meiburg, PhD
Charles M. Mendenhall III, PhD
Liston O. Mills, ThD (Deceased)
Jürgen Moltmann, ThD
Romney M. Moseley, PhD
Masamba ma Mpolo, PhD
Akbar Muhommad, PhD
Richard A. Muller, PhD
Tuntufye A. Mwenisongole, MAPC, MATS, DTh (Candidate)
Theron S. Nease, PhD
Christie Cozad Neuger, PhD
William Pannell, DD
Peter J. Paris, PhD
John Patton, PhD
Robert L. Pavelsky, PhD
Carol B. Pitts, PhD
George Polk, STM (Deceased)
Paul W. Pretzel, ThD
L. Rebecca Propst, PhD
Calvin Redekop
Daniel Rhoades, PhD
Horace O. Russell, DPhil
Irwin R. Sternlicht, PhD
Allison Stokes, PhD
Orlo Strunk Jr., PhD
Ronald H. Sunderland, EdD
David K. Switzer, ThD
Susan E. Vollmer, MA, MDiv, BCC
Peggy Way, PhD
Scott Cabot Willis, PhD
Patricia Zulkosky, PhD

1

Definitions

Every profession has a distinct language that is central to formation and practice in that profession. Pastoral care and counseling is informed and shaped by the discipline of pastoral theology, which seeks to provide the theological underpinnings and rationale for pastoral praxis. One of the historic methodological hallmarks of pastoral theology is to integrate the understandings of behavioral science, spirituality, and theology in providing operational definitions of praxis. These definitions reflect this integration in a way that helps define the uniqueness of pastoral care and counseling.

ACCEPTANCE. The therapeutic posture of receiving or taking in another person; an attitude of caring for and of holding in valued esteem another person as a person of distinct particularity.

Genuine acceptance is a primary characteristic of the therapeutic relationship in most forms of insight therapy. Carl R. Rogers considered it one of the six necessary and sufficient conditions for therapeutic change. Historically, Rogers developed acceptance in relation to, and as a correction of, the tendency of the counselor "to pass some type of evaluative judgment upon the client" (1951). Acceptance is not agreement or approval; rather, it is a warm and positive evaluation of the individual whether or not the person lives up to or conforms with the therapist's values or expectations. Acceptance is also not synonymous with appraisal. It does not evaluate the individual's experience in terms of what is important or worthy; instead it respects and cherishes the individual's experience for its own sake. In this sense, acceptance is permissiveness. It is a suspension of all judgment, but unlike permissiveness it does not come out of a laissez-faire attitude. Instead it is a deep and genuine affirmation of the individual in the totality of her or his experience.

Rogers emphasizes the unconditional nature of acceptance. He maintains that the therapist should prize every facet of the client's experience, whether negative or positive. In his later writings, Rogers prefers the phrase "unconditional positive regard" to the less radical term "acceptance" (1951).

Genuine acceptance serves several purposes in the therapeutic process. It is the *conditio sine qua non* of a positive and enduring relationship between client and counselor. Furthermore, it provides a safe atmosphere in which clients can explore and experience their inner world of feelings and meanings. Rogers believes that it also enables clients to achieve self-acceptance. As clients experience the acceptance of the therapist, they gradually begin to take the same attitude toward themselves, feeling a "dawning respect for, acceptance of, and, finally, even a fondness for" themselves (Rogers, 1951). The achievement of increased self-acceptance is crucial to Rogerian healing, for it represents a reunion with the depths of one's experiencing and an ability to live spontaneously out of the fullness of one's being.

Pastoral counselors recognize the importance of genuine acceptance for the same reasons that psychotherapists do. In addition, they emphasize the symbolic role of the pastor's acceptance as not only personal acceptance but as signifying an infinitely transcendent acceptance. Ultimately, the pastor witnesses to and makes concrete God's unconditional acceptance of the human being who is basically unacceptable. This paradoxical truth is crucial to Christian healing, for it frees individuals from the compulsive need to make themselves acceptable and assures them of God's unqualified love.

Bibliography. C. R. Rogers, *Client-Centered Therapy* (1951). For a theological discussion: T. Oden, *Kerygma and Counseling* (1966).

L. ADEN

ARCHETYPE. In analytical (Jungian) psychology, a primordial image representing psychic contents of the collective unconscious (as opposed to the personal unconscious) frequently manifest in dreams, myths, fairy tales, and symbols. As patterns of energy not directly experienced, archetypes yield an endless variety of distinct images shared by all people universally, for example, the mother or father imago, the hero, the tribe, or the deity.

I. R. STERNLICHT

BIBLICAL PASTORAL CARE AND COUNSELING. Biblical pastoral care and counseling is based on the primary belief in the Bible as an authoritative pastoral resource for interpreting, diagnosing, and responding to human problems and crises. Typically, the biblical counselor or caregiver represents the Bible with considerable pastoral authority, and often adopts a confrontational stance in relation to the parishioner or counselee, a stance believed to be an expression of care in the best interest of the person or persons involved.

1. Defining Characteristics of Fundamentalism. Biblical pastoral care and counseling is informed by Christian fundamentalism's central doctrine that affirms the absolute and inerrant authority of Scripture for life, faith, and theology. Other characteristics of fundamentalism derive from this tenet. Another distinguishing characteristic of fundamentalism is the doctrine of holiness or separation that influences fundamentalists to avoid dialogue and cooperation with those perceived to be willful disobeyers or deniers of Scripture. Mainly because of this, biblical counselors shun any use of modern behavioral science or "secular psychology" in addressing human problems.

2. Jay Adams as Representative. Jay Adams is the most widely known and influential theorist for biblical counseling. Adams emerged after a long period during which the social sciences had decisively influenced mainline pastoral care. He expressed several criticisms of this development: that pastoral care was losing its identity in relationship to the church, ministry, the Bible, and theology; that private practice counseling had little accountability to the church; and that the social sciences had more authority than the Bible as a guide for pastoral care. In response to these criticisms, Adams offered his own alternative, "nouthetic counseling," or more inclusively, a nouthetic pastoral method that makes explicit in an innovative way the traditional fundamentalist pastoral method.

a. Nouthetic counseling. "Nouthetic" is a transliteration of a Greek verb found eight times in the NT and for which Adams could find no adequate English translation, but which points to the basically spiritual character of Bible-centered counseling. Adams (1972b) insists that nouthetic counseling is the counseling theory and practice taught in the

Bible. In brief, nouthetic counseling aims at personal change from sin to faith and righteousness, "brought about by confrontation out of concern" for the counselee's benefit. At its core, nouthetic counseling perceives itself as biblical counseling, counseling that is to be taught by the inerrant, infallible, and authoritative Word of God and empowered by God's Spirit. It evolves from a literalistic and legalistic biblical hermeneutic and is a rational, problem-centered, behavior-oriented approach.

b. Pastoral counseling in general. Adams understands pastoral counseling to be one aspect of the pastoral ministry. Indeed, he understands it to be akin to shepherding in its efforts to put "new life into one by convicting and changing, encouraging and strengthening after trial, defeat, failure, and/or discouragement" (1975, 14). Pastoral counseling is a ministry of the church, done by representative persons of the church, preeminently by the ordained pastor, but also by trained laity. As a ministry of the church, it takes place within the context of a body of believers who practice mutual edification and correction. In fact, the counseling session itself often includes other persons significantly related to the counselee in respect to the presenting problem.

c. Separatism. Adams strictly adheres to the doctrine of separation. First, Adams asserts that the best training for pastoral counseling is not to be found in a school of psychology or of medicine but in a seminary that provides a proper biblical and theological foundation. Second, Adams insists that one avoid all sources that do not hold biblical presuppositions. The Bible is the textbook for counseling. Admittedly, Adams does say that science may illustrate, fill in generalizations, and challenge human interpretations of the Bible. However, except for occasional references to sleep studies, one finds little evidence that Adams acknowledges that he has been informed by other disciplines that he calls non-Christian. Further, Adams designates the evangelical view that all truth is from God as a ruse of Satan. Third, he perceives psychology and psychiatry as having incorrectly informed pastoral care and as having crossed into the turf of pastors who are the only true doctors of the soul (or psyche). Fourth, Adams is very concerned that the pastors protect their flock from those holding false doctrine.

Bibliography. J. E. Adams, *The Big Umbrella* (1972a); *The Christian Counselor's Manual* (1973); *Competent to Counsel* (1972b); *Pastoral Counseling* (1975). J. Barr, *Fundamentalism* (1977). D. E. Capps, *Biblical Approaches to Pastoral Counseling* (1981). J. A. Carpenter,

"Fundamentalism," in S. S. Hill, ed., *Encyclopedia of Religion in the South* (1984). S. G. Coles, *The History of Fundamentalism* (1931). N. F. Furniss, *The Fundamentalist Controversy, 1918–1931* (1954). G. M. Marsden, *Fundamentalism and American Culture* (1980). See also the website for the National Association of Nouthetic Counselors: http://www.nanc.org.

S. D. KING

BURNOUT. A syndrome, often occurring among individuals in helping professions, involving emotional and physical exhaustion, depersonalization, and a feeling of reduced personal accomplishment. Other symptoms include headaches; gastrointestinal disorders; lingering colds; weight loss; sleeplessness; shortness of breath; feelings of tension and anxiety; overuse of food, coffee, or chocolate; memory loss; irritability; daydreaming; tendency to blame; withdrawal; cynicism; marital dissatisfaction; impatience; feelings of inferiority; emotional flatness; loss of interest in hobbies; preoccupation with one area of one's life; and spiritual dryness.

1. Causes. There are several theories about the causes of burnout. C. Maslach (1982) and other social psychologists believe that burnout can be understood best by focusing on situational, environmental, and demographic factors, such as long working hours, little feedback regarding one's work, lack of family time, low salary, understaffing, life changes, unrealistic expectations, lack of time off, and inability to control one's schedule. This view supports the pastoral observation that people— whether church-school teachers or pastors—do not burn out from overwork so much as from lack of support.

Internal factors may also be involved, however. H. J. Freudenberger (1980) represents a psychoanalytic position that believes that intrapsychic or personality tendencies are a more reliable explanation of burnout. These include need for approval, workaholic qualities, authoritarianism, unassertive acts, overly sensitive reactions, "type A" personality, poor self-worth, and the "messiah" complex—the belief that only "I" can do everything best. Clinical pastoral experience along this line points also to identity issues, especially in pastors who attempt to fill diverse or conflicting roles and become confused about their pastoral identity in the attempt.

Instead of the linear causality of external or internal factors, a third model, proposed by L. Heifetz and H. Bersani (1983), understands burnout as a cybernetic interplay of situational, intrapsychic, interpersonal, physical, and spiritual factors. The combination of these five factors leads to burnout when the homeostatic balance among them is heavily weighted on one and not compensated by another. To illustrate, individuals feeling the pressure of unrealistic expectations imposed by others (an external factor) find it necessary to maintain homeostasis by drawing on internal self-confidence (internal factor) or spiritual resources. They may further enhance homeostasis by directly confronting the persons having the expectations (interpersonal variable). If these complementary efforts do not compensate for the external stress, the individuals are likely to experience burnout. This view assumes a holistic understanding of persons; each area affects the other, and it is the combination that leads to burnout.

2. Prevention. The following suggestions can enable pastors and other helping professionals to prevent burnout. (1) Gain a clear understanding of personal strengths and weaknesses; this helps one distinguish between external and internal sources of stress, and seek help when appropriate. (2) In order to gain a sense of purpose and priorities, carefully plan one's directions, focus on essentials, and learn to say no without feeling guilt or giving offense. (3) Structure changes in the environment that will relieve the stress, and adjust to factors that cannot be changed; such steps might include spreading unpleasant tasks between enjoyable ones, guarding productive time for creative pursuits, eliminating repetitive annoyances, learning to separate leisure activities from work, and attending workshops to gain new practical ideas. (4) Develop interpersonal relationships in which one can experience support and affirmation. (5) Take action to resolve interpersonal conflicts and differences. (6) Learn constructive ways of dealing with anger. (7) Achieve a balance between empathy for people and overinvolved sympathy, which diverts one from central issues. (8) Develop relaxation and recreational outlets by learning at least one relaxation technique, exercising, getting proper rest, having a balanced diet (with restricted sugars), making occasional retreats to nature, avoiding states of helplessness by taking control, and implementing a coping strategy in tough situations. (9) Seek professional help when that seems warranted.

The symptoms of burnout can be thought of as a built-in alarm system in the body signifying that life is out of balance. With proper attention to these symptoms, balance can be restored and burnout can be prevented.

Bibliography. K. Albrecht and H. Selye, *Stress and the Manager* (1979). E. Brachter, *The Walk-on-Water Syndrome* (1984). S. Daniel and M. L. Rogers, "Burnout and the Pastorate: A Critical Review with Implications for Pastors," *J. of Psychology and Theology* 9 (1981), 232–49. H. J. Freudenberger, *Burnout* (1980). L. Heifetz and H. Bersani, "Disrupting the Cybernetics of Personal Growth: Toward a Unified Theory of Burnout in the Human Services," in B. Farber, ed., *Stress and Burnout in the Human Service Professions* (1983). C. Maslach, *Burnout: The Cost of Caring* (1982). J. Warner and J. D. Carter, "Loneliness, Marital Adjustment, and Burnout in Pastoral and Lay Persons," *J. of Psychology and Theology* 12 (1984), 125–31.

D. G. CONGO

CARE OF SOULS (*Cura Animarum*). The traditional term for pastoral care. The primary meaning of the Latin word *cura* is "care," although it also includes the notion of "healing." The word *anima* was the most common Latin translation of the Hebrew *nephesh* ("breath") and the Greek *psyche* ("soul"). "Soul" has many shades of meaning in Scripture. In Gen. 2:7, when God breathed into his nostrils, the man became "a living being," yet the same word, *nephesh*, is used in Gen. 2:19 to describe animals (though translated "living creature"). In the NT "soul" stands for the essential human being, with emphasis on its transcendent destiny. The care, or cure, of souls, then, is distinguished from other helping enterprises by its consistent reference to ultimate meaning.

The term "care of souls" is used in three ways. First, its broadest use sums up the work of the office of priest, including leading worship, preaching, visiting, and organizing parish life. In this sense, "care of souls" acknowledges that all acts of ministry have as their ultimate aim the salvation and perfection of persons under God. In the Roman Catholic and Episcopal traditions a "curate" was one who had received the cure of souls by legitimate appointment to the office of parish pastor or assistant pastor. The bishop, likewise, exercised this care toward the diocese, and the pope toward the whole church.

Second, in a narrower sense, "care of souls" describes a particular strand of pastoral care tradition, *Seelsorge*, stemming from the Reformation and especially prominent in Lutheran pastoral theology. According to J. T. McNeill (1951), Lutheran practice rejected the compulsory nature of the confessional, but maintained it as a searching personal conversation on religious problems. Pastors gave priority to visiting the sick, the dying, and prisoners. Most important, they implemented Luther's recovery of the NT idea of mutual correction and encouragement, the "care of all for the souls of all," states McNeill.

Third, the "care of souls" is sometimes used as a synonym for pastoral care. W. A. Clebsch and C. R. Jaekle (1975) define the care of souls as "helping acts done by representative Christian persons directed toward the healing, sustaining, guiding, and reconciling of troubled persons whose troubles arise in the context of ultimate meanings and concerns."

The goals and methods of pastoral care have varied according to the age and culture. In a review of three hundred years of Protestant pastoral care in America, E. B. Holifield (1983) concluded that Pietism's preoccupation with the welfare of the individual soul became the seedbed for the growth of popular psychology. In turn, the new psychology reshaped the Protestant vision of the self, so that the goal of pastoral care moved "from salvation to self-realization" under God.

The ancient term "cure of souls" reminds contemporary pastors of their apostolic forebears who, in the spirit of Jesus, met human pain with compassion and human guilt with grace and forgiveness.

Bibliography. W. A. Clebsch and C. R. Jaekle, *Pastoral Care in Historical Perspective* (1975), 1, 4. F. Greeves, *Theology and the Cure of Souls* (1962). S. Hiltner, *Preface to Pastoral Theology* (1958), 82–172. E. B. Holifield, *A History of Pastoral Care in America* (1983), 356. J. T. McNeill, *A History of the Cure of Souls* (1951), 189–90. See also J. R. Haule, "The Care of Souls: Psychology and Religion in Anthropological Perspective," *J. of Psychology and Theology* 11 (1983), 108–16.

A. L. MEIBURG

EMPATHY. The ability to identify with and experience another person's experiences. This is accomplished by (as much as possible) suspending one's own frame of reference in order to enter the perceptual and emotional world of the other. Empathy is vital in the counseling situation. If a counselee feels that the counselor empathically and truly understands him or her, the counselee is more likely to trust the counselor with deeper feelings and enter the therapeutic process more deeply and productively.

D. E. MASSEY

GUIDED IMAGERY TECHNIQUE. A method that utilizes a person's ability to create images in one's own mind for a specific therapeutic purpose. Guided imagery has been used to facilitate relaxation, change physiological states (e.g., lower blood pressure, reduce anxiety), solve problems, overcome fears, resolve conflicts, and bring healing to past traumatic events. Basically, psychotherapists have used guided imagery as a method to simulate reality. The counselee might be asked to use his or her mind to imagine or picture a particular situation. The therapist would then use various techniques, such as questions, directives, or descriptions (Shorr, 1983), to guide the counselee through the image and toward a helpful or meaningful resolution. Currently, there are a number of different therapies or specific ways in which the technique of guided imagery is used. Systematic desensitization and implosion therapy are two very successful behavioral techniques that have utilized guided images.

Pastoral counselors and Christian therapists have used the guided imagery technique in the healing of memories (Linn and Linn, 1974) or inner healing (MacNutt, 1974). Quite often, a very traumatic event in someone's past will have long-lasting and far-reaching effects in that person's life. The goal sought after in the healing of memories is to replace the traumatic material in the memory with new material that can become a source of healing for the individual (Stapleton, 1976). Briefly, the method is for the counselor to ask the person to imagine in his or her mind a returning to that particular traumatic event. Once the person has imagined that event or situation and can describe it, then, instead of reliving the event as the person remembers it happening, the person is also asked to visualize Christ entering into that situation and remaining there with him or her (Stapleton, 1976). Christ can now become an experiential source of forgiveness, strength, compassion, love, or any other kind of healing for that person in that particular situation. This new reexperiencing of a past event, situation, or relationship transforms the way in which that event, situation, or relationship is preserved in memory. Thus, Christ and all his healing power are now a part of what is remembered.

Bibliography. D. Linn and M. Linn, *Healing of Memories* (1974). F. MacNutt, *Healing* (1974). J. Shorr, *Psychotherapy through Imagery*, 2nd ed. (1983). R. Stapleton, *The Gift of Inner Healing* (1976).

S. C. WILLIS

HANDICAP AND DISABILITY. A permanent condition of limitation in the ability to perform essential tasks. The cause may be congenital, or the onset may be gradual or sudden, by disease, accident, or war. Language usage varies, but it is clear that persons are not defined by a condition that limits some part or dimension of their activity. Persons with handicapping conditions include those whose disability or difference in appearance or behavior creates a problem of mobility, communication, intellectual comprehension, or personal relationships, that interferes with their social activity or participation.

The World Health Organization clearly delineates three widely used terms: (1) impairment, the loss or abnormality of a psychological, physiological, or anatomical structure or function, causing functional limitations to perform those activities usually carried out by the organ or systems affected; (2) disability, any restriction or lack of ability to perform an activity in the manner or within the range considered normal for a human being, that is, disturbances within areas of task, skill, behavior; (3) handicap, a disadvantage resulting from an impairment or disability that limits or prevents the fulfillment of a role that is normal for that individual. Thus an impairment is the cause; a disability is what a person cannot do; a handicap is the social barrier, attitude, or condition that restricts participation.

1. The Community Context of Care. Care must overcome a social/cultural and ecclesial community's negative response to disability and blemish. Through historical attitudes that have related sin to disability, and Western cultural attitudes that emphasized independence, persons with disabilities have frequently been viewed with fear, threat, or awkwardness. Because they have been named by their disability (i.e., the blind, the deaf, the lame, the dumb), rather than their personhood (i.e., persons with a disability or persons with handicapping conditions), they have been viewed as objects or recipients of care. Such attitudes can make a disability worse, as they lead to exclusion, invisibility, or being viewed solely as recipients of services provided by others.

Care begins with visibility, access, and invitation to full participation in community, recognizing that the disability is just one dimension of personhood. Thus the goal of pastoral care for persons with disabilities is their full equality and participation in community as whole persons. Agents of care must work with the attitudes of the whole community as they have led to physical and attitudinal barriers to full access and participation. As stewards of access, care providers thus invite partnership and reciprocity with persons with disabilities. Within the context of total community, recognition is also developed that disabilities cut across racial, social, sexual, ethnic, and age populations, and that no one is free from disability at some point of the life cycle.

2. Special Care and Counseling Considerations. As with any special population, a whole range of situations and feelings and a great diversity of responses must be expected. Consideration must be given to matters of onset and their differing meanings, namely, congenital, gradual, or sudden. Persons with disabilities must cope with personal and physical barriers and limits without surrendering their possibilities of finding alternatives, creative participation, and social usefulness. There may be feelings of grief, anger, and mourning over lost capacities or possibilities, as well as negative feelings about self-concept and body image. There may be ambivalent feelings about independence or premature dependency, as well as those of vulnerability, loneliness, and frustration.

The person with a disability is a social person, and the family context must be considered. Dynamics of overprotection or guilt within the disabled person or family member(s) may be present. The person may experience difficulties in personal relationships and with feelings and expressions of sexuality. There may be dynamics within the person or family that have developed through isolation, exclusion, or social invisibility, or from experiences of having been pitied or patronized. As in any counseling, attention must be paid to the differing meanings of individual and family narrative, including their broader social matrix.

The varying conditions of disability may call for slow, sustained efforts to find alternatives to normal social intercourse, in which care may focus on sustaining and supportive systems and standing by. The person or family may disclose needs for ethical reflection or moral guidance in matters of sexuality, marriage, having children, and issues of life and death. In broader social context, pastoral care and counseling for persons with handicapping conditions is interprofessional, and it is probable that pastoral caregivers will work with members of other helping professions, for example, doctors, physiotherapists, nurses, social workers, other mental health professionals, and technicians in facilitating the use of mechanical helps. It is important that the pastoral helper have knowledge of the particular disability, its prognosis, and related emotional effects. The caregiver should also be aware of self-help groups and advocacy organizations of persons experiencing the disability and their families as rich community resources.

3. Related Theological Issues. Christian community is not complete without the full participation of persons with handicapping conditions, whose past isolation must be reconciled within the wholeness of the family of God. God's love is not contingent upon physical perfection, and historical ties between faith and wholeness, sin and disability—which have led to fear, threat, and resulting isolation—must be corrected. Issues of suffering, finitude/limitation, and meaning, when there is no apparent physical healing, must be addressed. Mature understandings of the suffering servant and the finding of perfection through weakness may be helpful. Theological understandings of the nature of God's power and love, as well as of the meaning of healing, will be relevant.

The full inclusion of persons with physical limitation within Christian community invites the sharing of their gifts of ministry with full equality, and makes indispensable witness to all persons who accept finitude/limitation while refusing unnecessary barriers to the possibilities of their full personhood with human community.

Bibliography. L. G. Colston, *Pastoral Care with Handicapped Persons* (1978). J. Cox-Gedmark, *Coping with Physical Disability* (1980). J. van Dongren-Garrad, *Invisible Barriers: Pastoral Care with Physically Disabled People* (1983). N. Eiesland, *The Disabled God* (1994). T. Gould, "A Guide to Eliminating 'Handicappism' in Language," *New World Outlook* (May 1983). W. Kern, *Pastoral Ministry with Disabled Persons* (1985). G. Müller-Fahrenholz, ed., *Partners in Life: The Handicapped and the Church*, Faith and Order Paper No. 89, World Council of Churches (1979). H. O. Ohlsberg, *The Church and Persons with Handicaps* (1982). H. H. Wilke, *Creating the Caring Congregation: Guidelines for Ministering with the Handicapped* (1980); *Strengthened with Might* (1952); "Is Our Theology Disabled?: A Symposium on Theology and Persons with Handicapping Conditions," Health and Welfare Ministries Division, General Board of Global Ministries, The United Methodist Church (1982) or "God's Power and Our Weakness," Task Force of Persons with Disabilities of the Consultation on Church Union, G. F. Moebe, ed. (1982).

P. WAY

HOMEOSTASIS. Literally meaning "to stay the same," homeostasis has become a familiar concept in the behavioral sciences most commonly applied to interpersonal systems (viz., the family and the marital dyad). Secondary applications refer to larger social systems (i.e., organizations, communities) and to intrapsychic and physiological systems.

Physiologist Walter Cannon coined the term in 1932 to characterize the self-regulation demonstrated by organisms to maintain states of relative physiological constancy, such as body temperature and blood sugar. A parallel example from the mechanical sciences is the thermostat, a self-contained, error-activated device designed to regulate temperature. Both may be classified as operating systems involving a reciprocal relationship of self-contained and environmental elements.

According to general systems theory, a constant state of action-reaction exists between two or more associated components in relationship. This ongoing relationship is characterized by a fluid balance or equilibrium (homeostasis). The homeostatic principle dictates that patterns of relating, once established, will persist in the relatively balanced state, and variation or change will automatically be resisted as part of the system's survival.

The fundamental process involved in a system's homeostasis is the feedback loop, a reciprocal sequence in which system output is reintroduced into the system as information about the output's consequences. Feedback may be either positive or negative; both are vital to any organic system. Negative feedback typifies homeostasis and is often used synonymously with it. Negative, or constancy feedback, functions to decrease the system's deviation from a set norm or pattern, and thus maintains equilibrium, while positive, or variation feedback, amplifies systemic deviation. If uncontrolled, positive feedback will lead to systemic breakdown and disorganization.

In any interpersonal system, behavior and communication may be viewed as feedback loops, insofar as the behavior and communication of each person are affected by that of the other person or persons. Interactional psychology considers interpersonal relationships (particularly marital dyads and families) as open, adaptive, information-processing systems, functioning in accord with various general systems principles. Thus it is postulated that, for example, the family system's established interactional patterns represent a delicate balance, or homeostasis, that is intrinsically resistant to change.

Although less well developed, the idea of intrapsychic homeostasis also has been advanced. Psychiatrist Nathan Ackerman brought the homeostasis model to bear on the dynamics of the individual personality system as well as the group interpersonal system (i.e., family and society). He viewed homeostasis as a life-protecting principle for creative adaptation, which assures a control to prevent organisms being overwhelmed by traumatizing stimuli. Ackerman's discussion implies that personality consists of an integration of homeostatic processes, as a holistic organism, and that the environmental systems overarch and embrace this integration. In the same vein, psychiatrist Karl Menninger and associates (1963) have constructed a major theory of mental health and illness based on a hierarchy of homeostatic "levels of control."

Bibliography. N. Ackerman, *Family Process* (1970). W. B. Cannon, *The Wisdom of the Body* (1967 [1932]). K. Menninger, M. Mayman, and P. Pruyser, *The Vital Balance* (1963).

W. BECKET

HOSPICE. A program of health care delivery designed to control and relieve the emotional, physical, and spiritual suffering of the terminally ill. A hospice program may provide services primarily in the person's home, on an inpatient basis, or as a combination of inpatient and home care. An interdisciplinary team provides physical symptom management and psychological, sociological, and spiritual services as they are needed. Family members as well as the dying person receive care, and the bereaved are supported through the recovery period. The purpose of hospice care is to create an environment in which one can maintain quality of life to the fullest extent and then die peacefully without actively prolonging life or accelerating death.

Components of hospice philosophy are: (1) low technology, focusing on the appropriate use of machines or equipment, (2) respect for individual choices and personal dignity, (3) focus on quality rather than quantity of life, (4) attention to physical comfort, especially the relief of pain, (5) attention to psychosocial and spiritual needs, and (6) involvement of and support of the family or significant others.

Hospices extend their services to the family during bereavement, frequently by utilizing bereavement groups or one-to-one support. Provision of services is usually based on need rather than ability to pay.

C. BRAINERD

IDENTIFIED PATIENT. The member of the family self-designated, or designated by the family, as the cause and location of the family problem. Systemic family theory conceptualizes dysfunctional family transactional patterns as the cause of family problems and therefore views the identified patient only as the family symptom bearer.

B. J. HAGEDORN

INDIVIDUATION. A process of differentiation having as a goal the development of a conscious, complete, unique individual personality capable of successful outer (social) as well as inner (collective) relationship. In analytical psychology, individuation occurs as the self emerges and the person develops the various functions of personality.

I. R. STERNLICHT

LAY PASTORAL CARE AND COUNSELING. Pastoral care and counseling that (1) pertains to the laity, as distinguished from the clergy, and (2) does not belong to nor is connected with a profession; nonprofessional.

1. Lay Pastoral Care. There is a widely held presumption that the congregation's pastoral ministry is the responsibility of the clergy. Visits by laity to fellow members are only infrequently identified as pastoral visits.

When the function of pastoral care is limited to work performed by the clergy, the scope of the pastoral function is also limited. In most congregations, clergy discharge this function through visits to members who are hospitalized or bereaved, and the provision of more or less formalized pastoral counseling. In any event, clergy pastoral care often is limited to crisis response and may exclude any general home visitation.

E. E. Shelp and R. H. Sunderland (1981) suggest two reasons for this trend. On the one hand, pastoral education in the United States has emphasized that clergy have a special function in pastoral care for which specialized training was designed, located almost exclusively in health care settings. On the other hand, opportunities for ministry were surrendered by individual members of congregations and assigned to the professional clergy.

It is regrettable that this development has limited the religious community's perception of pastoral care to response to illness, bereavement, or family crises. The congregation's responsibilities to its members should be perceived in the broadest possible terms, and include such ministries as regular pastoral contacts with each family, with children as well as adults, and on occasions of celebration as well as consolation.

If it is to be effective, lay pastoral care must be characterized by the same intentionality that religious communities have come to expect of clergy. Expectations of lay ministers include adequate training, a system of accountability, and the provision of support for those people whose pastoral gifts have been recognized and who are called to exercise them in the service of the church. A. V. Campbell (1981) noted that the untrained helper's chief distraction is an overwhelming desire to be helpful. Effective ministry will result only when the caring person has accepted the discipline of training.

Second, it is essential that caring ministry be characterized by a level of accountability that reflects a self-consciousness of the importance of the task and the fact that the ministry is offered as an act of the caring community. Third, lay pastoral ministry is likely to be spasmodic and ineffective unless the caring minister receives support that both expresses the community's care for its own ministers and provides oversight, or supervision, by the community of its lay pastors.

2. Lay Pastoral Counseling. Pastoral counseling is usually regarded as a professional function requiring of the practitioner a higher level of training and supervision than that expected of ordained and lay ministers who are responsible for the more general ministry of pastoral care. The American Association of Pastoral Counselors has established standards concerning both education and services. Many states require professional counselors to qualify for state licensure before they are permitted to practice. When these standards have been met, pastoral counseling centers may employ social workers, clinical psychologists, and psychiatric nurses whose professional education has equipped them to provide counseling services.

In these instances, the efficacy of lay pastoral counseling will be determined by three factors: (1) evidence of call and gifts for the pastoral counseling ministry, (2) the adequacy of the counselors' training and the quality of supervision, and (3) the degree to which counselors have resolved issues relating to identity and spiritual formation. In pastoral counseling centers that utilize lay counselors under such circumstances, training for the counseling profession and resolution of pastoral identity are the necessary preconditions that must be met for both clergy and lay members of the congregation's staff.

Bibliography. A. V. Campbell, *Rediscovering Pastoral Care* (1981). C. Gerkin, *An Introduction to Pastoral Care* (1997). M. Kornfeld, *Cultivating Wholeness* (1998). E. E. Shelp and R. H. Sunderland, eds., *Biblical Basis for Ministry* (1981).

R. H. SUNDERLAND

LIVING HUMAN DOCUMENT. A term first used by Anton T. Boisen (1936, 1960), the founder of clinical pastoral education, to state that individual human experience, especially of people in crisis, should be "read" by theological students and pastors alongside the classical texts of theology and biblical study in order to test theological assumptions and develop a complete, holistic theological understanding. Boisen (1945) also studied social conditions and movements, with the assumption that collective religious experience would inform and enrich theological understanding as well.

Bibliography. A. T. Boisen, *The Exploration of the Inner World* (1936); *Out of the Depths* (1960); *Religion in Crisis and Custom* (1945).

G. H. ASQUITH JR.

NARRATIVE THERAPY. One of a group of contemporary therapies often categorized as "postmodern," although its founders prefer to locate it more specifically as post-structuralist.

1. History. Postmodernism, especially as it is relevant to psychotherapy, questions the existence of grand narratives or universal explanations and, instead, values the particular, the local, and the importance of difference. Post-structuralism does not assume that there are deep structures or fixed truths that explain "human nature," "personality," or human difficulties. Therefore, therapists who operate out of a poststructuralist perspective tend to reject pathologizing or diagnostic approaches to people's problems and, instead, rely on counselees' explanations for and meanings of the problems they bring to counseling.

Michael White, an Australian social worker, and David Epston, a Canadian-born anthropologist and family therapist working in New Zealand, are generally understood to be the cofounders of this approach, although many of the ideas that undergird narrative therapy also have been emerging in various streams of therapeutic thought (most specifically in feminist, other liberationist, and some constructivist approaches). Narrative Therapy became widely known after the 1990 (U.S.) publication of the book *Narrative Means to Therapeutic Ends* by White and Epston. It is fast growing in popularity around the world, with different contexts and theorists emphasizing different elements of the theory(ies) including social constructionism, postmodernism, social justice, and post-structuralist philosophies (especially those of Michel Foucault and Jacques Derrida). White and Epston have said that they would prefer the name of this approach to be "narrative therapies."

2. Principles and Values. The word *narrative* has multiple meanings and legitimately could be applied to many forms of therapy. After all, most therapy is about telling stories in one form or another. Yet, narrative therapy as a post-structuralist approach uses the notion of "narrative" in a very particular way. In this context "narrative" refers to the way that language is constitutive of our lives and meanings, not merely descriptive or reflective of them. Narrative therapists propose that people make sense of their lives through a narrative form. We have varieties of experiences in our lives. We take some of those experiences and attach meaning to them and we ignore or render meaningless other experiences. Those experiences to which we give significant meaning are joined together in story strands and arranged in time to generate the narratives through which we understand and create meaning around ourselves, others, values, and our futures. Those experiences to which we don't assign meaning get left out of those narratives and play little role in our identities, values, and relationships. We tend to render meaningful those events in our lives that support our primary narrative plots and ignore those that don't fit. Our lives are multiply storied in this theory. We each have many linking and overlapping narratives. We also have subjugated knowledges and discounted experiences that stand outside of our primary narratives. Narrative therapists are interested in helping people find these subjugated or hidden knowledges that might well serve as resources for deconstructing and disempowering the problem stories of their lives and offer new options for identity, meaning, and agency (Tarragona, 2008).

A key assumption in narrative therapy is that the "stuff" of our stories is shaped largely by the dominant cultural discourses that serve as "truths" for our contexts. Dominant cultural discourses are the assumptions and frameworks of a culture, shaped by those in power, that assign value to certain ways of being and knowing, and "prescribe the good, thereby implying how one should live" (Tarragona, 2008). The deconstruction of dominant discourses and taken-for-granted knowledge is a key element in narrative therapy, sometimes causing it to be categorized as a "political" therapy. Deconstruction, in this case, is the work of revealing dominant culture assumptions and frameworks as partial or untrue for particular people or groups. Cultural discourses are about power and credibility (racism, sexism, classism, and other structures that label people as outside of the norm). These discourses become embedded in institutions, bodies of knowledge/power, authoritative practices, and people's personal stories and identities. "Normal" becomes narrowly defined and reflects the characteristics of the group given credibility and access to power. The problems that people bring to counseling are always seen by narrative therapists as shaped in the context of dominant cultural discourses.

Narrative therapists believe that the counselees who consult them are the experts on their own lives and values. The counselor does not represent expert knowledge about health or normalcy. Rather, the counselor brings a certain level of expertise in how to generate and structure therapeutic conversation in such a way that deconstruction of problem stories and reauthoring of alternative stories can occur. White (2007) has characterized the narrative therapist as "de-centered but influential." This kind of therapeutic conversation is grounded in a set of values that are common to narrative therapy practitioners. Those values include a respect for the local knowledge and particular contexts of the counselee, a commitment to transparency and accountability in the counselor, a non-pathologizing and non-labeling approach to the counselee's situation, and a deep commitment to therapeutic collaboration between counselor and counselee.

3. Therapeutic Processes. A fundamental premise in narrative therapy is that the problem story is separate from the counselee. The person is never seen as the problem. Because of this commitment, narrative conversations may begin with an externalization of the problem through the use of externalizing questions. This creates distance between the counselee and the problem, and makes visible other, non-problem-saturated aspects of the counselee's life. As White and Epston have noted, when people have a significant problem in their lives they tend to see all of their experiences through the lens of the problem story. The problem story becomes definitive of the person for both the counselee and the counselor (e.g., "I am depressed" or "She is a borderline personality"). This is what White and Epston (1990), drawing from the work of Clifford Geertz, define as a "thin" description of the person's identity. Thus, if the problem story can be viewed and described as separate from the person (often through the simple linguistic move of shifting an adjective ["I am depressed"] to a noun ["I am struggling with depression"]) and be descriptive rather than labeled, then identities and experiences that aren't described by the problem story can become more available. Not all narrative therapy consultations begin in this way, but for those situations in which the problem story has become a "totalizing descriptor" of the counselee, this is the usual starting point. White has called this an "externalizing conversation."

White (2007) has described three major therapeutic conversational categories in narrative therapy. They are (1) externalizing conversations, as described above; (2) re-authoring conversations, where an experience that would not be predicted by the problem story (unique outcome) is richly described and connected with other similar experiences to form an alternative narrative; and (3) remembering conversations where engagement with the perspectives and memories of other significant people contribute to an emerging alternative narrative. All three of these therapeutic strategies have both deconstructive and reconstructive elements. White has proposed frameworks, or maps, for each of these conversational forms through which alternative narratives can be richly developed. He has written,

> Maps shape a therapeutic inquiry in which people suddenly find themselves interested in novel understandings of the events of their lives, curious about aspects of their lives that have been forsaken, fascinated with neglected territories of their identities, and, at times, awed by their own responses to the predicaments of their existence. (White, 2007)

Other typical elements of narrative therapy include (1) outsider witnesses and definitional ceremonies—where other people join the therapy session to help retell the alternative story from their own perspectives and thus "thicken" its description; (2) documents and rituals—certificates, pictures, declarations, and ceremonies through which the alternative story and its effects are noted, honored, and celebrated; (3) therapeutic letters—letters written to the counselee lifting up significant aspects of the counseling session where alternative knowledges and narratives occurred; and (4) letter-writing campaigns—where people who have experienced similar problems (e.g., anorexia, racism, troubled reputations, etc.) may exchange letters with one another where they share ideas, deconstruct dominant discourses, and join in generating descriptions of alternative narratives.

Narrative therapy theories and practices are continuing to develop in a variety of directions. The Dulwich Centre in Australia (founded by Michael White) sponsors training opportunities, the exchange of ideas through papers and conversations, and an increasing focus on narrative therapy's role in justice-making and community work. There are many other training and service centers in narrative therapy around the world and a rich network of Internet websites.

Bibliography. J. Freedman and G. Coombs, *Narrative Therapy* (1996). G. Monk, J. Winslade et al., *Narrative Therapy in Practice* (1996). A. Morgan, *What Is Narrative Therapy?* (2000). M. Tarragona, "Postmodern/Poststructuralist Therapies," J. Lebow, ed., *Twenty-first Century Psychotherapies* (2008). M. White, *Maps of Narrative Practice* (2007). M. White and D. Epston, *Narrative Means to Therapeutic Ends* (1990). J. Winslade and G. Monk, *Practicing Narrative Mediation* (2008).

C. C. NEUGER

NEAR-DEATH EXPERIENCE. A transcendent alteration of consciousness, similar to religious mystical states, occurring in a significant minority of persons close to death. The common pattern of near-death experiences (NDEs) includes one or more elements: ineffability, an out-of-body episode, movement through a dark void or tunnel, encounter with a sometimes-personified light of indescribable radiance, meeting "spirits" of loved ones, a feeling of encompassing all knowledge, life review, sense of boundary, decision, and a return to the physical body.

1. History. Although NDEs were known in antiquity (cf. Book X of Plato's *Republic* and the *Tibetan Book of the Dead*), recent centuries have dismissed them as occult phenomena. In the early 1970s they were brought to public attention by Drs. Elisabeth Kübler-Ross and Raymond Moody, and have since received serious study as a legitimate area of consciousness research.

2. Research Findings. Systematic studies by K. Ring, M. Sabom, G. Gallup Jr., and others indicate that 35–40 percent of persons who come close to death report NDEs; 8 million adult Americans may be experiencers. The NDE occurs across categories of age, sex, race, education, religious belief, national origin, and precipitating clinical event. The studies substantiate earlier reports of differentiation from dreams or hallucinations, and document profound aftereffects. There is no generally accepted theory of causation or explanation for the nonreporting of NDEs by a majority of persons near death.

3. Aftereffects. Immediate aftereffects vary widely, including anger at being "brought back," euphoria, or anxiety about insanity. Many experiencers are unable to talk about the NDE at first for fear of being thought insane, because it seems too sacred, or because "no one could understand."

Permanent aftereffects include loss of the fear of death; pronounced shifts in values from materialistic striving toward agape, service, and acceptance of others; increased interest in spirituality, though not necessarily in formal religious observances; psychic abilities; and a powerful sense of life purpose.

4. Counseling Implications. Many who have had an NDE become more self-actualizing, interpreting the experience as a powerful personal revelation of God's loving purposefulness. Those who have attempted suicide appear less likely to repeat the attempt. Conversely, as values shift, lifestyles and relationships are often disrupted. Families may need help; divorce is not uncommon. Many are bewildered by the advent of psychic phenomena or worried because their "mission" is unclear. A sense of deep isolation is frequent.

Counseling interventions may be needed for these issues, for continuing anger, and to discover new perceptions of religious belief. Careful, receptive listening is important in enabling the person to assimilate this powerful experience and to understand its implications for relationships and future decisions. After an NDE, persons often develop intuitive gifts for parish visitation or counseling, especially with the sick, the dying, or the bereaved.

Bibliography. G. Gallup Jr., *Adventures in Immortality* (1982). C. R. Lundahl, *A Collection of Near-Death Research Readings* (1982). R. Moody Jr., *Life after Life* (1975). D. M. Moss III, "Near-Fatal Experience, Crisis Intervention and the Anniversary Reaction," *Pastoral Psychology* 28 (1979), 75–96. K. Ring, *Life at Death* (1980). M. Sabom, *Recollections of Death* (1982). See also publications of the International Association for Near-Death Studies.

N. E. BUSH

OVERFUNCTIONING/UNDERFUNCTIONING. These terms describe reciprocal roles within the family or other social system. The overfunctioning person feels responsible for the emotional well-being of others and acts to compensate for real or imagined deficits in others' functioning. The underfunctioning person depends upon the overfunctioning of another to (1) do things that she or he is reluctant to do, or (2) to tell her or him how to think, feel, and act. The overfunctioning person may or may not experience this as a burden. Clergy often complain about being stuck with too much responsibility and fail to recognize that they are overfunctioning and that this promotes underfunctioning as an adaptive response.

Bibliography. E. Friedman, *Generation to Generation* (1985). M. E. Kerr and M. Bowen, *Family Evaluation* (1988).

C. B. PITTS

PASTORAL CARE AND COUNSELING (Comparative Terminology). In contemporary American usage, "pastoral care" usually refers, in a broad and inclusive way, to all pastoral work concerned with the support and nurturance of persons and interpersonal relationships, including everyday expressions of care and concern that may occur in the midst of various pastoring activities and relationships. "Pastoral counseling" refers to caring ministries that are more structured and focused on specifically articulated need or concern. Counseling always involves some degree of "contract" in which a request for help is articulated and specific arrangements are agreed upon concerning time and place of meeting; in extended counseling a fee may also be agreed upon, depending on the institutional setting and other considerations.

"Counseling" generally implies extended conversation focused on the needs and concerns of the one seeking help. "Care" in many of its expressions is also conversational, though briefer and less therapeutically complex than counseling, as in supportive or sustaining ministries like visiting the sick. The term is also applied to nonconversational ministries in which a significant caring dimension may be present, as in administering communion, conducting a funeral, or pastoral teaching.

In earlier, postwar pastoral literature, "care" and "counseling" were often used synonymously; their gradual distinction no doubt reflects the emergence of pastoral counseling as a specialized ministry. Today there is a question as to what extent, and in what respects, the general ministry of care should be guided by the methods and principles of specialized counseling, which have heavily influenced its modern development.

R. J. HUNTER

PRESENCE, MINISTRY OF. The ministry of presence has come to mean a form of servanthood (*diakonia*, ministry) characterized by suffering alongside of and with the hurt and oppressed—a *being*, rather than a doing or a telling. The articulation or celebration of faith goes on within the individual or community that chooses these circumstances, but does so in the form of *disciplina arcani*, the "hidden discipline," with no program of external testimony. Further, Christian presence is sometimes contrasted to Christian social action—suffering with the victim rather than seeking to alter the circumstances by systemic change. However, there are examples of the fusion of the ministries of presence and action, and also proclamation, as in the Taizé Community.

The ministry of Christian presence is grounded in the doctrine of the Incarnation, sometimes in its kenotic form, and/or in the doctrine of the Atonement, especially the priestly office. The identification of the ministrant with the condition of those in need is viewed as a continuation of the ministry of Christ who "emptied himself, taking the form of a servant...and became obedient unto death" (Phil. 2:7a-8a). This ministry of participation follows that of Christ, who "partook of the same nature, that through death he might...be made like his brethren in every respect, so that he might become a merciful and faithful high priest in the service of God.... For because he himself has suffered and been tempted, he is able to help those who are tempted" (Heb. 2:14a, 17a, 18). The ministry of presence can be voluntary or involuntary, as when verbal proclamation in the public sector is forbidden.

The ministry of presence in the pastoral office means vulnerability to and participation in the life-world of those served. The sharing of existence, satisfactions, and burdens may take the specific form of silent witness, as in the vicarious involvement of the counselor in the joys and pains of the counselee, or the change agent in the circumstances of the victim of poverty and injustice.

Another usage of the phrase is appearing in movements encouraging the ministry of the laity. Here Christian presence refers to the exercise of ministry by the people of God in the secular world, preeminently the workplace. Just as the clergy continue the prophetic, priestly, and royal work of Christ in their preaching and teaching, liturgical and pastoral acts, and leadership role in the church, so the laity carry forward this "threefold office" in the secular setting by their solidarity with the needs therein and their ministry of deeds thereto (not precluding, however, a verbal witness when appropriate). In counseling, for example, exponents of the ministry of the laity would view the arena of secular therapy as an opportunity for the continuation of Christ's priestly work through a lay ministry of presence, complementary to the pastoral exercise of the priestly office in the church.

Bibliography. G. Fackre, "Ministries of Identity and Vitality," *Theology Today* 36 (1979), 375–82. J. F. Six, ed., *Spiritual Autobiography of Charles de Foucauld*, J. H. Smith, trans. (1964). J. V. Taylor, *The Go-Between God* (1973). B. B. Zikmund, "Christian Vocation—in Context," *Theology Today* 36 (1979), 328–37.

G. FACKRE

PRESENTING PROBLEM. Refers to the originally stated concern that the parishioner or counselee brings to the pastor. There may be a deeper or more important issue related to the presenting problem, but pastoral responsibility requires that a careful and understanding hearing be given to the presenting problem, even when the pastor suspects that there is a more important concern.

J. PATTON

PSYCHOPHYSIOLOGICAL THERAPY. A term used to describe therapeutic modalities whose underlying theories are based on the interactive and reciprocal relationship between the psychological and physiological in both symptom formation and the capacity of the human brain-body to heal. The psychophysiological therapies are informed by Western, Eastern, and Native American medicine and meditative traditions; ethological observation; interpersonal neurobiology; adjunctive somatic therapies; and traditional forms of psychotherapy. Most are supported by an expanding body of research. Other terms used to describe these modalities include *Somatic Psychotherapy* and *Mind-Body Therapy*.

Psychophysiological therapies occur in the context of an interpersonal therapeutic relationship. Their goal is the client's deepest psychological *and* physical healing, sense of wholeness, and ability to function well in relational, vocational, and practical areas of life. Issues of faith and spirituality often emerge spontaneously in these therapies, and tend to elicit a maturing of the client's faith commitments. While all psychophysiological therapies may be used adjunctively, some have developed into comprehensive treatment approaches.

The following psychophysiological therapies may be of particular interest to pastoral counselors and caregivers:

1. Sensorimotor Psychotherapy (SP). Developed in the 1980s by Pat Ogden and evolving since then, SP intentionally integrates psychotherapy and body-therapy. It helps clients stabilize, release, and heal the physiological symptoms of trauma, attachment failure, grief and loss, and developmental arrest by using a wide range of somatic interventions woven seamlessly into the psychotherapeutic process. Sensorimotor psychotherapy emphasizes the need of the client to maintain a neurophysiological "window of tolerance" (Siegel in Ogden, Minton, and Pain, 2006) between hyper- and hypoarousal of the nervous system, in order for verbal interventions to be effective. Sensorimotor psychotherapy uses both "top-down" (cognition initiated) and "bottom-up" (sensory initiated) interventions in order to help the client maintain and expand that window. It also stresses the role of physical movement, stillness, and collapse in symptom formation, and therapeutic use of both physical movement and stillness in the healing process.

Sensorimotor psychotherapy uses a three-phase treatment approach: (1) development of somatic resources for stabilization; (2) trauma processing, primarily through the implicit memory systems; and (3) integration and success in normal life. In phase 1, the therapist assesses the client's physical being and teaches the client cognitive and somatic techniques for affect and arousal regulation. In phase 2, trauma and its effects are processed. If the client's emotional and physiological arousal level begins to move outside the window of tolerance, the therapist may instruct the client to "drop the content/emotion" and stay in the "here and now" of the body sensation. Processing is slow, and likely to proceed in micro-movements as body sensations lead the way to more positive cognitions and a sense of the event being in the past. In phase 3, the client addresses issues of daily living that arise in the absence of direct trauma symptoms by tracking and studying emergent micro-movements of the body, with positive shifts in cognition and affect arising out of the work.

2. Eye Movement Desensitization and Reprocessing (EMDR). Discovered and developed in 1987 by Francine Shapiro, EMDR is based on an adaptive information-processing model, which posits that most pathology emerges from the impact of earlier life events "held in the nervous system in state specific form" (F. Shapiro, 2001), and blocking the brain-body's natural and adaptive capacity to process sensory experiences from the environment, and from the body itself. Eye Movement Desensitization and Reprocessing is hypothesized to remove these blocks and to engage the body's innate healing processes. Neurobiologically, EMDR's effectiveness is speculated to be related to an activation of areas of the thalamus impaired by trauma, that activation resulting in a resumption of normal thalamus-cortical functioning and repaired neural integration (Bergmann, 2008).

Eye Movement Desensitization and Reprocessing can be used with people of all ages; rapid healing effects with children have been noted. Eye Movement Desensitization and Reprocessing is recognized by the American Psychological Association and the U.S. Department of Defense as an effective treatment for post-traumatic stress disorder. It is also effective in treating many other conditions, including anxiety, depression, phobias, eating disorders, and addictions (F. Shapiro, 2001; R. Shapiro, 2005, 2009).

Eye Movement Desensitization and Reprocessing uses an eight-phase protocol within a three-pronged structure (past, present, future). Central to the EMDR treatment process are (1) the use of alternating ("right-left") bilateral stimulation (BLS) of the brain through sensory means, such as eye movements, from which the therapy derives its name; and (2) the client maintaining dual attention between the issue being addressed and the present setting of the therapy and relationship with the therapist. Other forms of BLS include sounds moving from ear to ear, and tapping or pressing gently on the client's hands, in an alternating manner. The protocol elicits images, negative and desired positive self-cognitions, current emotional responses and their felt sense in the body, and assesses the client's degree of distress; BLS is then begun. Processing continues until the client has no felt sense of distress and the positive cognition is felt to be true. Completion of processing is evaluated in a future session.

3. Brainspotting. Brainspotting was discovered and developed in 2003 by David Grand, who explored reflexive movements and other irregularities occurring in eye movement BLS by having clients hold their eyes in the particular location of the irregularity. He and his clients noted profound, deep, rapid, and positive results. Grand hypothesizes that Brainspotting may stimulate the processing of disturbing material at a core reflexive or cellular level in the nervous system, while simultaneously activating the body's innate healing and self-integrative capacity. Brainspotting is appropriate for people of all ages; remarkably rapid effects have been noted with children and adolescents. A wide range of psychophysiological conditions can be treated effectively with Brainspotting, in a variety of settings of care.

In Brainspotting, one or more specific eye positions are located, with one or both eyes, in relation to the client's felt sense of distress. This may be done by the therapist initiating various eye movements and noting the reflexive movements and/or tracking irregularities of the client, or by the therapist and client together in a collaborative process of exploring the client's three-dimensional visual field. A "Brainspot" is defined as the neurophysiological system, identified through the client's eye position, in which the client's disturbing experience is held. This system is hypothesized to be located in the amygdala, the hippocampus, and/or the orbitofrontal cortex of the limbic system (Grand, 2009).

When the Brainspot is identified, the client holds her or his gaze on that spot in the visual field while silently focusing mental attention on the somatic and/or sensory experience of the issue, symptom, or problem being addressed. Guided by the client's reflexive movements, the therapist periodically asks for the client's report of what is being experienced, with particular attention paid to the client's bodily sensations. Processing continues until the client no longer experiences distress on each Brainspot identified in relation to the issue. This is hypothesized as indicating a down-regulation of the amygdala and a restored homeostasis of the nervous system (Scaer in Grand, 2009).

Brainspotting is also used to identify, access, and develop the client's internal resources, and to enhance the client's positively "felt" experiences. Resource Brainspots provide therapist and client with a means to moderate the intensity of the healing process to that which the client can safely manage. The effectiveness of Brainspotting may be enhanced with the use of bilateral sound stimulation provided by BioLateral Sound CDs.

Additional psychophysiological therapeutic modalities of note include Pesso-Boyden System Psychomotor, Somatic Experiencing, Eye Movement Integration, and Somatic Archaeology.

Bibliography. U. Bergmann, "The Neurobiology of EMDR: Exploring the Thalamus and Neural Integration," in *Journal of EMDR Practice and Research* 2(4) (2008). R. Gibson, *My Body, My Earth* (2008). D. Grand, *Brainspotting Training Manuals* (2005–9); *Emotional Healing at Warp Speed: The Power of EMDR* (2001); "What Is Brainspotting?" www.brainspotting.pro (2009). P. Levine with A. Frederick, *Waking the Tiger: Healing Trauma* (1997). P. Ogden, K. Minton, and C. Pain, *Trauma and the Body: A Sensorimotor Approach to Psychotherapy* (2006). A. Pesso and J. Crandell, *Moving Psychotherapy* (1991). S. Pinco, *Is It the Talking That Cures?* (2008). F. Shapiro, *Eye Movement Desensitization and Reprocessing: Basic Principles, Protocols, and Procedures*, 2nd ed. (2001). R. Shapiro, *EMDR Solutions I* and *II* (2005, 2009). D. Siegel, *The Mindful Brain* (2007).

M. S. JACOBI

RATIONAL-EMOTIVE PSYCHOTHERAPY. One of the best-known cognitive therapies, in which irrational ideas are considered to be the cause of emotional disturbance. Originated by Albert Ellis, rational-emotive psychotherapy (RET) shares with other cognitive therapies the assumption that maladaptive feelings are often caused by maladaptive thoughts. However, RET helps individuals challenge the core of irrational ideas that all troubled individuals are assumed to hold, whereas other cognitive therapies focus on an individual's idiosyncratic thought patterns.

L. R. PROPST

SHAMAN. A specialist in the well-being of the human soul who restores and maintains its health by means of archaic techniques of ecstasy.

Through ecstatic experiences the shaman can "see" the soul's wanderings, and by means of magical techniques is able to recover it when it has been stolen or lost.

In the strict sense, shamanism is a religious phenomenon of Siberia and Central Asia, where ecstatic experiences and soul restoration are considered to be central religious rituals. By cultural diffusion, it came to be one of the dominant religious expressions, if not *the* dominant religious expression, among the Eskimo of Asia and North America, among many of the North and South American Indians, and among certain peoples in Tibet and China. Similar phenomena are found in Southeast Asia and Oceania.

Shamanism is commonly associated with a religious worldview in which there are several cosmic regions. The shaman knows the mysteries that enable him or her to break through from one such plane to another in pursuit of the soul—from the earth to the sky or to the underworld. This the shaman does by passing through an opening found in central sacred places associated with such symbols as a cosmic mountain, world tree, or central pole.

Both men and women may be shamans. The chief methods of their recruitment are heredity or special calling. The validation of their new status as a person "chosen by the spirits" comes through an ecstatic experience that involves their suffering, "death," and "resurrection." Commonly this takes the form of an illness that brings the novice close to death, followed by an encounter with a spirit and a miraculous healing. In other cases, the initial ecstatic experience may be sought by means of a quest involving a period of seclusion in the wilderness, a symbolic burial and descent into the underworld, ordeals, or drug-induced hypnotic sleep. Through this encounter the shaman acquires a tutelary spirit, and knows that he or she has been "called" for the new office.

Through the initiation the shaman acquires the ability to have immediate concrete experiences with spirits and gods. Since the shaman's soul can safely abandon its body during an ecstatic rite, the shaman can enter their world and talk with them face-to-face. Because the soul is seen as a precarious psychic unit that is inclined to leave the body, it is an easy prey for demons and sorcerers. The resulting soul loss leads to illness and even death. In his or her ecstatic state, the shaman diagnoses the case, goes in search of the patient's soul, captures it, and returns it to animate the body it has left. If the shaman finds it near the village, its retrieval is easy, but if it is at the bottom of the sea, or in the realm of the dead, the shaman must make a dangerous and exhausting journey with the aid of the tutelary spirit to retrieve it. When death occurs, it is the shaman who conducts the soul safely to the underworld.

Bibliography. M. Eliade, *Shamanism: Archaic Techniques of Ecstasy* (1964). I. M. Lewis, *Ecstatic Religion: A Study of Shamanism and Spirit Possession* (1989). J. McCown, "Shamanism: The Art of Ecstasy," *Encounter* 39 (1978), 435–46.

P. HIEBERT

SOUL. Term referring to the spiritual side of human existence. It indicates both the life principle that animates the body and the individuality of the person as expressed in thought, will, and emotion. Soul is, thus, the seat of human activity and the source of moral judgment.

1. Biblical Usage. The scriptural view of human nature points away from a radical body-soul dualism toward a "psychosomatic unity." Nevertheless, the human being is a creature of polarities! The imagery of the OT can describe clay animated by "breath" (*ruah*) and can term the nonphysical pole of humanity "spirit" (*nephesh*). The *nephesh* can be described as going down to Sheol or Hades upon the death of the person; those in Sheol are "shades" (*rephaim*). *Nephesh* can also, by extension, refer to the whole person. The OT presents a fairly clear picture of the human being as an animated being, an embodied life. That the OT contains a holistic anthropology but equally a sense of physical-spiritual polarity is seen from passages like Ezekiel 37, where bones and flesh come together but live only when the animating *ruah* comes upon them. *Ruah* tends to indicate the animating principle, *nephesh* the animated being.

In the intertestamental literature a sense of duality is reinforced. The Wisdom of Solomon in particular argues the distinction of soul and body as well as the preexistence and immortality of souls (2:23; 3:1-4; 7:17, 20; 8:20). This is usually viewed as the result of Greek influence upon Hebrew thought, but it is also the result of a meditation on the problem of *rephaim* in Sheol and the presence, even there, of God (cf. Pss. 86:13; 139:8; Prov. 15:11).

The NT turns still more clearly toward the Greek usage of "body and soul" (*soma* and *psyche*) but also uses the more Hebraic phrases "flesh and spirit" (*sarx* and *pneuma*) or "body and spirit" (*soma* and *pneuma*). The dualistic direction of the intertestamental literature has, however, been arrested and the NT points toward the human being as a unity: redemption does not refer to soul as abstracted from body but to the whole person. In many instances psyche indicates "life," or the human person, rather than "soul" (cf. Mt. 6:25; Mk. 3:4; 8:35-37), while the more Greek meaning "soul," appears in Rev. 6:9. There is no indication in the NT that the soul or "life" escapes by nature the corruptibility of the body. Immortality of soul rests, like resurrection of the body, on God. There is no implication, moreover, of a trichotomous humanity composed of body, soul, and spirit in the NT: the human being is a unified, though bipolar, being, an embodied life.

2. Soul in Greek Philosophy. The more detailed speculation concerning soul that influenced the development of Christian thought came from the Greeks. We note two basic positions: the Platonic, which was most influential during the patristic period, and the Aristotelian, which shaped later medieval theology. Plato, drawing both on Socrates and on Orphic theology with its doctrine of the immortality of the soul, taught that human beings were composed of body and soul, the latter being the immaterial guide or ruler of the body. Soul, or psyche, consisted in the rational function, the moral courage, and the appetites or affections with only the rational function being immortal. This essentially dualistic sense of body and soul carries over from Plato into Neoplatonism, the church fathers, and (in modern philosophy) the Cartesians. The tendency in all these thinkers was to identify soul with mind and its functions.

Aristotle offers a radically different perspective: he viewed the human being as a composite and identified psyche as the animating principle, the consciousness and life of the body. The soul, thus, is immaterial or spiritual. In contrast to Plato, however, no dualism of body and soul is implied: the body is the matter of which the soul is the form. Soul is the real "substance," the formal principle, the source of physical motion, and the final cause or inward goal-regulator (*entelechy*) of the body. In the case of humans, the soul is also the intellectual or rational function of the individual.

Neither the biblical writers nor the Greek philosophers will permit the view of soul as mere epiphenomenon of the body. Soul is a spiritual, immaterial reality that is essentially simple and indivisible, identifiable with the life of the human being and the intellectual functions. It need not be located at any point in the body since it is the life or, for Aristotle, the form of the body.

3. Soul in the History of Christian Thought. The fathers of the first five centuries of the Common Era recognized three theories of the origin of the soul: preexistence, creationism, and traducianism. The first is essentially

Platonic. The soul, as a spiritual substance neither created nor destroyed, preexists the created body and must be embodied—perhaps because of a premundane fall of souls from divine perfection. This view, as denying the doctrine of creation *ex nihilo,* was rejected by all but the most platonizing of the fathers (e.g., Origen). The majority were creationists, arguing that souls are created by God for bodies and are joined with the body at conception. A smaller number, including Tertullian, held that the soul, like the body, is inherited from the parents: this view is termed traducianism. In both of these latter views, the Platonic dualism of body and soul is modified in favor of a view approaching that of Scripture.

If the fathers believed in the separation of body and soul at death, they viewed this as unnatural, as the result of sin, and they held to the doctrine of the Resurrection as descriptive of the destiny intended by God for humanity: both body and soul were destined for immortality since the person functions as a living whole. This latter point is particularly dear in the thought of Justin Martyr, Athenagoras, Tertullian, and Augustine. In addition to their modification of Platonism, the fathers must also be credited with the addition of a strong emphasis on the faculty of will to the doctrine of soul.

In the Middle Ages, after the rediscovery of Aristotle and the incorporation of Aristotelian thought into Christian philosophy by Thomas Aquinas, the Aristotelian notion of soul as *entelechy* prevailed over the Platonic position, and the view of the human being as a living unity received a powerful philosophical impetus. The creationist view of the origin of soul became normative in Roman Catholicism and among the Reformed at the time of the Reformation, while the traducian position was favored by Lutheranism. Return to an essentially dualistic view occurs in the thought of Descartes, who identified soul with thought and body with "extension." The great philosophical problem faced by Cartesianism, and one of the reasons that Descartes' philosophy was not readily accepted by theologians, was the difficulty it encountered in explaining the interaction of body and soul.

A renewed interest in "soul" is manifest in nineteenth-century German philosophy and theology, together with a preference for trichotomy on the part of authors like Lotze and Delitzsch. A distinction is here made between soul (*psyche, Seele*) and spirit (*pneuma, Geist*), according to which spirit is a higher principle than soul; soul is merely the life principle, spirit is the "unity of our being," or our "ego." This form of trichotomy does not, therefore, deny but rather presses the unity of the per-son under the three forms of body, soul, and spirit. The importance of this philosophical development for theology, philosophy, and the new disci-pline of psychology is that, for the first time in the history of thought, it identifies fully the issue of an ego, of the individual as conscious self, and maintains the polarity of the human being as a psychosomatic unity that cannot simply be reduced to protoplasm and its functions. Soul and spirit now become the seat of personality as well as the locus of intellect, will, and affections.

The concepts of ego and self deriving from this philosophic history have been widely employed in certain branches of modern psychology (especially psychoanalysis and humanistic psychology), but "soul" has been almost universally rejected with the primary exception of Carl Jung and his school. Jung disavowed the religious and the philosophical mean-ings that "soul" has had in the West, which he regarded as projections, but found the term psychologically valuable and often employed it. His intent was to assert the nonreductive reality and mystery of psychic life, especially the unconscious, against the materialistic and rationalist spirit of modern psychology. He also made a technical distinction in some writ-ings between soul, as a "soul-complex" in the unconscious (related to the *anima*), and *psyche*, the latter referring to the whole of psychic life (Jung, 1953, 201).

In modern clinical pastoral care and counseling and pastoral theology, "soul" has also been generally replaced by the more psychological "ego" and "self," though the growing influence of Jung's psychology may lead to a recovery of its use and importance. From a more psychoanalytic and theological perspective, Charles V. Gerkin (1984, ch. 5) has proposed a revised concept of soul, similar to the modern concept of spirit, related to hermeneutical process.

Bibliography. G. C. Berkouwer, *Man: The Image of God* (1962). G. S. Brett, *The History of Psychology*, 3 vols. (1912–21); abr. ed., 1 vol. (1965). C. Brown, "Soul/Spirit," in *New International Dictionary of New Testament Theology* 3, 676–709. F. Copleston, *A History of Philosophy*, 9 vols. (1946–74). F. Delitzsch, *Biblical Psychology* (1875). R. K. Fenn and D. Capps, eds., *On Losing the Soul* (1995). C. V. Gerkin, *The Living Human Document* (1984). C. G. Jung, *Two Essays in Analytical Psychology* (1953). H. W. Robinson, *The Christian Doctrine of Man*, 3rd ed. (1926). E. Rohde, *Psyche: The Cult of Souls and Belief in Immortality* *among the Greeks* (1925). R. Seeberg, *Text-Book of the History of Doctrines*, ET, C. Hay (1956).

R. A. MULLER

TOUCHING/PHYSICAL SUPPORT. *Touching* is physical contact between persons, usually for the purpose of communicating positive attitudes, values, and intentions toward the person touched. *Physical support* may be alternately defined as: (1) an expanded form of touching expressed in carrying, embracing, assisting, or holding; or (2) the provision of material resources such as money, food, shelter, and clothing to persons in need.

Developmental studies of infancy and childhood clearly demonstrate the importance of reliable touching and physical support on the part of the caretaker as a basis for trust in the goodness of life, and for the capacity to love and to hope for a meaningful future. In some cases, physical survival itself depends upon the satisfactory experience of touching and physical support. There is evidence that even for adults the lack of human companionship and its expression in touching may contribute significantly to the onset of life-threatening illness, while the presence of touch and physical support may contribute positively to human health and to the recovery of the sick.

The therapeutic use of touch is disputed. Some dismiss it because it fosters inappropriate dependencies, sexual expectations, and magical thinking such as that connected with certain forms of faith healing. Others see it as central to the therapy process, regarding it as an important means to establish rapport, communicate acceptance, overcome repressions, and promote self-disclosure and openness to therapeutic exploration.

Pastoral care draws heavily upon touching and physical support in ministering to persons suffering from major material and interpersonal losses, acute anxiety and depression, and serious illness. By these and other means, pastoral care transcends an exclusive reliance upon the written and spoken Word in making present and furthering a sense of hope and of God's providence, by which a capacity to love and certain forms of healing and religious fellowship may emerge.

Guidelines for the pastoral use of touching include awareness of the purpose for which the touching is intended, naturalness of expression, responsiveness to the community standards in which touching occurs, freedom to refuse touching and to allow touching to be refused or discontinued, exploration of the meaning of touching (or not touching) to the parishioner, chastity and emotional fidelity to primary relational commitments, and public accountability.

Bibliography. J. J. Lynch, *The Broken Heart: The Medical Consequences of Loneliness* (1977). E. E. Mintz, "On the Rationale of Touch in Psychotherapy," *Psychotherapy: Theory, Research and Practice* 6 (1969), 232–34. J. Pattison, "Effects of Touch on Self-Exploration and the Therapeutic Relationship," *J. of Consulting and Clinical Psychology* 40 (1973), 2:170–75.

L. K. GRAHAM

VERBATIM. A document, written from memory, recording a conversation in approximately the dialogical form in which it occurred. Typically a verbatim also includes: (1) description of the setting, the persons involved, and the expectations for the conversation; (2) the dialogue; and (3) reflection on the relationship. Current usage identifies a product, "the verbatim," but early usage recognized a process synonymous with Cabot and Dicks's "note-writing": "verbatim recording of visits" or "recording of direct discourse as it took place during the call" (Guiles, 1945).

Akin to the data employed in clinical-pathological conferences in medicine, verbatims are the characteristic learning instruments of clinical pastoral education and of much contemporary pastoral theology (theological reflection on pastoral acts; Hiltner, 1958) and pastoral psychology. Throughout the world, nascent pastoral care movements have employed collections of verbatims to display and interpret the new pastoral care.

Russell Dicks initiated modern verbatim-writing, making notes on his pastoral calls and recording his prayers. According to A. P. Guiles, Dicks introduced it into pastoral education, its current *Sitz im Leben,* to solve a problem: "The student's description of his calls failed to preserve the overtones and undertones, the veiled emotion or intentions of the patient, a sort of double-talk, which was fully as significant as the patient's outright pronouncements" (1945, 47). By 1945 "note-writing" had become part of the standards of clinical pastoral training (57).

Audio and video recording provide closer access to the nuances of live caregiving and to the complexities of systems, yet verbatims remain ideal for brief or public encounters or for situations that discourage technological recording. Although verbatims bring the frustrations of incompleteness and inaccuracy, they teach students that they can learn from what they imperfectly remember. In fact, one pillar of contemporary pastoral care is the study of incomplete and partially distorted memories of pastoral caregiving.

Verbatims disclose not only the pastoral partner but also the pastor. In verbatims, students reveal their problems in caregiving. Verbatims produce anxiety, particularly about self-exposure; hence the eye of a censor, not altogether unconscious, guides discourse-recording. Nevertheless, verbatims are like expressionistic paintings, which reveal how painters have experienced themselves and their world (Zijlstra, 1971, 40). In verbatim-writing, Cabot and Dicks (1936) identify some of the moral rigor and low-keyed spirituality of modern pastoral care, calling verbatim-writing self-criticism, self-revelation, preparation for self-improvement, meditation made effective, and sometimes prayer—noting that writing entails "new acts of forgiveness, of one-hundred-percent veracity with ourselves."

Bibliography. R. Burck, "Pastoral Expressionism: Verbatims in the Pastoral Paradigm," *J. of Supervision and Training in Ministry* 3 (1980), 39–56. R. C. Cabot and R. L. Dicks, *The Art of Ministering to the Sick* (1936), 24–61. A. P. Guiles, in S. Hiltner, ed., *Clinical Pastoral Training* (1945), 47–57. S. Hiltner, *Preface to Pastoral Theology* (1958). W. Zijlstra, *Seelsorge-Training—Clinical Pastoral Training* (1971).

J. R. BURCK

2

HISTORY AND BIOGRAPHY

Knowing the religious and theological history of pastoral care and counseling is essential to understanding its method and identity in the contemporary interdisciplinary world. Pastoral care and counseling has a long history that is rooted in ancient biblical faith and tradition. Following are articles that spell out the significant people, traditions, and practices that built the foundational "root system" of pastoral care and counseling. An important addition to this collection of articles is a brief analysis of "Pastoral Care and Counseling in a Postmodern Context," which completes the story of the philosophical and methodological influences on pastoral care and counseling from the first edition of the *DPCC* (1990) up to the present (2010) time.

AMBROSE OF MILAN, ST. (ca. 339–97). Roman Catholic bishop of Milan, Italy; one of the great church fathers.

Pastoral care permeated the life, works, and ministry of Ambrose in many ways, perhaps best summarized with five modern regions of pastoral care: (1) *counseling and soulcare* for the bereaved and mourning, the misguided, those seeking perfection, the virgins dedicated to God; (2) *worship and homiletics*: lively and inspiring, singing-oriented services; well-crafted, Bible-based preaching; (3) *outreach/social ministry*: giving funds (including his personal wealth) to the poor, special care for the helpless, patron of the orphans; (4) *pastoral care and ethics*: criticizing the excesses of the upper classes, holding the state morally accountable; insisting on separation between church and state, submission of state to church in matters of faith; practical application of morality; stress of four virtues; and (5) *congregational ministry*: a strong emphasis on a sense of community among believers, care of the common good against trouble-makers, assistance to the needy, affirmation of good members.

N. F. HAHN

BAXTER, RICHARD (1615–91). English Presbyterian divine, famed for his innovative pastoral work in the parish of Kidderminster, Worcestershire. Baxter's fame as a pastoral writer rests largely on his *Gildas Salvianus*, or *The Reformed Pastor* (1656). The book described in detail the public duties of pastors—preaching, discipline, and the administering of the sacraments—and exhorted the clergy to lead exemplary lives of faithfulness and humility. But Baxter's primary interest was in persuading English pastors to devote more of their time to "private conference," the instruction of families, and the teaching of the catechism. It was through such methods that he transformed his Kidderminster parish during his ministry of fourteen years there.

He wrote voluminously, producing treatises on such varied pastoral topics as meditation, patience, preparation for the sacrament, sickness, melancholy, assurance, joy, and death. He once said that his own bodily weakness and pain prompted him to study how to die—and hence how to live. His classic devotional treatise, *The Saints' Everlasting Rest* (1650), provides a distinctive insight into seventeenth-century Puritan attitudes toward death and dying.

His contention that the main part of pastoral care consists of teaching and guidance within a local church—and that pastors must "take heed to themselves" before they attempt such a task—has deeply influenced Protestant conceptions of ministry.

E. B. HOLIFIELD

BLANTON, SMILEY (1882–1966). American psychiatrist. Blanton's chief contribution to pastoral care and counseling was his service as director of the American Foundation of Religion and Psychiatry, which was affiliated with the Marble Collegiate Church in New York City. Having long wished to create a training center for clergy, he joined with Norman Vincent Peale in 1937 to establish a psychiatric clinic as a free service of the church, and with the aid of Frederick Kuether, a minister of the Evangelical and Reformed Church, he and Peale expanded the clinic in 1953 into a foundation that offered psychiatric services and Clinical Pastoral Education (CPE).

Though he was associated by the public with Peale's ideas about positive thinking, Blanton was a Freudian therapist who had studied with Freud and been psychoanalyzed by him in Vienna. A graduate of Vanderbilt University and Cornell Medical School, he studied at the Royal College of Physicians and Surgeons in London and completed a residency in psychiatry under Adolph Meyer at Johns Hopkins before serving as a psychiatrist for the U.S. Army during World War I. After teaching speech and mental hygiene for ten years at the University of Wisconsin, he organized the Minneapolis Child Guidance Clinic and taught psychiatry at the University of Minnesota Medical School. He was forty-seven when he went to Vienna to study with Freud, in search of therapeutic aids for stutterers. He was on the faculty at Cornell when Peale sought his guidance about counseling. They subsequently published *Faith Is the Answer* (1940), the book that helped launch Peale's public career. Blanton's *Love or Perish* reflected his distinctive merging of suggestive therapy and Freudian analytic ideas.

E. B. HOLIFIELD

BOISEN, ANTON (1876–1965). Founder of clinical pastoral training for ministers and theological students. After graduating from Union Theological Seminary, Boisen served as a Presbyterian minister in rural parishes, a member of the YMCA Expeditionary Force, and supervisor of the rural survey of the Interchurch World Movement, before becoming the chaplain at Worcester State Hospital in Massachusetts and Elgin State Hospital in Illinois. During those years, he also earned a master's degree at Harvard and studied under Macfie Campbell at the Boston Psychopathic Hospital. He lectured for two years at the Boston University School of Theology and for fifteen years at Chicago Theological Seminary.

Boisen is revered as the chief founder of Clinical Pastoral Education (CPE)—a program of professional training through the long-term supervised encounter of ministers and theological students with men and women in crises in hospitals, prisons, and social agencies. After conversations with Richard Cabot, with whom he had studied social ethics at Harvard and from whom he learned the value of the firsthand study of "cases," he established the first clinical group in 1925 at Worcester State Hospital. In 1930, he and Cabot joined with others in the formation of the Council for the Clinical Training of Theological Students.

In his clinical teaching, Boisen hoped to lead students toward deeper theological insight by teaching them to view the patients in the mental hospital as "living human documents" whose pain and healing could illuminate the nature of religious experience. In his book *The Exploration of the Inner World* (1936), he argued that emotional collapse is a chaotic encounter with God that could lead either to a new integration of the personality or to a fall into total inner disarray. He thought that certain forms of mental illness manifested the existence of a "power that makes for health," immanent within the purposive movement of the natural order. His autobiography, *Out of the Depths* (1960), revealed with scrupulous honesty his attempt to interpret and learn from his own episodes of mental illness.

A student of George Albert Coe, Boisen was concerned with what he called "the basic psychology of religion," and he thought that the mental hospital offered a setting in which to study, firsthand, "the problem of sin and salvation." His interest in turbulence and chaos within the personality deeply informed the methods and presuppositions of the Council for Clinical Training. Coe's teaching also directed Boisen's attention to the social nature of religion, and he eventually adopted Josiah Royce's notion of loyalty, which he interpreted with the aid of George Herbert Mead's descriptions of the way we form our conscience by internalizing social standards. Boisen believed that mental illness exposed the failure to grow into higher social loyalties, as well as the effort to transcend that failure. He found the insights of Freud to be useful but excessively narrow; he distrusted the effort to locate the source of mental illness primarily in childhood experiences, and he disliked any use of psychological theory that minimized the importance of ethical ideals. He also felt uneasy when the clinical traditions seemed to turn their attention to the psychological dynamics and therapeutic needs of the students themselves, insofar as that detracted from the primary task of achieving greater theological understanding.

Boisen knew Elwood Worcester at the Emmanuel Church in Boston, and his work represented in part a point of continuity with the older Emmanuel Movement. But it was the depth and intensity of his own personality, as well as the force of his ideas, that ensured his profound influence on the Clinical Pastoral Education movement. His emphasis on the "living human document" has periodically reappeared as a guiding theme for clinical supervisors and Protestant pastoral theologians.

Bibliography. A. T. Boisen, *Out of the Depths* (1960).

E. B. HOLIFIELD

BONNELL, JOHN SUTHERLAND (1893–1992). Presbyterian pastor and pastoral theologian. As the pastor of the Fifth Avenue Presbyterian Church in New York City, Bonnell (1938) proposed that pastors become adept in "pastoral psychiatry," which he defined as a ministry directed to the "healing of the soul." He believed that the goal of pastoral counseling was to bring the parishioner in touch with God and the spiritual resources that flowed from God. Impressed by his father's vocation as a staff member of the Falconwood Hospital on Prince Edward Island, Bonnell familiarized himself with the work of the European therapists, especially Alfred Adler and Karen Horney, and in 1935 began a counseling program at his Fifth Avenue Church. In his *Pastoral Psychiatry* and other, similar works, he drew on the theme of "adjustment" in order to develop a method of counseling that reflected both psychological theory and a Christian theology.

Bibliography. J. S. Bonnell, *Pastoral Psychiatry* (1938).

E. B. HOLIFIELD

BUCER, MARTIN (1491–1551). German Protestant Reformer and pastor. His book, *Von der wahren Seelsorge*, contains the first biblically and theologically grounded theory of the care of souls. No longer is the care of souls determined by sacramental penance or aimed at comforting tempted consciences. Bucer's new key word is *improvement* (*Besserung*), his central theological image is the church as the body of Christ, and his intent is the establishment of Christ's reign in the church. This means the serious realization and earnest practice of Christianity in daily life, particularly in the care and concern of Christians for one another. Thus, each individual Christian is entitled, indeed obligated, to engage in the care of souls in a holistic fashion. To that end, Bucer combines the spiritual and the material, the ecclesial and the internal form of faith, addresses individuals as well as the faith community as a whole, upholds the law in its strictness while superseding it with the gospel. He combines toughness with consideration, a biblical basis with practical pastoral experience. He extends his pastoral concern to include soul care for "healthy" members of the community as well as for the poor and for the "heathens, Jews, and Turks" (Bucer, 1538).

Bibliography. M. Bucer, *Von der wahren Seelsorge* (1538).

N. F. HAHN

CABOT, RICHARD C. (1868–1939). American physician and ethicist. A hematologist and cardiologist at the Harvard Medical School, Cabot pioneered in the use of the case method and established the first clinical pathological conferences in medical education, founded Harvard's Department of Medical Social Work, and assisted in the early development of Clinical Pastoral Education (CPE). After resigning his post at Massachusetts General Hospital in 1920, he taught social ethics at Harvard University and later at Andover Newton Theological Seminary.

Cabot's 1925 article "A Plea for a Clinical Year in the Course of Theological Study" helped stimulate interest in CPE, and he assisted Anton Boisen in the organization of the first clinical program, implemented at Worcester State Hospital. In 1930 he became a founder and first president of the Council for the Clinical Training of Theological Students; he also helped establish the Theological Schools' Committee on Clinical Training in 1938.

In 1936 Cabot and Russell Dicks published a book that helped to change the understanding of pastoral care in American Protestantism. *The Art of Ministering to the Sick* popularized Cabot's notion that creative listening by the minister could help patients discover the direction in which God—defined as "the power in ourselves that makes for health"—was leading them. By helping men and women discover their "growing edge," the minister could foster healing and health (Cabot and Dicks, 1936).

His ethical vision and clinical methods remained important in the Clinical Pastoral Education movement, especially at the Institute for Pastoral Care organized in Boston in 1944.

Bibliography. R. C. Cabot and R. Dicks, *The Art of Ministering to the Sick* (1936).

E. B. HOLIFIELD

CLINEBELL, HOWARD (1922–2005). An internationally recognized author, teacher, leader, pastor, counselor, supervisor, and consultant in the field of pastoral psychology. He was professor of pastoral psychology and counseling at the Claremont School of Theology. His major clinical and academic training was received at DePauw University (BA), Garrett Theological Seminary (BD), William A. White Institute (Certificate of Applied Psychiatry for Ministry), and Columbia University (PhD,

Psychology of Religion). He wrote or edited more than thirty books and fifty articles, several of these with his wife, Charlotte Ellen.

Clinebell profoundly shaped the growth of contemporary pastoral psychology. He was the first president of the American Association of Pastoral Counselors. His book *Basic Types of Pastoral Counseling* (1966, revised 1984), perhaps the most widely used seminary textbook for pastoral counseling in its time, helped to expand the scope of pastoral approaches from individual/intrapsychic dynamics and nondirective methods to a more inclusive focus on interpersonal dynamics and more directive human potentials approaches.

Clinebell's emphasis on human potential—the aspirations, possibilities, and strengths of the human soul and psyche—led him to develop a "Growth Counseling" approach to actualizing and liberating human life. In the field of pastoral psychotherapy, this "Growth Counseling" orientation has been one of the few to address human development in relation to feminist, social, political, and global consciousness-raising. Clinebell's lifestyle, as well as his pastoral theory, embodied a creative zest for embracing human thoughts, emotions, actions, spirituality, and relationships in a holistic way.

C. M. MENDENHALL III

COE, GEORGE ALBERT (1862–1951). American religious educator and psychologist of religion. A professor of religious education at Union Theological Seminary and Teachers' College, Columbia, Coe helped organize and direct the Religious Education Society of America.

Coe's efforts to appropriate the New Psychology for the churches contributed not only to a revised appraisal of the traditional Protestant Sunday school but also to a renewed appreciation for methods of pastoral care and counseling that were grounded in psychological research. His own research into the psychology of religion convinced him that the functionalists were right when they turned their attention from isolated states of consciousness to the interests and preferences of concrete persons. He believed, too, that such functional psychologists as John Dewey were correct when they argued that growth, occurring within a network of social relationships, was the highest ethical end. Hence he concluded that the aim of religious education was "the growth of the young toward and into mature and efficient devotion to the democracy of God, and happy self-realization therein" (*A Social Theory of Religious Education*, 1917, 55).

He believed that religious education was ideally a form of "social interaction" that would alter the individual's outlook toward the social good. He thought also that such a progressive conception of education had clear therapeutic implications. "Cooperative thinking" could release the personality from its self-imposed limitations by forming the "habit of being free and freely cooperative" (*The Motives of Men,* 1928, 209).

Such insights confirmed Coe's belief that the care of souls, like education itself, could become "a system of organized and proportioned methods based upon definite knowledge of the material to be wrought upon, the ends to be attained, and the means and instruments for attaining them" (*The Spiritual Life,* 1900, 21). It was no surprise that religious educators offered the first modern classes in pastoral counseling in the American Protestant seminaries.

Coe worked for a "scientific" understanding of pastoral care, a Sunday school informed by functional and developmental psychologies, and a recognition of the therapeutic capacities of free interchange within small and intimate groups. Many of his views failed to survive the neoorthodox revolt against liberalism in the early 1930s, but the Protestant pastoral care traditions in the United States remain indebted to some of his central insights.

Bibliography. G. A. Coe, *The Motives of Men* (1928); *A Social Theory of Religious Education* (1917); *The Spiritual Life* (1900), 21.

E. B. HOLIFIELD

DICKS, RUSSELL (1906–65). American pastoral theologian. A Methodist minister, Dicks served as a hospital chaplain at Massachusetts General Hospital and other hospitals, as well as a professor of pastoral care at Duke University Divinity School.

As one of the first chaplain supervisors of Clinical Pastoral Education (CPE) in a general hospital, Dicks pioneered in the supervisory use of written "verbatims"—word-for-word transcriptions—of pastoral conversations. He believed that study of the direct encounter between a student and a patient could reveal whether or not the student understood what was happening in the interchange. His method represented a departure from Anton Boisen's technique of having students in clinical settings write detailed case histories of the patient's physical and emotional development.

Dicks was a prolific writer, and in 1936 he and Richard Cabot published *The Art of Ministering to the Sick,* an influential study of the "directed listening" through which the minister could elicit in patients an awareness of the power within themselves that made for good health. In subsequent years, he wrote devotional material for the sick, along with numerous books on pastoral counseling. The analysis of pastoral conversations in his 1939 publication *And Ye Visited Me* popularized the use of verbatim material in textbooks on pastoral care. Dicks was active in the early development of the Institute of Pastoral Care, which was founded in Boston in 1944, and he also served for several years as the editor of the journal *Religion and Health*.

Dicks was important primarily because of his pioneering use of the verbatim transcript as an instrument of clinical supervision and as an illustrative device in textbooks on pastoral care and counseling.

E. B. HOLIFIELD

DUNBAR, HELEN FLANDERS (1902–59). Pioneer in psychosomatic medicine and a founder of Clinical Pastoral Education (CPE). A woman who dazzled many with her keen intelligence, academic degrees, driving ambition, formidable style, and beauty, Dunbar dropped her first name early in her career to mislead readers into thinking that she was male.

After her graduation from Bryn Mawr (1923), Dunbar earned an AM and PhD from Columbia (1924, 1929), a BD from Union Theological Seminary (1927), and an MD from Yale (1930). She managed simultaneous studies in philosophy, theology, and medicine by employing two secretaries. During her final year of medical school she assisted in clinics in Vienna and Zurich, and visited the shrine at Lourdes to observe the relation of faith to healing.

In 1925, the year that Anton Boisen began introducing clinical training for divinity students, Dunbar worked with him at the Worcester State Hospital. In 1930 she became director of the newly formed Council for the Clinical Training of Theological Students, and later hired Seward Hiltner as executive secretary. Under their leadership, clinical training became established in theological seminaries.

Dunbar is remembered chiefly for her work in psychosomatic medicine. She compiled a massive bibliography, *Emotions and Bodily Changes*, a standard reference work updated several times, and popularized her research in *Mind and Body* (1947) and other publications. Dunbar also founded the journal *Psychosomatic Medicine* (she served as editor-in-chief from 1938 to 1947), and the American Psychosomatic Society (1942).

Dunbar's first husband, Dr. Theodore Wolfe, brought orgone therapist Wilhelm Reich to America and was his English translator. Her second husband, George Henry Soule Jr., an editor of *The New Republic*, fathered her only child, born in 1941. In Dunbar's later years the quality of her work deteriorated as she relied on alcohol to deal with stress and emotional pain. Some interpreted her death by drowning as a suicide.

Bibliography. R. C. Powell, *Healing and Wholeness*, unpublished doctoral dissertation, Duke University (1974). A. Stokes, *Ministry after Freud* (1985).

A. STOKES

EMMANUEL MOVEMENT. An organization formed in 1904 with the general aim of bringing together the forces of medicine and religion to promote healing both mind and body under the conviction that Jesus Christ heals in the contemporary world as he did in NT times.

In 1904 Elwood Worcester, rector of the Emmanuel Episcopal Church in Boston, in cooperation with several prominent New England physicians, established a clinic for spiritual healing. The clinic's activities, housed in Worcester's church, were dubbed the "Emmanuel movement" by the press. Spectacular reports of healings drew national attention. In 1908 Worcester, in collaboration with his ministerial associate, the Reverend S. McComb, and Dr. I. Coriat, a prominent physician on the faculty of Tufts Medical School, published *Religion and Medicine*, a volume that set down clearly the philosophy undergirding the movement. The book drew mixed reviews, but its influence was enhanced when it was included in the Surgeon General's *Progress of Medicine during the Nineteenth Century*.

Unlike other healing cults of the time, the Emmanuel movement built on enlightened and sophisticated notions in both medicine and religion. Its approach to healing was based on four principles: (1) the person is a composite of mind and body; (2) religion should clearly and emphatically value the therapeutic efficacy of medical treatment of organic disorders; (3) the relation between organic and functional disorders should be a legitimate domain for spiritual healing; and (4) the contributions of the medical profession to health and welfare are in no sense to be minimized. As Worcester (1931) was later to summarize it: "What distinguishes this work from all healing cults...is its frank recognition of Religion and Science as the great controlling forces of human life and the attempt to bring these two highest creations of man into relations of helpful cooperation."

Despite these serious intentions to relate high scholarship in both medicine and religion to the area of praxis, the movement was sputtering by the early 1930s and dead by 1940. Edward Thornton (1970) suggests three reasons for the movement's demise: (1) it failed to train ministers; (2) Worcester did not himself grow and change with the rapid developments in psychiatry; and (3) the relationships between physicians and clergy, integral to the movement, broke down.

As an item in the history of the medicine-religion dialogue, the Emmanuel movement holds a minor but nevertheless important place, particularly in the development of holistic tendencies in medicine and health care. Perhaps of equal significance, from the perspectives of the pastoral care and counseling movements, were its spin-offs in regard to later developments in the mental hygiene movement, the hospital care offered by chaplains, and the establishment of Clinical Pastoral Education (CPE) as a part of theological education.

Bibliography. C. J. Scherzer, "The Emmanuel Movement," *Pastoral Psychology* (1951), 27–33. E. E. Thornton, *Professional Education for Ministry* (1970). E. Worcester and S. McComb, *Body, Mind and Spirit* (1931). E. Worcester, S. McComb, and I. Coriat, *Religion and Medicine* (1908).

O. STRUNK JR.

GUILES, AUSTIN PHILIP (1894–1953). American theological educator. He assumed a leading role in the formation of the Council for Clinical Training of Theological Students (1930), the New England Theological Schools Committee on Clinical Training (1938), and the Institute of Pastoral Care (1944).

Envisioning clinical training as a discipline to produce professional competence, Guiles argued that clinical experience should be a regular part of the education of ministers within the theological seminary. At a time when there was still tension between clinical educators and seminary faculties, he introduced clinical training to Andover Newton Theological Seminary, and he helped, in 1938, to form the committee that would reinforce the growing amity between clinical supervisors and theological faculties in the Boston area.

Guiles received his own clinical training under the supervision of Anton Boisen and then served as a chaplain at Massachusetts General

Hospital. He lost his chaplaincy when he began to write—and to insert in the medical records—psychiatric evaluations of some patients. He then became the first field secretary and interim director of the Council for Clinical Training of Theological Students, before joining the faculty of Andover Newton in 1931 as director of Clinical Training. After a policy dispute with Helen Flanders Dunbar, he left the council and worked closely with Richard Cabot in the effort to expand clinical training to the seminaries of New England. Because of Cabot's distrust of psychiatry, Guiles tended to promote general hospitals, rather than mental hospitals, as the settings for clinical pastoral training. But the Institute of Pastoral Care, which he helped establish in 1944 to promote clinical education within theological schools, soon began to use both mental and general hospitals.

He also founded pastoral counseling centers under the auspices of Andover Newton. Guiles tried to promote interest in what he called "clinical theology," but he remained influential primarily as an organizer and administrator of clinical programs.

E. B. HOLIFIELD

HILTNER, SEWARD (1909–84). American Presbyterian minister and pastoral theologian. A prolific writer who published at least ten books and more than five hundred articles on pastoral care and pastoral theology, Hiltner served as executive secretary of the Council for Clinical Training of Theological Students (1935–38), executive secretary of Pastoral Services for the Federal Council of Churches (1938–50), professor of pastoral theology at the University of Chicago Divinity School (1950–61), and professor of pastoral theology at Princeton Theological Seminary (1961–80).

No pastoral theologian has had more influence than Hiltner on the development of pastoral care traditions in modern America. He helped establish a style of counseling that attracted widespread interest. In his *Pastoral Counseling* (1949), Hiltner advocated an "eductive method" that would help the pastor distinguish moralistic exhortation and ineffectual advice from a style of counseling that drew on "the creative potentialities of the person needing help." Hiltner's method was similar to the client-centered methods of psychotherapy proposed by Carl Rogers, and Hiltner's book helped introduce Rogerian themes to the American clergy. But Hiltner developed his ideas independently and always retained a sensitivity to the need for ethical clarification and pastoral identity on the part of the pastoral counselor. In later years, he emphasized the ecclesial setting for pastoral counseling and the importance of the pastor's "pre-counseling" relationships in the parish. He also discouraged the assumption that pastoral counseling and pastoral care were synonymous.

Always seeking a basic theory of ministry and of pastoral care, Hiltner published *Preface to Pastoral Theology* (1958), in which he argued that the task of pastoral theology was a disciplined inquiry into the healing, sustaining, and guiding activities of the minister and the church. He distinguished three overarching "perspectives" on pastoral activity— shepherding, communicating, and organizing—and insisted that the pastoral theologian was to find, within the shepherding activities of healing, sustaining, and guiding, a theological wisdom that could illumine all the church's functions and its theological doctrines. He believed that a pastoral counselor's struggle with a marriage problem or a family conflict could provide new insight into the gospel—an insight perhaps available through no other source.

Convinced of the power of social and cultural pressures to shape human perceptions, Hiltner made several cultural studies of pastoral issues. He helped stimulate interest in the problems of older people, the pastoral implications of the Kinsey Report on sexual behavior, and ministry to alcoholics. He also served on the National Committee for Mental Hygiene and urged the churches to support the mental health movement.

As a clinical student of Anton Boisen and an early proponent of Clinical Pastoral Education (CPE), Hiltner worked closely with the Council for Clinical Training of Theological Students, always with the aim that CPE should be understood as a part of pastoral and theological training, not as a substitute for it or a general training in counseling methods. He also labored to define the chaplaincy, constructing, in alliance with Russell Dicks, the first statement of standards for chaplains in hospitals and other institutions.

As a teacher, he was among the first to combine the use of case histories, which he learned from Anton Boisen, with close attention to verbatim transcripts of pastoral conversations.

He served as the consultant for the journal *Pastoral Psychology,* and his many articles in that journal helped ensure his influence among American clergy who were especially interested in pastoral care and counseling.

E. B. HOLIFIELD

OATES, WAYNE E. (1917–99). Baptist pastor, chaplain, pastoral theologian, and clinical educator. Oates taught pastoral theology at Southern Baptist Theological Seminary and served as professor of psychiatry and behavioral sciences at the School of Medicine, University of Louisville.

A product of a South Carolina mill town, Oates remained sensitive throughout his career to the problems of pastoral care in the rural South. He also maintained a strong interest in the "symbolic role of the pastor" as the representative of a specific community and tradition. The result was a conception of pastoral counseling as "spiritual conversation," a dialogue between a pastor and a parishioner marked by trust, understanding, covenantal engagement, and concern for persons within community. In his *Protestant Pastoral Counseling* (1962), he attempted to define the precise character of pastoral care within the Protestant free church tradition and found its defining marks to be theological: an affirmation of the lordship of Christ, of the personal dialogue between Creator and creature, of the priesthood of believers, and, above all, of the power of the Spirit. Such criteria enabled Oates to draw on modern psychotherapeutic theories, but to modify them in the light of the specific social and ecclesiastical setting within which the pastor worked.

Using a notion of "social role" derived in part from the social psychology of Gardner Murphy, Oates urged ministers to be sensitive to a community's ways of expressing its expectations of the clerical role. He thought that ministers could learn to use communal expectations in understanding why people would come to them in search of aid, rather than to other counselors. He also felt that the ministerial "role" properly affected the minister's method of counseling. On occasion, the minister might well simply help men and women interpret their feelings, but ministers should also acknowledge certain broad objectives and therefore assume a measure of initiative in counseling.

As a theologian, he stood in a neoorthodox tradition that reasserted the importance of Christology as the clue to understanding human existence. In his *Christ and Selfhood* (1961), he argued that "the claim to uniqueness of the Christian understanding of the personality resides wholly in the Person of Jesus Christ." He also shared the prevailing neoorthodox fascination with the destructive power of "idolatry," the misdirected focusing of ultimate loyalties on conflicting finite values. And he worried that psychology itself could become still another idol, so he warned against the tendency of pastoral counselors to seek a "borrowed identity" derived from psychotherapy. He always maintained a deep interest in psychoanalytic traditions, developmental psychologies, and social psychology, but he also wanted pastors to find within their own religious traditions the imagery and language to guide their pastoral practice.

Oates helped introduce Clinical Pastoral Education (CPE) into the South. He had undergone clinical training at Elgin State Hospital under the auspices of the Council for Clinical Training, but he eventually founded his own clinical program at Kentucky State Hospital in Danville and forged links with Southern Baptist Theological Seminary.

A prolific writer, Oates published dozens of books and hundreds of articles on theology, pastoral care, and pastoral theology. He was one of the leading figures of the postwar pastoral counseling movement in the United States.

E. B. HOLIFIELD

PASTORAL CARE (History, Traditions, and Definitions). Pastoral care derives from the biblical image of shepherd and refers to the solicitous concern expressed within the religious community for persons in trouble or distress. Historically and within the Christian community, pastoral care is in the cure-of-souls tradition. Here "cure" may be understood as "care" in the sense of carefulness or anxious concern, not necessarily as healing, for the soul, that is, the animating center of personal life and the seat of relatedness to God.

Designating this care as pastoral may refer either to the person of the religious leader or to the motivation/attitude characterizing the caregiver. In the first instance, pastoral care refers to ordained or acknowledged religious leaders who bring the resources, wisdom, and authority of the religious community to bear on human distress. But pastoral care may also be understood to be provided by any representative of the religious community who is perceived to stand for or reflect the values and commitments of the group.

Just as *pastoral* may reflect different understandings, so *care* has both broad and narrow meanings. It may refer to any pastoral act motivated by a sincere devotion to the well-being of the other(s). In this sense liturgical forms and ritual acts may reflect care as may education and various forms of social action. Usually, however, pastoral care refers to the more intensive dimension of the larger tasks of ministry, to conversation with persons or groups who seek interpersonal, moral, or spiritual guidance.

Seward Hiltner (1958) and W. Clebsch and C. Jaekle (1964) suggest that the content of care includes the pastoral functions of healing, sustaining, guiding, and reconciling, and specify a precise content to the care. They also limit pastoral care to instances in which there is some sense of individual need and willingness to accept help. Further, Clebsch and Jaekle insist that the care must include matters of "ultimate concern," that is, the troubles must be meaningful in relation to Christian faith in that they foster a deeper faith and relation to God. To follow these writers leads to the conclusion that not all helping acts of mercy, love, and charity are pastoral care.

What becomes apparent rather quickly in any survey of the history of pastoral care are the diverse understandings of the endeavor. Simply stated, what constitutes pastoral care is rooted in the basic religious convictions of the community. But it is also rooted in the historical, political, and social fabric of a given time and place. Thus christological, soteriological, and ecclesiological convictions define our sense of obligation for each other and to some degree determine what constitutes helping. Even so, the political climate, cultural values and ideals, economic factors, and various forms of secular knowledge enter to determine in part the shape and intent of pastoral care.

Only a few efforts have been made to trace this history. Apart from John McNeill (1951), Clebsch and Jaekle, C. Kemp (1947), and, to a lesser degree, T. Oden (1983) and Hiltner, the history of pastoral care is largely unclaimed and unknown. Yet members of religious communities have always sought out those whom they perceived as wise or mature or holy for assistance in life. And the perplexities, uncertainties, and efforts to understand, which plagued the caregivers, are recorded in a rich treasure of literature on the human quest for relatedness to God and the successes and failures of those seeking to help.

The purpose of this essay is to offer a glimpse of this history and its varied understandings of pastoral care.

1. From Beginnings to Establishment. Any definition of pastoral care has at its core a way of understanding our relatedness to God and the ingredients or acts that may serve to enhance or detract from that relatedness. Despite its diversity, the NT reflects a view of Christian life rooted in an inner transformation resulting from faith in Christ as God and as the inaugurator of a new age. In the Gospels and Letters, the task of the shepherd is "to create an atmosphere in which the intimate exchange of spiritual help, the mutual guidance of souls, would be a normal feature of Christian behavior" (McNeill, 1951, 85).

Paul reflects this concern when he confesses his "daily anxiety" for the churches. He seeks to express the meaning of the Christian life and to have the churches reflect this meaning. The form his anxiety takes is first instruction, then rebuke, later exhortation, and always encouragement and compassion. He guides the churches in disputes, answers questions about marriage, and wants them to settle disagreements among themselves. He wants sinners restored, the weak strengthened, and love to prevail. He reminds them of his weakness while seeking their prayers and encouraging them to utilize their gifts for the welfare of the community and as a sign of faithfulness.

This quest for mutual edification and care has both individual and corporate dimensions. They should live quietly, bearing one another's burdens without shirking responsibility for themselves. Anxiety about themselves should foster contemplation about what is honorable and true and of good report. At the same time they should wait on and encourage each other with "brotherly affection." The needs of the saints should be attended to, especially the need for mutual confession, prayers and visitation for the sick, and contributions to the homeless, hungry, and destitute.

By the close of the first century the emphases in care within the church began to change. Second- and third-generation Christians sought to preserve the genius that had sustained them while at the same time attempting to come to terms with themselves as a separate community. The results were a somewhat different view of the Christian life, one that placed more emphasis on its form than its content.

The Shepherd of Hermas reflects this shift. The overriding concern of Hermas is sin committed after baptism. Baptism remitted sin, but since Christ's return was delayed, Christians began to question whether there could be a second repentance. In the vision that constitutes this book, Christ as grace and forgiveness falls into the background before the demands for moral conduct on the part of the believer. What is stressed is the laxness of the church in its attachment to the world, the ambition, discord, and misconduct of church leaders, and a representative table of virtues and vices. Hermas paves the way for the strong ascetic tendency in the early church. He begins to exchange the Pauline emphasis on justification for moralism and legalism. Finally, he concludes that one additional repentance is possible for less grievous sins provided the believer demonstrates true repentance and has paid for his or her error. Pastors, in turn, are to regulate both repentance and penance.

The shift to reconciliation became a dominant theme of pastoral care during the persecutions (ca. 150–300 C.E.). Questions as to what kinds and degrees of renunciation of the faith were forgivable led to strife in the church over efforts to reconcile apostates. The controversy, finally resolved by Cyprian, led to the definition of bishops as the determiners of church membership and served to standardize the practice of one penance even for those guilty of the three capital sins of murder, unchastity, and idolatry.

Although this debate dominated the time of the persecutions, care continued to be exercised in other modes in the church. For example, Augustine suggested a list of pastoral duties:

> Disturbers are to be rebuked, the low-spirited to be encouraged, the infirm to be supported, objectors confuted, the treacherous guarded against, the unskilled taught, the lazy aroused, the contentious restrained, the haughty repressed, litigants pacified, the poor relieved, the oppressed liberated, the good approved, the evil borne with, and all are to be loved. (McNeill, 1951, 100)

Another example of other modes of care is seen in the continuation of the consolation literature of the classical era. Cyprian reworked topics from pagan treatises adding Christian doctrine to support those undergoing persecution and reminding them that "Christ was the companion of his soldiers in flight and hardship and death." Others such as Gregory of Nazianzus, Jerome, and Ambrose addressed letters to individuals for sympathy and consolation. The Christian faith, said Ambrose, will only be discredited by excessive sorrow so the grief-stricken should allow themselves to be comforted.

When Constantine converted to the Christian faith in 313 C.E., the focus of the church's pastoral energies shifted once more. Two early church fathers reflect the pastoral effort to assume their place as "semi-official educators, as dispensers of state welfare funds, as leaders of an imperially endorsed religion, [and as interpreters] of the troubles that beset people" (Clebsch and Jaekle, 1964, 19). In his *Treatise on the Priesthood*, John Chrysostom described the mark of the true pastor as his readiness to perish for his sheep. In caring for souls, Chrysostom presented himself "as a physician dispensing medicaments to those who voluntarily submitted to his art and of the church as a hospital whither the sinner might have to repair for more than one serious sin" (Niebuhr and Williams, 1956, 70). Perhaps his most important pastoral contribution was his search for an alternative to the humiliating act of public penance. His understanding of inward sinfulness caused him to advocate the iteration of penance in a diversified fashion. "It is not right to take an absolute standard and fit the penalty to the exact measure of the offense, but it is right to aim at influencing the moral feelings of the offenders, [since] no one can, by compulsion, cure an unwilling man" (Niebuhr and Williams, 1956, 70).

In the West, Ambrose was Chrysostom's counterpart. His *On the Duties of Clergy* was also published in 386 C.E., and exemplifies efforts to accommodate lofty pagan virtues with the spirit of Christianity. Relying upon Cicero, he found biblical examples of the classical virtues of prudence, justice, fortitude, and courage and joined them with Paul's faith, hope, and love.

2. From Gregory to the Renaissance (500–1300). The soul care of the church fathers was codified and transmitted by Pope Gregory the Great. The invasion by the Slavic and Teutonic peoples and the collapse of Roman society left the church, its priests, and its monasteries, as the primary vehicles for order. Gregory's *Book of Pastoral Rule* became the guide for centuries of priests in their attempts to provide care. It is without question among the most valuable classics in the cure of souls.

Gregory regarded the "government of souls [as] the art of arts." Priestly authority should be exercised with humility by one who acts as a compassionate neighbor. In the midst of social and political transition, Gregory sought order by guiding troubled souls into faith and moral uprightness. By encouraging the distraught to bring their concerns to the church, he was able to introduce the Christian tradition and to impose rites and practices on the nature-paganism of the folk cultures.

Part 3 of the book might prove the most interesting to today's pastor. Gregory sought to adapt his advice to individual cases, all the while assuming that care provided in depth would invariably involve deeper spiritual issues. He noted different personality types, for example, the simple and the insincere, the impudent and the bashful, as requiring special concern and called attention to situational differences affecting persons. With each type he enumerated the particular temptation to which they were subject and sought to strengthen their resolve. Later he spoke more carefully of different treatments for sins of intention and of impulse, for sins abandoned as opposed to those one clings to, and so forth. Physicians of the soul must be discerning and have medicine "to meet moral diseases by a varied method."

The Celtic penitential literature represented another source of guidance for the medieval priest. One of these, *Corrector et medicus*, explained:

> The book is called "the Corrector" and "the Physician" since it contains ample corrections for bodies and medicines for souls and teaches every priest, even the uneducated, how he shall be able to bring help to each person, ordained or unordained; poor or rich; boy, youth, or mature man; decrepit, healthy, or infirm; of every age; and of both sexes. (Clebsch and Jaekle, 1964, 24)

A vast array of this literature was in use, offering instruction on every aspect of soul care. The literature's attention to detail, to modes of interviewing, to penances prescribed for various sins, to exceptional cases, and so forth, meant that the priest could provide guidance on life as the church saw it in every circumstance.

By 1200 the church had codified the sacramental system and had essentially standardized pastoral care practices. The parish priest, as the most educated person in the community, was regarded as counselor, lawyer, teacher, doctor, and friend. His foremost function was the provision of the sacraments, for therein lay the cure for human disease and distress. Thus baptism was essential for salvation and removed the taint of original sin. The other sacraments came as propitious events in the life cycle. Confirmation sanctioned the move to adulthood, holy matrimony the joining with a mate, and unction vouchsafed one's death.

For adults, however, the two great sacraments of healing were the Mass and penance. The Mass provided a dependable grace during the common ventures of life. Here the faithful partook of the very life of God, strengthening them to endure and withstand temptation, illness, bereavement, indeed every joy or vicissitude of life. The penance, involving as it did contrition, confession, and satisfaction, offered the priest opportunity to conduct a thorough spiritual examination. No one escaped faultless, yet hope, not despair, was the outcome. Penitents emerged with clean slates and an assured relation to God.

3. The Reformation. John McNeill begins his chapter on the Reformation with the statement: "In matters concerning the cure of souls the German Reformation had its inception" (1951, 163). The sale of indulgences aroused Luther's indignation; simple people were deceived to believe that the purchase of the certificates assured salvation. Luther himself had undergone a long and arduous personal conflict over repentance and justification. For him repentance meant "coming to one's sense," "a change in our heart and our love" as response to God's grace (McNeill, 1951). Thus Luther's objection was not against either confession or absolution but against the notion that the remission of sins depended on confession and not the goodness of God. He objected, second, to the authority to bind and loose sin being restricted to priests. All Christians, he said, have authority to hear confessions and absolve; we share a common priesthood just as we share our spiritual gifts. Thus, to Luther only two things mattered: "the Word of God and faith." Or as he put it: "The sum of the Gospel is this: who believes in Christ, has the forgiveness of sins" (Niebuhr and Williams, 1956, 111).

The key to relatedness to God, then, is a trusting faith in God's mercy. For Luther "spiritual counsel is always concerned above all else with faith—nurturing, strengthening, establishing, practicing faith" (Tappert, 1955, 15). Luther's pastoral practice is characterized by warmth, conviction, and identification with the distressed. At Worms, a few hours before his second appearance before the Diet, he went at dawn to the bedside of a dying knight to hear his confession and administer the Sacrament. The *Table Talk* shows him convening in a friendly fashion and asking questions about the state of body and soul of his companions. His letters of consolation, his concern for the young women who had left the nunneries, his correspondence with friends, and his response to plague and persecution reveal him as always attentive to the distressed. And he took his own advice. When his beloved thirteen-year-old daughter was near death, he comforted his wife with the words, "I rejoice in the spirit, but sorrow in the flesh" (McNeill, 1951, 172).

John Calvin shared Luther's concern for justification by faith, the priesthood of all believers, and his commitment to the cure of souls. But Calvin's emphasis on repentance was broader than Luther's, and this was reflected in his pastoral approach. Calvin's repentance "embraces the soul's progressive appropriation of the obedience, holiness, and goodness that mark the restoration of man's lost or obscured image of God" (McNeill, 1951, 198). Thus he, like Luther, has a place for confession and absolution. But the fruit of this confession is transformation. There was no requirement for private confession but ministers were encouraged to interview each communicant prior to communion. Here the power of the keys was exercised by Christ's ambassador and the grace of the gospel was confirmed and sealed.

Calvin's genius at organization also influenced his pastoral care. The elders watched carefully over the citizens of Geneva and sought to protect and to correct them. Ministers met regularly to admonish and sustain one another. Deacons visited the sick, the imprisoned, the widows and orphans and were charged to catechize the children. And Calvin himself by means of a voluminous correspondence sought to strengthen, encourage, and embolden the persecuted and comfort the bereaved.

Neither Luther nor Calvin wrote specifically on the care of souls. However, two prominent Reformation figures did. Ulrich Zwingli in *Der Hirt* (*The Pastor*) distinguished between the true and false shepherd. Proclamation, he said, must be followed by instruction and service, since the sheep that are healed should not be allowed to fall again into sickness. In love pastors do everything to upbuild the people. In *On the True Cure of Souls*, Martin Bucer describes a fivefold ministry in soul care. In public and by visitation ministers draw the alienated to Christ, lead back those drawn away, restore those who fall into sin, strengthen weak and sickly Christians, and preserve those who are whole and strong (McNeill, 1951, 192).

Reformation pastoral care may be characterized in several ways. The confessional as institution was abandoned and the pastor emerged as a central figure. However, the pastor's ordination did not set him apart. A married clergyman emphasized his identification at every point with his people. Moreover, though the primary acts of care were preaching and communion, the message of reconciliation symbolized in these events was felt to be central to the life of the entire community. Pastors and laypersons alike were mutually to comfort, correct, and sustain one another. The mark of a transformed life lay in mutual ministry with the end of being reconciled to God and to one another.

4. Traditions. Until the Reformation, the course of pastoral care followed a well-marked path in the Roman Catholic Church. Disagreements were always present but the tradition itself was clear. Since the Reformation a number of somewhat different understandings of relatedness to God have fostered a variety of traditions of pastoral care. Brooks Holifield in *A History of Pastoral Care in America* enumerates four: Roman Catholic, Lutheran, Anglican, and Reformed. To these one might add the Congregational or Free Church tradition. These same traditions existed in Europe, although they assumed a particular shape in America. It is impossible to trace these streams in any detail, but it is informative to attend individual representatives of each.

a. Roman Catholic. Roman Catholic pastoral care continued to revolve around the sacramental system after the Reformation. The Council of Trent in 1552 sought to correct the abuses of the penitential discipline and made great strides in that regard. Thus penance was defined as a sacrament for the baptized and consisted of contrition, confession, and satisfaction. But an *entire* confession was required by Christ for *all* sins after baptism. This of course emphasized sin as an act of transgression and reflected the conviction that original sin was covered by baptism. Mortal sins, then, must be confessed and the confession of venial sins was commended. The confession was to priests and bishops only. They alone could remit sins and their absolution was effected by the Sacrament. Penalties and penance remained both as remedy and as "an avenging and chastisement for past sin" (McNeill, 1951, 288).

This careful redefinition of sacramental penance fostered an immense literature on problems of conscience. The Jesuits were among the more attentive to these matters of casuistry and, when they were suppressed, a Redemptorist priest, Alfonso de Liguori, took up some of their tasks in moral theology and ascetic piety. A confessor, he said, must be a father, physician, teacher, and judge. "Confession must be: vocal; secret; true; and integral" (McNeill, 1951, 292). He sought particular remedies for various faults and warned confessors that to hear confessions without sufficient knowledge (of laws, bulls, decrees, other opinions) is to be subject to damnation. Liguori became the accepted authority for confessors, so that by 1831, all priests were advised or permitted to follow his opinions.

In the seventeenth century the vocation of spiritual director emerged. This role was distinct from that of confessor in that the goal was the pursuit of higher spiritual attainments. St. Francis de Sales, St. Vincent de Paul, and St. François Fénelon provide a treasure of correspondence on the spiritual life. Fénelon urged the quest for a pure and disinterested love reflected in quietism. His letters are replete with a subtle awareness of the capacity for self-deceit, the exhortation to attend devotions, and a rare courage to remind court figures of their worldliness. All, he said, need to be humiliated by their faults, to lose hope in themselves, without losing hope in God.

Undergirding the sacramental system was, as Holifield notes, a metaphor of growth. Salvation is achieved in ascending stages and the sacraments nurture this process. The process is reminiscent of Benedict's *Twelve Step*

Ladder of Humility, which began with fear and culminated in a life of love. Such notions of growth had long since set the standards of morality for priest and laypersons. And though the laity could not attend the ascent as did priests and religious, the aspiration permeated the church. In this context, then, the sacraments provided the means, the grace, to feed the soul and to foster love of God for God's sake.

b. Lutheran. Throughout the seventeenth and eighteenth centuries Lutheran pastoral care was characterized by a formal orthodoxy on the one side and a pietistic reaction to it on the other. A voluminous pastoral literature appeared during this time, but it viewed the cure of souls narrowly and placed emphasis on confession to the pastor. Scholarly literature neglected pastoral care in the name of belief and behavior, and pastoral literature recommended limited visitation, a mechanical view of confession based on the catechism, and absolution by the pastor. Critics said, "The binding key is quite rusted away while the loosing key is in full operation" (McNeill, 1951, 182).

Pietism under the direction of Philipp Jacob Spener turned away from the scholastics and invited Christians to personal religion. Spener stressed regeneration and the cultivation of the religious life, utilizing small conferences as vehicles for mutual edification. Christian faith meant accepting responsibility for a spiritual priesthood that included sacrifice, prayer, and the Word. By the Word persons were empowered to teach, exhort, rebuke, and console others who gathered to study Scripture and for mutual encouragement.

Pia Desideria (Pious Longings) was regarded as the text of the movement. Here and in *The Spiritual Priesthood Briefly Set Forth,* Spener expressed his wish that every Christian stand in a special friendship with his or her pastor or another Christian. He stressed individual conferences and private conversations, visiting in homes, and calling on the sick. Moreover, such work did not belong to the pastor alone. Laypersons were to engage in mutual correction and encouragement. "The sum of Christianity," he said, "is penitence, faith, and a new obedience; true, inner, spiritual peace" is its fruit (McNeill, 1951, 184).

For the generation after Spener, August Hermann Francke and his associates at the University of Halle became leaders among the Pietists. Francke's experience of anguish and conversion caused him to value despair as the prelude to rebirth. Indeed, this agony, this "feeling of repentance," constituted the difference between the true believer and others. Personal interviews became an important pastoral mode so as to discern despair and to lead one through these negative feelings to hope. Preparation for the Lord's Supper frequently involved such conversations.

This stream of Pietism flowed into America through many channels. It influenced Zinzendorf and Wesley, New England Puritanism, and British and subsequently American Baptists. Among Lutherans Pietism came to the United States through Henry M. Muhlenberg and Theodore Frelinghuysen. It sought to turn persons away from controversy to fellowship and from scholastic argument over faith to faith itself. Muhlenberg brought with him the ideals of Halle and records in his journals the spiritual guidance he sought to provide. His psychological insight convinced him that a "sick body produces a sick soul," so that he frequently cooperated with physicians (McNeill, 1951). He sought to institute a clear discipline in his congregation and, like his predecessors, examined candidates before communion.

c. Anglican. Winthrop Hudson remarks that the Reformation in England was both less drastic and less systematic than on the Continent. The structure of the church was largely unchanged so that its dioceses, parishes, bishops, and priests remained. And the theological statement, the Articles of Religion, "avoided precise definition." Despite this lack of drastic reform, the view of ministry in Anglicanism was altered. "Formerly the clergy had been 'priests,' finding their primary responsibility at the altar; now they were 'ministers,' with preaching and pastoral care as their preeminent duties" (Niebuhr and Williams, 1956, 180).

During the seventeenth century the distinction between even Puritans and Anglicans was not great with regards to pastoral care. Their differences were more of mood and temperament than theology. The Puritan wanted reform and was more eager to obey God than men. "The Anglican was more cautious and moderate; more aware of the power of habit and custom...[remembering] Paul's counsel that due regard must be given constituted authority" (Niebuhr and Williams, 1956, 181).

These tensions seem important if one is to understand the Anglican tradition in pastoral care. No one represented the cautious and moderate mood better than George Herbert. His classic volume *A Priest to the Temple or, The Country Parson* presents the ideal pastor as devout, competent, gracious, and holy. On Sundays he preached in the morning and catechized in the afternoon. The rest of the day he reconciled quarreling neighbors, visited the sick, sometimes attempting to persuade them to confess, or exhorted those in his flock "his sermons cannot or do not reach." On weekdays he engaged in systematic parish visitation to examine and advise, to counsel, admonish, and to exhort. Mornings were for reading and mealtimes for inviting parishioners to dine so that within a year he had been with them all. He offered advice to pastors for assisting those in good spiritual condition and those in despair of God's grace. The goal of this activity, according to Henry Scougal, was "to advance the divine life in the world. . . . The world lies in sin, and it is our work to awaken men out of their deadly sleep" (Niebuhr and Williams, 1956, 184).

Throughout the seventeenth and much of the eighteenth centuries, an extensive literature on the cure of souls emerged among Anglicans. Jeremy Taylor's *Holy Dying* and Gilbert Burnet's *Discourses of Pastoral Care* are among the most important. Some, such as William Law, reflected a higher view of the authority of priests as guides of conscience. Law placed great emphasis on daily self-examination and confession of sins to God as a means of growth. It was this emphasis on an awakened conscience and the work of grace in the hearts of believers, together with the evangelical revivals personified in George Whitefield, that led finally to despair of reform of the church among Puritans and an affirmation of the sacraments among Anglicans. The Puritan strain appears in the Reformed and Free Church traditions. The Anglicans emphasized the Eucharist and the sacramental efficacy in the life of the community of the prayers and worship of the church.

It seems fair to observe that in the balance between tradition and experience, Anglican pastoral care finally leaned toward the tradition. The Evangelicals were an exception to this, but the Oxford Movement, as represented by Edward Pusey and John Keble, reacted to this strain with an emphasis on the confessional and spiritual direction that was finally persuasive. Yet in the midst of these differences, an enormous importance was attached to the cure of souls and an impressive literature on conscience and casuistry resulted. In the United States Philips Brooks personifies this devotion to pastoral guidance and spiritual intimacy between priest and people.

d. Reformed. Although a historical distinction must be made among Presbyterians, Puritans, and the Continental Reformed traditions, their pastoral care orientation reflects a common source. The source, according to Holifield, was John Calvin and his emphasis on the disobedience of an idolatrous heart as the core of human distress. What their physicians of the soul sought to cure was the idolatrous heart. What they sought to ensure was exemplary conduct. Their theology was rooted in experience, but their insistence upon constant and effective discipline and their watchful care to protect the communion from scandalous offenders gave this tradition a distinct character.

Scottish Presbyterian and Continental Reformed churches each reflected this orientation. The Discipline of the Reformed Church of France, for example, contained exacting codes of behavior for ministers, elders, deacons, and members, providing procedures for suspension and excommunication for those who refused to repent "after many admonitions and entreaties" (McNeill, 1951, 209). Although it was difficult to maintain order during the persecutions, elders were instructed to "teach, reprove, and comfort." Dutch ministers were to provide guidance for elders, deacons, and members, and elders were to visit so as to "instruct and comfort the members in full communion as well as to exhort others to the regular profession of the Christian faith" (McNeill, 1951, 210).

The Reformed Church in Scotland also placed great emphasis on discipline as pastoral care. John Knox's *Book of Discipline* carefully outlines the procedures for dealing with offenders. He intended to ensure a watchful firmness with patient consideration for human frailty, a desire "rather to win our brother than to slander him (McNeill, 1951)." Yet the discipline was difficult to maintain at a high level and frequently deteriorated to simple legalism. The purity of the congregation was carefully guarded by means of examinations by the elders prior to communion and by their general oversight of congregational life. At the same time, ministers and elders were enjoined to visit the sick, distribute goods to the poor, and to ensure that Bibles and other literature were available so that faithfulness could be engendered.

The record would be incomplete, however, if one neglected those seventeenth-century pastors whose efforts went beyond discipline. In Scotland, David Dickson tried to be a "prudent friend" to those caught up in doubt, depression, and temptation; he wanted to lead them to repentance, never despair (McNeill, 1951). In the Netherlands, Gijsbert Voet prescribed mental prayer and solitary devotion to strengthen the soul and restricted excommunication even for grave sins. Beyond question the Swiss Reformed pastor Alexander Vinet personifies most clearly this movement in the Reformed church. His *Pastoral Theology* became immensely influential and can be read with profit today. Vinet manifests great empathy for his friends and parishioners and cautions against too much "direction" and too little regard for liberty and responsibility in pastoral work. After visiting Vinet one parishioner told her pastor, "You judge me from above, but he...as my equal" (McNeill, 1951, 215).

Over the next two centuries Reformed churches relaxed discipline and placed more emphasis on the reclamation of souls and personal religion. The evangelical revivals influenced this change as did the secularization of certain of the church's functions, for example, the Poor Law in England in 1845. Vinet exemplifies this shift on the Continent. In Great Britain John Watson ("Ian Maclaren") wrote *The Cure of Souls* (1896) and emphasized visitation and private conversation, offering guidelines for interviewing and keeping confidences. A few years earlier Patrick Fairbairn in *Pastoral Theology* described the difficulty of knowing where discipline should begin and encouraged the cultivation of spiritual enlightenment and conviction as an alternative.

Reformed pastors in the United States adapted their pastoral practices to different conditions than those of Europe. Their convictions were the same and may be traced to their Scottish, Continental, and Puritan forebears. However, the absence of settled communities and parish structures made the institution of the procedures difficult. L. Trinterud (1949) notes, for example, that though "experimental religion" was the foundation, Gilbert Tennant insisted that "a continual renewal of repentance was...utterly essential" for Christian life. And William W. Sweet (1936) describes later Presbyterian congregations on the frontier seeking to enforce discipline and ensure church purity by examinations of conscience and "fencing the table." Seward Hiltner (1958) examined the work of the nineteenth-century Presbyterian pastor Ichabod Spencer as he sought through diligent visitation to lead anxious men and women to repentance and faith. Spencer possessed a keen sense of responsibility to guide persons in distress, yet reflected genuine compassion for their anguish.

English Puritanism's contribution to pastoral care in this tradition was extensive. They shared the basic theological ground with their colleagues and so emphasized codes of behavior and concern for offenses. However, since they never attained the status of an organized church, they lacked the institutional structures to enforce a discipline. Their pastors turned instead to casuistry and to the guidance of individuals and families. William Perkins expressed this goal of awakening and guiding conscience when he said, "As the lawyer is [a counselor] for their estates and the physician for their bodies," so the minister is the "counselor for their souls," who "must be ready to give advice to those that come to him with cases of conscience" (Niebuhr and Williams, 1956, 196). The fruition of this emphasis on conscience was an extensive literature on casuistry best represented in the works of William Ames, Jeremy Taylor, and Richard Baxter.

There is no doubt that the most important contribution to pastoral care in this era was Richard Baxter's *Reformed Pastor* (1656). The volume places great demands on pastors and suggests that for Baxter, care consisted of two concerns. First, it must reveal to persons that happiness or good which is their ultimate end. Second, it must introduce them to the right means to attain this end, help them utilize these means, and discourage any contrary efforts. His practice was to spend fifteen to sixteen hours each week instructing families in the faith, "searching men's hearts and setting home the saving truths." He also visited the sick and the dying "helping them prepare for a fruitful life or a happy death." Care also involved counseling, and lest unskilled counselors aggravate problems, he advised such persons "to have a care to qualify themselves." A host of manuals gave instruction on approaches to various questions of conscience and states of anxiety and depressions. A good counselor, it was said, would bear with peevishness and with "disordered and distempered affections and actions." He would share sorrows and tears, listen well, guard secrets, and not be censorious when conscience was "unduly disturbed." According to Baxter (1656), the pastoral office was more than those "men have taken it to be, who think it consists in preaching and administering the sacraments only."

In summary, it may be observed that established groups within the Reformed tradition were somewhat more compulsory in their emphasis on discipline in pastoral care than were the Puritans, at least for a time. At the same time, the Continental and Scottish groups also placed more responsibility on lay participation through elders and deacons. The entire tradition reflects the extension of the goal of preaching to pastoral care. Private interviews, consultations, corrections, and admonitions became extensions of the call to repentance and uprightness of life. The relief of anxiety and guidance to one's true destiny were the goals of both.

e. Congregational. One tradition emerged in Great Britain in the seventeenth and eighteenth centuries that has been prominent in the United States. McNeill describes it as non-Anglican British churches and their daughter communions. The theological roots of these groups were in Anabaptism, Pietism, and Puritanism, so that without exception they sought conversion and insisted on an upright life among their members.

Life, they said, was a brief interlude, a battleground in which the forces of evil seek to divert the believer from God and eternal rest. Their distinction was their emphasis on congregational care. In itself this was not new; "mutual edification" and "fraternal correction" served to characterize most Protestant congregational life. But the shift to a congregational church polity by Baptists and Congregationalists and geographical circumstances among Methodists meant that the laity assumed a larger role in pastoral care.

Such generalizations certainly appear true for British Baptists. With roots in Puritanism and Pietism, they maintained strict membership standards. Their small congregations provided a setting for intimate relations of watchful care, both with their pastors and one another. John Bunyan was the best-known representative of the era that continued until the Act of Toleration (1689) precipitated a diminution of discipline and communal life before these were renewed by the Evangelical revivals.

In the United States, Baptist life is linked with New England Congregationalism and frontier revivalism. Few of these churches had regular pastors, so the responsibility for pastoral care fell to the congregation. These groups were held together by covenants wherein they agreed to "watch over each other in brotherly tenderness, each endeavoring to edify his brother; striving for the benefit of the weak of the flock . . . (and) to bear each other's burdens" (Sweet, 1931). The records of early Baptist churches are largely a record of this care. Discipline was prominent, frequently over matters now regarded as trivial, but so was concern for the sick, widows, families, and the troubled.

British Independents also adopted a congregational polity after the Act of Toleration, though never so completely as the Baptists. Isaac Watts and Philip Doddridge, two of their best-known leaders, maintained an extensive correspondence reflecting spiritual guidance and concern for personal and family religion. Doddridge emphasized private religious exercises and directions for the spiritual life. As pastor, he put elders to work visiting prisoners and those in spiritual distress. They were to reprove wrongdoers and not to spare their pastor for offensive temper and behavior.

The American Puritans as successors to these British Independents are best known through the works of Cotton and Increase Mather and Jonathan Edwards. As with their British mentors, conscience was the theme of their preaching, conversation, and concern. Edwards encouraged his members to give themselves to mutual care and admonition and not simply to be preoccupied with their own souls. Neglect is "a failure of our duty of love and charity." Cotton Mather felt the personal care of souls neglected and instructed fellow ministers to visit, catechize, and distribute literature so as to enhance piety, aid in reproof, and provide consolation. By the end of the nineteenth century, Washington Gladden's *The Christian Pastor and the Working Church* revealed just how far Congregationalists had moved from these roots. He advised pastors that "the one thing needful is for them [parishioners] to know that he loves them and wants to do them good" (McNeill, 1951, 278). At the sickbed he suggested "a few pleasant and sympathetic words with the patient" (McNeill, 1951).

f. Wesleyan. From the beginning John Wesley organized Methodism in groups intended for mutual confession and discipline. His societies were subdivided into classes of some twelve persons according to sex and marital status. Together with their leader they were to "help each other to work out their salvation." They should bear one another's burdens and "do good of every possible sort"; they should feed the hungry, clothe the naked, visit or help the sick or imprisoned and "instruct, reprove, and exhort" (McNeill, 1951, 279). They should do business with one another, practice frugality, and attend worship. Wesley's groups owed much to Pietism and would have delighted Spener.

Wesley himself was a model for his followers. He talked constantly to the anxious, perplexed, and distressed, visited the sick, and attended prisoners condemned to death. His correspondence was voluminous, but its constant theme was the spiritual needs of persons. He wanted conversions, to be sure, but he was equally concerned to encourage the pursuit of holiness and to reclaim the lapsed.

In the United States Francis Asbury was Wesley's heir. He too traveled constantly, always ready to engage in personal counsel and guidance out of his Evangelical faith. Asbury insisted on maintaining the standards of the *Discipline*. "Our society," he wrote, "may be considered a spiritual hospital, where souls come to be cured of their spiritual diseases" (Mills, 1956). Basic to this cure was conversion. But the prospect of relapse demanded striving for "full salvation" and Wesley's class structure was the vehicle for this care.

It is apparent that certain theological assurances underlay the pastoral care practices of each of these traditions. Foremost among them was that persons were created in the image of God and that their true destiny was a meeting with God. In between, preparation was to be made for that meeting, and pastoral care was endemic to that process. By the end of the nineteenth century these affirmations were not so widely shared. The winds of secularism and technology offered the symbols of science as alternative understandings of both human distress and care and set the stage for the particular problems and possibilities of pastoral care in the twentieth century.

5. The Twentieth Century. Beyond question the single most important influence of the twentieth century on pastoral care was the emergence and prominence of the psychological sciences. On the one hand, their influence fostered an emphasis on pastoral care that led H. Richard Niebuhr to describe it in 1955 as the most important movement in theological education. On the other hand, their presence symbolized the diminution of theological understandings of human life and offered alternative, and at times competitive, conceptions of human distress and its alleviation. The efforts of pastors and theological educators to make their way amid uncertain theological affirmations and the secularization of care have shaped pastoral care's recent history.

Pastors and theological educators were quick to discern the significance of psychology and psychotherapy for ministry. Following the initiative of Anton Boisen in 1925, it took only two decades for most of the major theological seminaries to appoint full-time faculty versed in these disciplines to teach pastoral care, and for a substantial literature began to appear.

These teachers and authors undertook a difficult task. At the same time they sought to reinterpret the work of ministry as illumined by various psychological theories, especially by Carl Rogers (*Client-Centered Therapy*), and to maintain a tie to the traditions by defining ministry and pastoral care as distinct from other professions and forms of care. The literature reveals an interest in all the human dilemmas that have served as a focus for pastoral concern. Its distinction lay in the tentativeness of its normative theological judgments and in its misgivings about confrontation and discipline. Holifield describes this shift as occurring over three centuries and suggests it to be a move from the theological notion of salvation to the cultural ideal of self-realization as the goal of pastoral care. However, this assessment may be too easy. For to survey this literature certainly shows the leaders—for example, Anton Boisen, Seward Hiltner, Carroll Wise, Wayne Oates, Paul Johnson, Reuel Howe, William Hulme, Howard Clinebell—struggling with the issue of theological understanding. In any event, the practice flourished, producing specialists in clinical education (Association for Clinical Pastoral Education), pastoral counseling (American Association of Pastoral Counselors), and graduate programs in theological seminaries.

With the exception of the Roman Catholic Church and conservative Christian groups, these developments seem to have characterized pastoral care until 1970. More recently, an increasing number of persons, such as Don Browning, Edward Farley, and Charles Gerkin, suggested that pastoral care was too dependent on its auxiliary discipline, psychology, and had lost its theological mooring. The Roman Catholic tradition, contrary to the others, resisted the incursions of psychology and maintained itself until Vatican II. The work of this council laid the foundation for a broadened understanding of care and a reinterpretation of the sacramental tradition and has made possible an increasing participation by Roman Catholics in the broader understanding of pastoral care. Conservative Christians and groups tended to view the shifts in pastoral care with caution. They voiced concern that the innovators were forsaking the Bible and setting aside a proper understanding of Christian faith and life. In recent years these same voices have begun to articulate an evangelical pastoral care and to produce a significant literature.

When one inquires about the present state of pastoral care, several observations are in order. First, despite the uncertainties of definition, pastoral care continues as an essential activity of ministers and laypersons. The perennial concerns of illness, death, family conflict, and depression are now supplemented with divorce and a host of complex moral and ethical questions surrounding abortion, live-in mates, prolongation of life, and aging. Second, the emerging consciousness of the Black church and the increasing participation of its leaders in specialized pastoral care introduce new dimensions to pastoral care's self-understanding and definition. *Pastoral Care in the Black Church* by Edward Wimberly offers a sample of the contributions that may be anticipated. Also, an increasing number of women are finding their vocation in ministry in pastoral care. Literature by women promises to have a significant effect on the conceptualization and practice of pastoral care.

Finally, there appears to be a growing sense that pastoral care neglects its theological roots and intent to its peril. Serious efforts by Don Browning, Charles Gerkin, John Patton, James Lapsley, Don Capps, James Poling, and a host of others seek to attend the theological character of the endeavor. It seems that concerted efforts are underway to reclaim pastoral care's place in the cure of souls tradition and to understand its tasks as intrinsically theological. The hard-won gains of association with the psychological sciences are not being set aside, but these gains are being placed in relation to the heritage in the church. Thus pastoral care seeks its roots in a theological worldview at the same time that it comes to terms with the forces and contending voices of the contemporary scene. What is reflected in these more recent enterprises is a continuation of a long and honorable tradition. For the commitment to persons that pastoral care's history reveals and the effort to discern the meaning of life in relation to God remain as fundamental ideals in those who would care for souls.

[Editor's note: The founding of the Society for Pastoral Theology in 1985, under the initiative of Liston Mills and James Lapsley, has addressed this article's concern about reclaiming the theological roots of pastoral care and counseling. *The Journal of Pastoral Theology*, sponsored by the Society, is the primary forum for research and writing in this field.]

Bibliography. R. Baxter, *Reformed Pastor* (1656). M. Bucer, *On the True Cure of Souls* (1538). W. Clebsch and C. Jaekle, *Pastoral Care in Historical Perspective* (1964). G. Herbert, *A Priest to the Temple or, The Country Parson* (1632). S. Hiltner, *Preface to Pastoral Theology* (1958). E. B. Holifield, *A History of Pastoral Care in America* (1983). C. Kemp, *Physicians of the Soul* (1947). J. T. McNeill, *A History of the Cure of Souls* (1951). L. O. Mills, "The Relation of Discipline to Pastoral Care in Frontier Churches," *Pastoral Psychology* (December 1956). H. R. Niebuhr and D. Williams, *The Ministry in Historical Perspective* (1956). T. Oden, *Pastoral Theology* (1983); *Pastoral Counsel* (1989). P. J. Spener, *Pia Desideria* (1675); *The Spiritual Priesthood Briefly Set Forth* (1677). W. Sweet, *Religion on the American Frontier: The Baptists* (1931); *The Presbyterians* (1936). T. Tappert, *Luther's Letters of Spiritual Counsel* (1955). L. Trinterud, *The Forming of an American Tradition* (1949). A. Vinet, *Pastoral Theology* (1853). J. Watson, *The Cure of Souls* (1896). E. Wimberly, *Pastoral Care in the Black Church* (1979). U. Zwingli, *Der Hirt* (1524).

L. O. MILLS

PASTORAL CARE AND COUNSELING IN A POSTMODERN CONTEXT. During the first half of the twentieth century in the United States, mainline Protestants and Catholics enthusiastically explored the relationship of psychology to religion, especially in the areas of psychology of religion, religion and health, and psychotherapy as a nonmoralistic approach to personal healing for religious individuals. By the 1950s, psychologically sophisticated Protestant clergy were embracing the therapeutic techniques of Carl Rogers as a compassionate, nonjudgmental approach to pastoral care and counseling. At many mainline Protestant seminaries, pastoral care courses focused on the practice of pastoral counseling, drawing upon psychodynamic models of personality, existential theologies, and Rogerian therapeutic techniques. In addition, clinical pastoral education was recognized as a form of theological education and endorsed as a way of preparing for ministry. Pastoral counseling centers opened across the country, and the American Association of Pastoral Counselors was established as an organization that certified pastoral counselors and accredited pastoral counseling centers.

The clinical paradigm of pastoral care practiced in this pastoral counseling movement reflected many modern American values: personal autonomy, individual freedom, and a belief in progress, along with a nonmoralistic use of religion that focused on self-actualization and personal growth (Holifield, 1983; Myers-Shirk, 2009). During the 1960s, more theologically conservative Protestant clergy, seminary professors of pastoral care, and therapists (calling themselves Christian counselors and psychologists) rejected the clinical paradigm and retrieved a classical/clerical paradigm of pastoral care and counseling that focused on the authority of the Bible, a personal commitment to Jesus Christ, and a shared evangelically oriented theology. In many ways, this return to the so-called Christian fundamentals of faith represented an effort to emulate a simple understanding of premodern Christian pastoral care, in which Christian revelation could be interpreted without using biblical critical methods and progressive theologies developed during the twentieth century.

Challenges to the clinical paradigm of pastoral care also emerged from theologically progressive pastoral theologians and clinicians, beginning in the 1980s. While still embracing the liberal moral sensibility that gave rise to the clinical paradigm, these voices, primarily from within the academy, pushed pastoral theology and the practice of care in new directions. African American pastoral theologians (Smith, 1982; Wimberly, 1979) questioned the ways in which the clinical paradigm reflected Euro-American middle-class perspectives on personal development and healing through intensive one-on-one dyad relationships. They brought Black psychology into dialogue with Black liberation theology in order to reflect upon experiences of racism and the communal experience of pastoral care within African American churches. Drawing upon emerging feminist psychologies and theologies, feminist pastoral theologians and

71

counselors looked at the ways in which women's experiences as both caregivers and care receivers challenged traditionally male-oriented theologies, models of personality, theories of human development, and practices of care (Glaz and Moessner, 1991). Within the academy, practical theologians questioned the clinical paradigm's heavy reliance on psychological theories and therapeutic techniques, and proposed cross-disciplinary methods that gave equal voice to psychological and theological studies.

By the end of the twentieth century, challenges to the clinical paradigm by African American and feminist pastoral theologians, as well as practical theologians, were fueled by aspects of postcolonialism and post-modern approaches to knowledge that stressed the need for

- a relational and ecological understanding of life;
- a perspectival understanding of knowledge as socially constructed;
- an appreciation for the performative and constructive nature of theology;
- a self-reflexivity about how one's social location and social privileges shape one's experience and knowledge;
- a social, political, and theological analysis of the role of power and difference in human suffering and social injustice; and
- systemic strategies for pastoral and spiritual care in which individual, familial, and communal change is grounded in social justice.

Postcolonial approaches to knowledge decentered pastoral theologians and practitioners in the United States, making them look beyond their own borders, cultures, and predominantly Christian theologies. Within a global, religiously pluralistic horizon, the varieties of pastoral and spiritual care, with their indigenous practices and contextual theologies, were valued as distinctively unique. In a global, religiously pluralistic context, Lartey's (2006) proposal for an intercultural paradigm of pastoral and spiritual care provided a framework for spiritual care based on aspects of postcolonial and postmodern approaches to knowledge, as well as a phenomenological method of comparing religions of the world.

Given this global, religiously pluralistic context, pastoral theologians and practitioners now see the contextual need for multiple paradigms of spiritual and pastoral care as well as multiple methods of practical theology. During the 1980s, practical theologians, citing the seminal writings of Seward Hiltner (1958), challenged colleagues working within a clinical paradigm of care to redefine pastoral psychology as practical theology. Their method of practical theology was based on theologian David Tracy's (1975) revision of Tillich's correlation method, which brought the questions raised by cultural interpretations of human existence, like psychological studies, to Christian revelation for answers. In Tracy's revised critical correlational method, both the questions and answers arising from cultural interpretations of existence could be brought into dialogue with a critical interpretation of Christian claims about existence. The revised correlational method has been used extensively by practical theologian Don Browning and his colleagues (Browning and Cooper, 2004) to excavate the embedded theologies and ethics being enacted in a range of congregational and cultural practices, and to deliberate over these theological and ethical practices, using a range of cultural, sociological, psychological, biblical, and theological studies, in order to arrive at faith claims that can provide guidance for individuals, families, communities of faith, and public policy. When postmodern approaches to religious knowledge are used in a revised correlational method, truth claims are seen as provisional and contextual.

A second method of practical theology that explicitly uses postmodern approaches to knowledge has been proposed by Elaine Graham (1996), who describes theology as performative rather than propositional knowledge, and praxis as the way in which communities and persons embody and enact their beliefs. Her inductive method of contextual practical theology, described as critical phenomenology, begins with the concrete experiential theology that faith communities enact in their practices and enables faith communities to give a public, critical account of the faith claims embedded in their practices. Graham's method provides ways for pastoral theologians and practitioners to draw upon postmodern approaches of religious knowledge to reconceptualize pastoral care (Doehring, 2006), pastoral psychotherapy using psychodynamic approaches (Cooper-White, 2007), and narrative approaches to therapy (Neuger, 2001) and ethnography as a form of pastoral listening (Moschella, 2008).

One of the lasting influences of postmodern approaches to knowledge has been to make pastoral theologians and practitioners explicit about the methods by which theological, psychological, and cultural studies are related to one another and to the practices of spiritual and pastoral care. In addition, there is a growing awareness that multiple methods of practical theology are needed, especially within a global, religiously pluralistic context (Graham, Walton, and Ward, 2005). Pastoral theologians and practitioners are called upon to assess theologically whether one's practical theological method is contextually meaningful and whether it can be seen as part of a web of life-giving, life-limiting, or destructive relationships.

Bibliography. D. S. Browning and T. D. Cooper, *Religious Thought and the Modern Psychologies*, 2nd ed. (2004). P. Cooper-White, *Many Voices: Pastoral Psychotherapy in Relational and Theological Perspectives* (2007). C. Doehring, *The Practice of Pastoral Care: A Postmodern Approach* (2006). M. Glaz and J. S. Moessner, eds., *Women in Travail and Transition: A New Pastoral Care* (1991). E. Graham, *Transforming Practice: Pastoral Theology in an Age of Uncertainty* (1996). E. Graham, H. Walton, and F. Ward, *Theological Reflection: Methods* (2005). S. Hiltner, *Preface to Pastoral Theology: The Ministry of Theory and Shepherding* (1958). E. B. Holifield, *A History of Pastoral Care in America: From Salvation to Self-Realization* (1983). P. Lakeland, *Postmodernity: Christian Identity in a Fragmented Age* (1997). E. Lartey, *Pastoral Theology in an Intercultural World* (2006). M. C. Moschella, *Ethnography as a Pastoral Practice: An Introduction* (2008). S. Myers-Shirk, *Helping the Good Shepherd: Pastoral Counselors in a Psychotherapeutic Culture 1925–1975* (2009). C. C. Neuger, *Counseling Women: A Narrative Pastoral Approach* (2001). N. J. Ramsay, ed., *Pastoral Care and Counseling: Redefining the Paradigms* (2004). A. Smith, *The Relational Self: Ethics and Therapy from a Black Church Perspective* (1982). D. Tracy, *Blessed Rage for Order: The New Pluralism in Theology* (1975). E. Wimberly, *Pastoral Care in the Black Church* (1979).

C. DOEHRING

PASTORAL CARE MOVEMENT. A twentieth-century movement, prominent especially in Protestantism within the United States after 1945, that attempted to refine ministry by drawing upon the findings of modern medicine, psychotherapy, and the behavioral sciences. It produced innovative forms of pastoral practice, created new institutions, generated theological reflection, and influenced the training of ministerial students.

1. Historical Background. The reliance on secular wisdom in the modern pastoral care movement is no innovation. From the beginnings of church history, Christian theologians have enriched pastoral care by exploiting the resources of Western philosophy, medicine, and psychology. Even the letters of Paul reflect the philosophical tradition of "psychagogy" that defined pre-Christian Western methods of spiritual direction. Sixteenth-century casuists appropriated innovations in Renaissance philosophy and logic in much the same way that twentieth-century pastoral theologians read Freud, Adler, and Jung. Earlier pastoral writers also studied medical treatises to enrich their practice of the pastoral arts, as when seventeenth-century English Calvinists incorporated in their pastoral handbooks the standard medical analysis of such ailments as melancholia. From one perspective, the pastoral care movement simply represented a significant twentieth-century form of this time-honored practice of appropriating secular psychological and medical wisdom for a ministry of healing.

As early as 1808, moreover, when American Protestant seminaries began to offer lectures in "pastoral" or "practical" theology, these courses included attention not only to preaching but also to standard forms of pastoral counsel and visitation, as codified in such classics as George Herbert's *Country Parson* (1652), Richard Baxter's *Reformed Pastor* (1658), and Gilbert Burnet's *Discourse of the Pastoral Care* (1713). The pastoral theology lecturers hoped to help young ministers engender and recognize the marks of rebirth, partly by teaching them the categories of English and Scottish "mental philosophy"—the early nineteenth-century's version of what we call psychology. This tradition of pastoral theology continued through the later nineteenth century, introducing ministerial students not only to customary methods of exhortation and advice but also to changing conceptions of human nature formulated by philosophers and psychologists.

By the late nineteenth century, pastoral writers displayed an increasing awareness of the ways in which knowledge of psychology and medicine could instruct the pastor. In part this awareness reflected the influence of liberal theologians, whose doctrine of divine immanence assumed that God was manifest in the highest cultural attainments. Further stimulus for a new awareness came from innovations in medicine and the academic disciplines.

2. Psychology of Religion and Psychotherapy. One such new discipline was the psychology of religion. Its seminal figure, G. Stanley Hall at Clark University in Worcester, Massachusetts, emphasized the functional value of religious experience as a means of nurturing the development of the personality. When William James wrote *The Varieties of Religious Experience* (1902), he expanded this notion by arguing that religious experience put men and women in touch with a "wider self" through which they could be transformed. A few of the early psychologists of religion used these insights to promote methods of pastoral care designed to respect the natural processes of human growth. They also stimulated interest in notions of the unconscious or subconscious and deepened within the seminaries a growing interest in the practical applications of psychological research.

Equally important for pastoral practice was the expanding critique of medical materialism. After the English translation in 1905 of the *Psychic Treatment of Nervous Disorders* by Pierre DuBois, a professor of psychotherapy at the University of Bern, a few American physicians began to acknowledge the possibility of a "scientific mind cure." In 1906 the American index of medical papers listed *psychotherapy* as a separate topic, and in 1909 Sigmund Freud attended the first American Conference on Psychotherapy. The National Committee for Mental Hygiene, also founded in 1909, soon was attempting to apply the new understandings of psychotherapy to the reform of hospitals and the creation of institutions to advance mental health.

Both the psychologists of religion and the psychotherapists displayed a special interest in notions of subconscious or unconscious mental processes. By 1905, a few American pastoral writers began to explore those notions, some favoring a Freudian notion of the unconscious as a source of internal conflict, others preferring theories that attributed to the subconscious mind both rationality and creativity. Both ideas found proponents among the pastors, who in 1904 organized in Boston the Emmanuel Movement, whose founders, especially the Episcopal priest Elwood Worcester, argued that the cure of souls within the church should be guided by science, not tradition. Their journal, *Psychotherapy*, helped to popularize themes that would reappear in the later pastoral care movement.

3. Religious Education. Even more important than the Emmanuel pioneers in laying the groundwork for the pastoral care movement were the religious educators. In 1903 they formed the Religious Education Association, which became a channel for communicating to the churches many of the latest developments in psychological theory and research. Agreeing with George Albert Coe that religious education should be a "forming of the whole self," they taught some of the earliest pastoral counseling courses in Protestant seminaries. As early as 1921 Harrison Elliott taught such a course at Union Theological Seminary in New York; Gaines Dobbins at Southern Baptist Theological Seminary made similar efforts to "capture psychology for Christ" in the heartland of southern religious conservatism.

In the 1930s, religious educators and pastoral theologians began to publish guidebooks instructing pastors how to apply twentieth-century psychological theory to their pastoral conversations. In *The Cure of Souls: A Socio-Psychological Approach* (1932), Charles Holman of the University of Chicago, drawing partly on John Dewey's definitions of adjustment, described "soul-sickness" as inadequate religious or moral adaptation. In *Pastoral Psychology* (1932), Karl Stolz of the Hartford School of Religious Education also argued that the pastor's responsibility was to help persons adjust themselves to reality. John Sutherland Bonnell, a Presbyterian minister in New York, drew the ideas in his *Pastoral Psychiatry* (1938) from both Sigmund Freud and Alfred Adler, though he too contended that the goal of pastoral counseling was to help people make a right adjustment to God. The most influential book written during the 1930s came from the physician Richard Cabot and the hospital chaplain Russell Dicks, who published in 1936 *The Art of Ministering to the Sick,* which depicted the pastor's task in the hospital room as the discerning and nurturing of the patient's "growing edges."

4. Clinical Pastoral Education. It would not have been possible to refer during the 1930s to a pastoral care "movement." Interest in the newer understandings of pastoral care was still too diffuse and unorganized. But a few innovators in theological education had begun as early as 1923 to create new patterns of ministerial training—and some new institutions— that made it possible for a genuine movement to develop.

The Episcopal physician William S. Keller in 1923 founded a summer school in social service in Cincinnati, designed to deepen theological education by having students do casework in social agencies. Keller thought that the students would learn best through engagement in the practice of ministry with persons in need, followed by periods of reflection.

In 1925, Richard Cabot, a Boston neurologist and cardiologist, published "Plea for a Clinical Year in the Course of Theological Study," arguing that the exposure of theological students to people suffering in hospitals would enhance their capacities for ministry. Before the end of the year, the hospital chaplain Anton Boisen began, with Cabot's blessing, to train a handful of students at Worcester State Hospital. Boisen viewed clinical training as an occasion for introducing students to "living human documents" from whom they might derive insight into sin, salvation, and religious experience. His *Exploration of the Inner World* (1936) argued that mental illness represented a chaotic encounter with God, which could lead either to a new integration of the personality or a fall into total inner disarray.

In 1930, Cabot, Boisen, and others joined in the formation of the Council for Clinical Training of Theological Students, designed to make possible a long-term supervised encounter with men and women in crisis in hospitals, prisons, and social agencies. Known later as Clinical Pastoral Education (CPE), this new form of theological education was destined to alter dramatically the prevailing conceptions of pastoral care.

Almost from the beginning, the clinical pastoral educators split into two groups. Under the leadership of the psychiatrist Helen Flanders Dunbar, the Council for Clinical Training favored mental hospitals as training sites and tried to give students a clear conception of the place of psychoanalysis in psychotherapy. When Robert Brinkman became director in 1938, he turned to psychoanalytic doctrine not only to provide the students an understanding of "deeper motivation" but also to interpret traditional Christian images. Richard Cabot, scornful of psychoanalysis and skeptical of other forms of psychotherapy, then joined with Philip Guiles of Andover Newton and David R. Hunter, chaplain at Massachusetts General Hospital, in the formation of the New England Theological Schools Committee on Clinical Training.

The Theological Schools Committee lasted only a short time, but in 1944 Rollin Fairbanks, a professor at the Episcopal Theological Seminary in Cambridge, led in the organization of the Institute for Pastoral Care, which developed close relationships with seminaries in the Boston area. In contrast to the council, which preferred mental hospitals and prisons as training sites, the institute initially preferred general hospitals. While the council was sometimes perceived as interested mainly in educating chaplains, the institute emphasized its interest in training the parish minister. The council viewed itself as a focus of rebellion against rigid and oppressive moral conventions and religious legalism; the institute did not share that self-understanding.

The tensions between the two clinical programs dissipated slowly, but in 1967 they joined in a new organization: the Association for Clinical Pastoral Education, a group that also encompassed denominational clinical programs founded by Lutherans and Southern Baptists.

In 1932 Austin Philip Guiles had broken away from the Council for Clinical Training of Theological Students and established a program in clinical education at Andover Newton Theological Seminary. Within the next thirty years, clinical supervisors developed alliances with more than forty other theological schools; they also organized at least 117 regular centers for CPE, linked closely to medical centers and other institutions. By 1955 more than 4,000 Protestant students had undergone some form of CPE, and the National Council of Churches was offering scholarship aid for parish ministers who wanted the training. By this time, moreover, Anton Boisen, Russell Dicks, and the Presbyterian theologian Seward Hiltner had refined the pedagogical methods that would mark education in the centers: case studies and "verbatims," or word-for-word transcriptions of pastoral conversations.

5. Pastoral Counseling Centers. The expansion of CPE paralleled and stimulated a gradual proliferation of pastoral counseling centers staffed by ministers, psychiatrists, and social workers. Austin Philip Guiles typified the leadership of clinical educators in the formation of such centers: he opened one at the Wellesley Hills Congregational Church and another at the Old South Church in Boston. Other counseling centers came into existence independently of both the Council for Clinical Training and the Institute for Pastoral Care. The Religio-Psychiatric Clinic of Marble Collegiate Church in New York, founded in 1937, gradually developed into an extensive center for pastoral counseling, especially after 1951, when it was renamed the American Foundation of Religion and Psychiatry. In 1950 there were 10 such centers; in 1963, by one count, there were 149.

The emergence of the pastoral counseling centers helped to sharpen a new distinction between pastoral care and pastoral counseling. Some of the centers offered specialized training programs in counseling. For instance, shortly after Frederick Kuether, one of Boisen's early students, assumed responsibility for the clergy training program of the American Foundation of Religion and Psychiatry in 1954, he inaugurated such a program. The Institute of Religion in the Texas Medical Center in Houston became another popular center for the training of pastoral counselors.

6. Seminaries and Chaplaincies. Prior to World War II, few theological seminaries offered courses in counseling. During the war, however, the Chaplain's School at Harvard discovered that counseling skills were essential for military chaplains. The clinical programs and counseling centers also helped convince the seminaries to take counseling seriously, and during the 1950s almost all the North American theological schools developed counseling courses. More than 80 percent offered additional courses in psychology, and more than 80 percent listed at least one psychologist on the faculty.

Such courses proved especially enticing for students planning for institutional chaplaincies, and the postwar economy permitted increasing numbers of hospitals to hire full-time chaplains. In 1940, few openings had been available; by the end of the 1950s, almost 500 full-time chaplains served in general hospitals, and at least 200 more worked in mental hospitals. In the hospitals of the Veterans Administration alone, 240 clergy served in chaplaincy posts. As early as 1946, John M. Billinsky, who taught pastoral care at Andover Newton, and Russell Dicks, who would soon begin teaching at Duke Divinity School, formed a chaplain's section of the American Protestant Hospital Association. Two years later, Ernest Bruder, a chaplain at St. Elizabeth's Hospital in Washington, D.C., led in the formation of the Association of Mental Hospital Chaplains. Because hospital chaplains spent most of their time visiting and counseling patients and their families, the expansion of hospital openings deepened interest in counseling issues.

The new literature of the pastoral care movement reflected this interest in counseling. Clinical pastoral educators founded in 1947 the *Journal of Pastoral Care* and the *Journal of Clinical Pastoral Work*. In 1950, Simon Doniger became the first editor of *Pastoral Psychology,* which soon had more than 16,000 subscribers, most of them ministers. A small group of pastoral theologians assumed a position of intellectual leadership. Seward Hiltner, who had been associated with the Federal Council of Churches before joining the faculty of the University of Chicago, drew on social and cultural anthropology in preparing his *Pastoral Counseling* (1949), in which he proposed "eductive" methods of counseling that tried to elicit solutions out of the creative potentialities of the person needing help rather than offer advice and direction. Carroll A. Wise, a professor of pastoral psychology and counseling at Methodist Garrett Biblical Institute, based his *Pastoral Counseling* (1951) on personalist theology, dynamic psychology, and the nondirective theories of the therapist Carl Rogers. In *The Christian Pastor* (1951), Wayne Oates, a professor of pastoral care and the psychology of religion at Southern Baptist Theological Seminary, attempted to combine traditional Protestant language with a theory of "psychosocial role behavior" taken from the social sciences. Paul Johnson, a Methodist professor of psychology at Boston University, drew on the methods of Carl Rogers, interpersonal psychiatry, and personalist theology for his *Psychology of Pastoral Care* (1953).

The surge of interest in counseling stimulated reflection on the broader meaning of pastoral care. A few pastoral theologians reemphasized the distinction between pastoral care, the whole range of clerical activity aimed at guiding and sustaining a congregation, and counseling, a more narrowly defined relationship between a pastor and a person in need. Some argued that pastoral counseling was merely one dimension of pastoral care and that it made sense only within the context of the church. In 1955 a commission on the ministry sponsored by the New York Academy of Sciences observed that a minister's work was always "distinguished by the religious setting in which it is done" (Oates, 1955).

7. American Association of Pastoral Counselors. By 1961 a number of leaders in the pastoral care movement began to call for pastoral counseling specialists to work in counseling centers or even to carry on private pastoral practice. In 1963 Frederick Kuether and Arthur Tingue convened a conference in New York City that resulted in the formation of the American Association of Pastoral Counselors, a group designed initially for specialists in pastoral counseling. The conference, which elected Howard Clinebell of the Claremont School of Theology in California as its chairperson, generated controversy within the larger pastoral care movement. When Kuether challenged the idea that pastoral counseling belonged exclusively in the churches, both Seward Hiltner and Wayne Oates of Southern Baptist Theological Seminary criticized the association, arguing especially that the notion of private pastoral practice, which Kuether thought might sometimes be appropriate, was a contradiction in terms and a violation of the character of ministry. In 1964, however, the association, meeting in St. Louis, decided to admit parish ministers as members. It soon opposed any notion of private practice that failed to ensure some measure of accountability to an ecclesiastical judicatory.

The interest in pastoral care and counseling had other institutional consequences. By the end of the 1950s, at least seven universities offered advanced graduate programs in personality and theology, pastoral psychology, pastoral theology, or pastoral counseling. And pastors could also find resources at more than thirty-five institutes and seminars, such as Reuel Howe's Institute for Advanced Pastoral Studies, located in a suburb of Detroit, or Thomas Klink's Program in Religion and Psychiatry at the Menninger Clinic in Kansas.

The movement during the 1950s invested heavily in the nondirective methods of the American psychologist Carl Rogers, but during the 1960s the Rogerian style came under attack. Clinebell and Johnson began to argue that the presuppositions of Rogerian counseling were too individualistic, and Clinebell called in his *Basic Types of Pastoral Counseling* (1966) for a "relationship-centered counseling" aimed at enhancing a person's ability to form satisfying relationships with other people, and advocated an eclectic array of alternative pastoral counseling methods. Hiltner and Oates warned against the tendency of pastoral writers to seek a borrowed identity from psychotherapy, emphasized the importance of the church as the setting for pastoral care, and accented the distinction between pastoral care and pastoral counseling.

By the late 1970s, theologians of pastoral care were seeking greater clarity about the theological underpinnings of their discipline. Such theorists as Don Browning of the University of Chicago and Charles Gerkin at Emory University proposed new ethical and theological models for pastoral care. Gerkin's *The Living Human Document* (1984) drew on theological hermeneutics to reinterpret pastoral counseling, and Browning's *Religious Ethics and Pastoral Care* (1983) related psychology and the social sciences to moral theory.

The pastoral care movement flourished especially in America. This was owed partly to the profound influence of psychotherapy in American culture, partly to the strength of the institutional network established by clinical pastoral educators, who created and nurtured in theological students an interest in counseling issues, and partly to the capacity of the American economy to sustain a host of chaplaincy positions in hospitals and other institutions. The expansion of the movement also depended heavily on financial support from private foundations. The William C. Whitney Foundation gave the Council for Clinical Training its start; the Earhart Foundation provided the initial money for the rival clinical program in New England; a foundation funded by insurance magnate W. Clement Stone supported the American Foundation of Religion and Psychiatry and provided most of the initial money to start the American Association of Pastoral Counselors; the Old Dominion Foundation backed the new program in psychiatry and religion at Union Theological Seminary; and the Lilly Endowment undergirded a similar program at the University of Chicago.

8. European Movements. By 1963, Europeans had also developed their own revised views of pastoral care and counseling. In England, Leslie

Weatherhead began as early as 1922 to encourage ministers to learn from psychotherapists, and the former medical missionary Frank Lake began seminars in 1958 that introduced depth psychology to many English pastors. During the 1920s in Berlin, the "Doctor and Pastoral Counselor" group began conversations between ministers and psychoanalysts, and Otto Haendler introduced a later generation of German theological students to the writings of Freud, Adler, and Jung. In 1944, Gute Bergsten in Stockholm founded the Institute for Spiritual Counsel and Psychological Treatment under the auspices of the St. Luke's Foundation.

In 1966, Dutch and American pastors met together in the Netherlands, with the result that the American CPE movement soon gained strong adherents in that country. Six years later, Werner Becher in West Germany, who had studied at the Menninger Foundation, led in the organization of a European conference "Clinical Pastoral Education for Pastoral Care and Counseling" at Arnoldshain, the first of several such gatherings that preceded the first large international meeting at Edinburgh in 1979. Out of that meeting came not only the International Committee on Pastoral Care and Counseling but also a new consciousness of what came to be called the international pastoral care and counseling movement. This was the first international meeting in which there was significant Third World participation, with representatives from Africa, Asia, and Latin America.

Europeans who founded national organizations tended to follow the nomenclature that became standard in the international movement, which linked pastoral counseling closely to pastoral care. When the English, for instance, founded in 1972 their own Association for Pastoral Care and Counseling, they tended not to encourage a view of counseling as an autonomous activity. And the American debates over the accreditation of counselors and organizations, the nature of pastoral counseling centers, and the practice of pastoral psychotherapy have not attracted significant attention in Europe. In Third World countries the movement has developed indigenous forms emphasizing the force of social, political, and economic circumstances on human development and fashioning new forms of pastoral education and care in response to them.

Bibliography. R. Baxter, *Reformed Pastor* (1658). A. Boisen, *Exploration of the Inner World* (1936), *Out of the Depths* (1960). J. S. Bonnell, *Pastoral Psychiatry* (1938). D. Browning, *Religious Ethics and Pastoral Care* (1983). G. Burnet, *Discourse of the Pastoral Care* (1713). R. C. Cabot and R. Dicks, *The Art of Ministering to the Sick* (1936). H. Clinebell, *Basic Types* *of Pastoral Counseling* (1966). P. DuBois, *Psychic Treatment of Nervous Disorders* (ET 1905). C. Gerkin, *The Living Human Document* (1984). G. Herbert, *Country Parson* (1652). S. Hiltner, *Pastoral Counseling* (1949). E. B. Holifield, *A History of Pastoral Care in America: From Salvation to Self-Realization* (1983). C. Holman, *The Cure of Souls: A Socio-Psychological Approach* (1932). W. James, *The Varieties of Religious Experience* (1902). P. Johnson, *Psychology of Pastoral Care* (1953). W. E. Oates, *The Christian Pastor* (1951); "The Findings of the Commission in the Ministry," *Annals of the New York Academy of Sciences*, vol. 63, issue 3 Psychotherapy, 414–22 (1955). A. Stokes, *Ministry after Freud* (1985). K. Stolz, *Pastoral Psychology* (1932). E. E. Thornton, *Professional Education for Ministry* (1970). C. A. Wise, *Pastoral Counseling* (1951).

E. B. HOLIFIELD

TILLICH, PAUL (1886–1965). Protestant systematic theologian. After leaving Germany in 1933, Tillich taught at Union Theological Seminary (New York), Harvard University, and the University of Chicago. In his sermons, his writings on the theology of culture, and his systematic theology, he often sought to find correlations between theological and psychological themes.

One of Tillich's most important contributions to the pastoral care tradition was his method of correlation, according to which the philosophical or psychological analysis of existence and the questions it raised shaped the form of the Christian answer presented by the theologian. Since 1929, when the neurologist Kurt Goldstein and the psychologist Adhemar Gelb at the University of Frankfurt encouraged Tillich to study psychiatric theory, he had incorporated a psychological vocabulary into his thought. His method of correlation permitted him to seek the inner continuities between the psychological language and traditional theological concepts. Hence the Protestant notion of justification by grace could be reinterpreted, in the light of clinical psychiatric experience, as the insight that the unacceptable were accepted. The psychoanalytic method, Tillich said, had taught him what it meant to speak of accepting the unacceptable. And that knowledge, in turn, provided a new insight into the notion of justification. Yet at the same time, the method of correlation also redefined acceptance by locating it within a wider theological vocabulary that deepened its significance. It enabled Tillich to say that the acceptance offered by counselors represented and embodied a "power of acceptance" that transcended any finite relationship.

Tillich also enhanced the understanding of pastoral care by his careful exploration of such notions as anxiety, freedom, guilt, and courage. His work influenced the existential and phenomenological psychologists who sought to understand such themes without simply retracing them to childhood origins or viewing them as merely surface manifestations of deeper psychic processes. Tillich's single most important contribution to the theory of pastoral care might well have been his *Courage to Be* (1952), in which he explored, among other topics, the relationships between ontological and pathological anxiety.

After moving to New York, Tillich took an active part in the New York Psychology Group, which contained theologians, psychologists, sociologists, and psychoanalysts. The group, which sometimes met in Tillich's apartment, served as an important resource for some of the leaders of the modern pastoral care movement, including Seward Hiltner, David Roberts, Rollo May, and Harrison and Grace Elliott. He also became an influential theological consultant for the journal *Pastoral Psychology* and often wrote for it. Tillich carried on a continuing dialogue with psychologists and psychoanalysts, always urging them to recognize the ontological—and ultimately theological—implications of their psychological categories.

Indeed, during the two decades following World War II, no theologian exercised more influence than Tillich on the theological and theoretical interpretation of pastoral care, especially in North America.

E. B. HOLIFIELD

WILLIAMS, DANIEL DAY (1910–73). A Congregational Church minister, author, lecturer, and a theology professor at Chicago Theological Seminary and the University of Chicago, 1939–54, and Union Theological Seminary (New York), 1954–73. Influenced by the process philosophy of Whitehead and Hartshorne, his early writing (*God's Grace and Man's Hope*, 1949) struck an intermediate position between the liberal and neoorthodox traditions. Later he produced what has been called the first systematic process theology (*The Spirit and the Forms of Love*, 1968). His continuing concern to interpret the Christian faith in relation to human thought and experience led to a particular emphasis on theology and psychotherapy (*The Minister and the Care of Souls*, 1961). A sensitive pastor and counselor, Williams's most significant contribution to pastoral counseling has been in the area of theological methodology. Specifically, he calls for a pastoral method that goes beyond a simple linguistic linking of theological and psychological cate-gories to a deeper exploration of the metaphysical realities that inform them both.

C. M. MENDENHALL III

WISE, CARROLL A. (1903–85). Methodist chaplain, pastor, clinical educator, and pastoral theologian. As one of the theological leaders of the American pastoral care movement, Wise explored the function of reli-gious symbols for the integration of personality and developed an inter-pretation of pastoral care as the art of communicating the inner meaning of the gospel to persons at the point of their need through relationships in which deep feelings could find expression and acceptance.

Such a conception of pastoral care led Wise to adopt the methods of client-centered counseling proposed by the therapist Carl Rogers. He thought that communication in counseling occurred more through the pastor's acceptance and understanding of the parishioner than through any efforts at verbal reassurance. In his *Pastoral Counseling: Its Theory and Practice* (1951) and *The Meaning of Pastoral Care* (1966) he argued that the condition for success in pastoral counseling was the quality of the relationship between the pastor and the person in need, and he therefore urged that pastors consider their "general pastoral relationships" as the setting within which effective counseling could take place. Wise devel-oped his views partly through his work as a counselor for the YMCA, through a four-year appointment as the counseling minister of the Hennepin Avenue Methodist Church in Minneapolis, and through his teaching as professor of pastoral psychology and counseling at Garrett Biblical Institute.

Having received clinical pastoral training under Anton Boisen at Worcester State Hospital, Wise became Boisen's successor in 1931 as chaplain and clinical training supervisor at that institution. He worked within the Council for Clinical Training and defended its use of mental hospitals for purposes of clinical training. He also supported the psycho-dynamic orientation that characterized the work of the council. He later became the president of the council and a supporter of plans for its merger with the Institute for Pastoral Care. Thus he contributed to the formation of the Association of Clinical Pastoral Education in 1967. He also sup-ported the creation of an American Association of Pastoral Counselors in 1963.

The publication of his *Religion in Illness and Health* (1942) stimulated interest in the therapeutic functions of religion. Impressed by the work of Helen Flanders Dunbar and Walter B. Cannon in psychosomatic medicine, Wise explored the function of religious symbolism in the understanding of illness and the promotion of health. He believed that an appropriate religious worldview would lead toward the integration and growth, and hence the health, of the personality. He had an interest, as well, in the unhealthy use of religious symbols as means of self-deception and concealment. The book represented the growing acceptance of psychodynamic theories among Protestant pastoral writers.

Wise had studied theology at Boston University, and his work represented an expansion and modification of theological personalism. Arguing that the gospel was revealed through a person and could be communicated only through personal relationship, Wise was critical of any moralism or intellectualism that imposed static categories on dynamic relationships. He urged pastoral counselors to value the person rather than attempt to change the person's values.

Wise was among the most influential of the American pastoral theologians after World War II. His emphasis on interaction and relationship found wide acceptance in seminaries and clinical centers.

E. B. HOLIFIELD

3

ISSUES OF POWER AND DIFFERENCE

In the 2004 expansion of the original *Dictionary of Pastoral Care and Counseling*, Nancy Ramsay notes that, in the latter twentieth century, the pastoral care and counseling field, and the organizations in which its leaders serve, were at the point of "assimilation" of difference and "leveling the playing field," but had not reached the important stage of redefinition of dominant norms that is now a primary frontier (and necessity) in this field and in today's world. Most of the articles in this chapter were written during that earlier "assimilation" stage, and yet they still point us toward the challenges of redefinition of norms still being faced by the theological seminaries, churches, health care institutions, and other organizations in which readers of this volume work. Contextual theologies (including black, feminist, and liberation theologies) provide a theological basis for this movement. Racism, sexism, and abuse of power are still "alive and well" in many groups and organizations, including those that claim to be faith-based, and this points all the more to the needs for pastoral care and counseling to address social justice and social systems as well as care for individuals.

Included in this chapter are contemporary (2009) commentaries from the gay and lesbian community and from sub-Saharan Africa regarding struggles particular to those contexts.

BLACK THEOLOGY AND PASTORAL CARE. Black theology represents the religious dimension of a significant cultural revolution that was forged by black Americans in the mid-1960s as a new development in their struggle for racial justice. Black theology boldly asserts that a racist cultural bias in the Euro-American theological tradition has distorted the true meaning of Christianity. Assuming a prophetic stance, Black theology wages an unrelenting battle against the ideological assumptions of ecclesiastical authorities and academic scholars by advocating the identification of the mission of Jesus with the liberation struggles of oppressed peoples in general, and black Americans in particular. In fact, Black theology argues that solidarity with the black American struggle is a fundamental requirement of all American Christians desirous of being faithful to Jesus Christ.

1. Historical Development. In the midst of the activities of Christian activists in the Black church–related civil rights movement of Martin Luther King, Jr., and the events stimulated by the Black Power movement, the National Committee of Negro Churchmen (NCNC, later called the National Conference of Black Churchmen) published a Christian theological justification for the phrase "Black Power." During that period blacks found themselves alienated not only from white conservatives but also from their former allies, white liberals. Accordingly, the NCNC statement launched the first attempt since the Marcus Garvey movement of the 1920s to separate Black Christianity from the theology of the white churches. It strongly affirmed black consciousness and Black Power as necessary elements in the quest for liberation.

The publication of James H. Cone's book *Black Power and Black Theology* in 1969 marked the first major explication of a Black theology. As the progenitor of this new movement, Cone describes his own work as an attempt to develop a systematic explanation of the contents of a gospel of liberation that will be a motivational force and a Christian justification for the liberation struggle against racism. In other words, Black theology contends that the Bible must be read in light of the struggles of oppressed black Americans whose social condition establishes for them a place of hermeneutical privilege in grasping the will of God.

Black theology is integrally related to Black liberation politics. Its subject matter is the God of the black American experience, that is, the One in whom black Americans have trusted throughout the period of slavery up to the present time. This identification of the "Jesus of the black experience" with the "Jesus of Scripture" is the principal way whereby Cone establishes common ground between the social realities of the black American experience and the claims of the NT record. But (according to many) herein lies Black theology's chief vulnerability, namely, a tendency to identify political ideology with Christian theology. Not surprisingly, some of its strongest critics have been sympathetic theologians trying to persuade Cone to avoid the idolatry implicit in every cultural theology.

In his book *God of the Oppressed* Cone responds to his critics by drawing upon the resources of the sociology of knowledge in order to show the necessary relationship between the theologian's social situation and his or her theological enterprise. Further, he argues that the identification of God with the particularity of oppressed black Americans implies no exclusive election of blacks by God but, rather, represents a specific instance expressive of God's solidarity with all oppressed peoples. In fact, Cone and other Black theologians appeal to the biblical claim of God's identification with the Israelite struggle for liberation as a primary ground for demonstrating the relationship between the social condition of oppressed peoples and the activity of God.

Cone argues further that God's solidarity with the black struggle for racial justice in the twentieth century is similar to his solidarity with the Israelites in effecting their deliverance from slavery. In short, Black theology contends that it is consonant with the biblical understanding that God's activity in history is always seen in the liberation struggles of oppressed peoples. In this respect, Black theology has made a creative contribution to theological inquiry by tracing the bias within the Bible (viz., God's identification with the oppressed), thereby clarifying a theological symbol that has been obscured by the Euro-American theological tradition.

Clearly, Black theology represents a revisionist method in theological scholarship that is typified by a move away from the universal realm of absolute ideation as the starting point for the theological task and toward the historical context of concrete reality. Hence, like all liberation theologies, Black theology does not seek theological solutions for theoretical problems but, rather, theological understandings that are relative to the liberating desires and activities of oppressed peoples. Nevertheless, Black theology is dogmatic and like every form of dogmatism it claims possession of absolute truth, aims at its systematization, and assumes for itself an authoritative posture on all normative matters of thought and practice. The general ambivalence of the black churches to the Black Theology movement is caused in large part by the latter's dogmatic orientation.

Black theology may be described best as radical social criticism for three reasons: (1) its wholesale condemnation of Euro-American theology's uncritical appropriation of the prevailing racist values implicit in its cultural milieu; (2) its methodological focus on praxis (i.e., the liberation struggle) as both a descriptive and normative principle: descriptive in its portrayal of the nature of human experience with which the inquiry begins, and normative in both its theological identification with Jesus the Liberator as well as its moral imperative for political action; and (3) its revolutionary aim to provide theological grounds for a liberating praxis that aims at effecting radical change in all societal structures of racial oppression.

2. The Implications of Black Theology for Pastoral Care. The novelty of Black theology's inductive approach to theological inquiry lies in its explicit affirmation of the experiences of oppressed peoples as the starting point for an understanding of God's activity in the world. This distinctive approach has constituted a radical challenge to an older style of scholarship that was interested primarily in measuring the impact of oppression on the oppressed, implying thereby that the latter were merely victims of external forces acting on them. Consequently, that older form of scholarship failed to discern those self-initiating and constructive activities of oppressed peoples. In fact, it assumed that the oppressed were incapable of exercising any agency whatsoever. Hence, the results of such scholarship were predictable: that is, pervasive levels of pathological disorder permeating the social, psychological, political, and cultural dimensions of life among the oppressed. In fact, for a long while, it was not uncommon for scholars in all fields (black and white alike) to view the thought and practices of black religion as aberrations of their white counterparts.

The emergence of Black theology has afforded blacks a perspective with which they might make a distinctive methodological contribution to all areas of religious scholarship, including that of pastoral care. Since Black theology represents the religious dimension of a cultural revolution among black Americans, all areas of the humanities and the social sciences have felt its impact to some degree. Hence, most recent research in the area of black American studies assumes a high measure of cognitive, moral, religious, social, and political agency on the part of oppressed blacks throughout their history: agency that has enabled them (then and now) to gain significant levels of transcendence over the crippling conditions of their lives.

Black theology's efforts in identifying the liberating activity of blacks with the acts of God have hastened the demise of all feelings of racial inferiority that had plagued blacks for so many generations. Black theology has given renewed impetus to such principles as racial self-respect, self-reliance, self-initiative, self-determination, and self-fulfillment; principles that formerly relied on various pragmatic arguments for their justification are now grounded theologically.

For its continuing enlightenment, however, Black theology must rely on the findings of all the areas of study, including the resources provided by the field of pastoral care. Further research on the psychology of oppressed peoples both as victims and as agents of liberation can help Black theology in its reflections. Further, the psychology implied by Black theology needs clarification and critical evaluation.

Finally, Black theology's focus on the self-initiating activities of the black oppressed must be brought into relationship with the immense suffering that results from the conditions of oppression. Both the capacity to transcend those conditions and the capacity to undergo them represent two poles of the black experience that must not be separated from each other. Black theology's tendency to focus on the former and pastoral care's tendency to concentrate on the latter must be challenged by the insights of each such that both might strive for a more holistic approach to the black American experience.

Bibliography. J. H. Cone, *Black Power and Black Theology* (1969); *God of the Oppressed* (1975). V. L. Lattimore, "The Positive Contribution of Black Cultural Values to Pastoral Counseling," *J. of Pastoral Care* 36 (1982), 105–17. G. S. Wilmore and J. H. Cone, eds., *Black Theology: A Documentary History, 1966–1979* (1979).

P. J. PARIS

CONTEXTUAL THEOLOGY. Theology that is constructed with maximal concern for its relevance to the cultural context in which it occurs. Contemporary attempts at theological contextualization frequently carry such labels as "Black theology," "Liberation theology," "African theology," "Melanesian theology," and the like.

All theologizing is done from a particular point of view, in terms of the perspectives (including the biases) of the producers of the theology. Those who are doing the theologizing have particular questions in their minds arising from their life experience within the culture in which they participate. As they study and reflect on the Scriptures (and other sources to which they look for assistance) they seek to discover and formulate answers to those questions. In this way, theology comes into being.

The term "contextualization" was defined by Shoki Coe (1973) as preferable to the term "indigenization," which has been widely used as a label for the ideal toward which cross-cultural witnesses to Christianity strive in non-Western contexts. To many missiologists, the latter term has come to connote too static an understanding of what should happen when Christianity is introduced into a given culture. A term like "contextualization" is felt to have a more dynamic meaning (see Taber, 1979).

Since its introduction, the term has gained fairly wide currency among missiologists in both liberal and conservative camps. Anthropologically oriented conservatives have largely embraced the concept and sought to point out its relevance both in missiological contexts and in describing the process by means of which Western theologizing is done (see Kraft, 1979; Taber, 1978). Conservative theologians tend to be suspicious of both the term and the process, perhaps due to the fact that the term originated within the liberal camp (see Henry, 1980; Nicholls, 1979). H. M. Conn (1977), a conservative theologian-missiologist with cross-cultural experience, is a notable exception.

1. Historical Use. Advocates of contextualization see this process as part and parcel both of the NT record and of the theologizing activity of all subsequent interpreters of Christianity. This is the process that the Apostles were involved in as they sought to take the Christian message that had come to them in Aramaic language and culture and to conceptualize it for those who spoke Greek. In order to contextualize Christianity for Greeks, the Apostles gave themselves to the expression of Christian truth in the thought patterns of those to whom they spoke. Indigenous words and concepts were used to deal with such topics as God, church, sin, conversion, repentance, initiation, and most other areas of Christian life and practice.

The early Greek churches were in danger of being dominated by Hebrew theology, just as many non-Western churches today are in danger of being dominated by Western theologies. The Apostle Paul and others, however, struggled against the Hebrew Christians to develop a contextualized Christian theology for those who thought according to Greek conceptual patterns. In doing this they had constant conflict with many of the Hebrew church leaders, who felt it proper to simply impose Hebrew theological concepts on new converts (see Acts 15). These conservative Hebrews were, as D. von Allmen (1975) points out, the heretics against whom Paul fights for the right for Greek-speaking Christians to have the gospel contextualized in their language and culture.

It was a similar battle that Martin Luther and the other reformers fought in the sixteenth century for the rights of Christians to think theologically in German rather than in Latin. Later, the Anabaptists and others struggled against the Lutherans for the right to contextualize Christianity in their own cultural forms. The history of denominationalism in Europe and America is full of such struggles. A like situation exists in many missionized countries today, where peoples of non-Western cultures are finding that the theological formulations of generations of Western theologians are often irrelevant to the pressing problems that they need to deal with. Contextualization becomes, therefore, the way to escape the conceptual domination of the West (Boyd, 1974) just as political independence has become the way to escape political domination.

2. Method. Some might feel that the intensive investigations of generations of Western theologians must surely have produced a once-for-all set of theological understandings that can simply be passed on from culture to culture. Those who have been involved in attempts to contextualize Christian theology in non-Western cultures have not, however, found this to be true. The questions addressed by Western theologians (particularly academic theologians) are very often quite different from those being asked by village Africans, Asians, Latin Americans, and even non-academic North Americans. It is discovered, rather, that

> any authentic theology must start ever anew from the focal point of the faith, which is the confession of the Lord Jesus Christ who died and was raised for us; and it must be built or re-built (whether in Africa or in Europe) in a way which is both faithful to the inner thrust of the Christian revelation and also in harmony with the mentality of the person who formulates it. There is no short cut to be found by simply adapting an existing theology to contemporary or local taste. (von Allmen, 1975, 50)

The contextualization of Christian theology is, therefore, not simply the passing of a "product" that has been developed once for all in Europe or America. It is, rather, the imitating of the process that the early apostles went through. Since the materials from which the theologizing is done are the same biblical materials, the essential message will be the same. The formulation of that message, the relative prominence of many of the issues addressed, and, indeed, the presence or absence of certain issues will, however, differ from culture to culture. New Testament teaching concerning the superiority of the power of Christ to that of evil spirits is, for example, a much more prominent part of contextualized African or New Guinean theology than of American theology. Advocates of theological contextualization frequently draw a parallel between contextualization and the Incarnation of Jesus Christ (Coe, 1973). They suggest that just as in Christ God participated fully in a given human culture, though his origin lay outside of that culture, so in contextualization the theologizing process participates fully in the cultural realities in which the formulations take place, even though the stimuli (e.g., the Bible and other revelatory activity on the part of God) have their origins outside of the receiving culture. Incarnation, of course, involves more of life than thinking, articulating, and writing.

Incarnational/contextualized theologizing is seen, therefore, as an activity that embraces all of living rather than something relegated to small portions of living (such as thinking behavior). Non-Western and nonacademic theologizing even in Western contexts is seen more as something that is lived than as something that is merely written. It is also seen as something that everyone does rather than simply the activity of a few academically trained specialists. Theologizing is, therefore, seen as expressed through ceremony, ritual, singing, informal conversation, and all other aspects of life. Indeed, persons may formally articulate theological beliefs that are different from those beliefs that they practice or express in ceremony, ritual, and so forth.

Contextualization of theology is, therefore, something that is always happening whenever people ponder or otherwise express their faith. It takes many forms, only some of which are recordable in writing. It may be done formally (as by those with academic training in theology) or informally (as by everyone, including academics, in the living, ritualizing, and so forth, of the faith). Even academic theologizing may be done in terms of perspectives other than those traditionally recognized as Theology. (See Kraft, 1979, for an appeal for and exemplification of this contention.)

Bibliography. R. H. Boyd, *India and the Latin Captivity of the Church* (1974). R. M. Brown, "The Rootedness of All Theology," *Christianity and Crisis* (1977), 170–74. S. Coe, "Authentic Contextuality Leads to Contextualization," *Theological Education* 9 (1973), 24–25. H. M. Conn, "Contextualization: Where Do We Begin?" in C. E. Armerding, *Evangelicals and Liberation* (1977), 90–119. C. F. H. Henry, "The

Cultural Relativizing of Revelation," *Trinity J.* (1980), 153–64. C. H. Kraft, *Christianity in Culture* (1979); "The Contextualization of Theology," *Evangelical Missions Quarterly* (1978), 31–36. B. Nicholls, *Contextualization: A Theology of Gospel and Culture* (1979). C. R. Taber, "Contextualization: Indigenization and/or Transformation," in D. M. McCurry, ed., *The Gospel and Islam* (1979), 143–54; "Is There More Than One Way to Do Theology?" *Gospel in Context* (1978), 4–10; "The Limits of Indigenization in Theology," *Missiology* (1978), 53–79. D. von Allmen, "The Birth of Theology," *International Review of Mission* (1975), 37–55.

C. H. KRAFT

FEMINIST THEOLOGY AND PASTORAL CARE. Theology that seeks to empower women to personal creativity and self-confidence by enabling them to remember that they too are created in the image of God. Feminist theology takes women's experience into account when interpreting Scripture, ritual, and dogma. Frequently it criticizes aspects of "patriarchal religion" such as the "maleness" of God in imagery, language, and function, the origin of sin, the history of human origins, hierarchical structures, and the dualities of good/evil, mind/body, transcendent/immanent, inner/outer, heaven/earth, sacred/secular, and male/female. Conventional thought frequently associates men with the first term in each of the dualities and women with the second. From this follows the popular belief that "men are to women as God is to humankind" (Schaef, 1981). Historically, these unquestioned assumptions have been used to justify the political, economic, and social inequalities of the sexes. In addition to unveiling such hidden "patriarchal" assumptions, feminist theology pays particular attention to how the male orientation of Scripture, theology, and religious practice manifests itself in language, imagery, doctrine, and ritual, and what effect these have on women's identities and roles in the church. It advocates female images of God, reinterpretation of Scripture, and inclusive language.

1. Directions and Contributions to Theological Discussion. Feminist theology has developed in both exodus and reformist/liberationist formulations. Many women find the traditional religious structures too confining and too slow to change, so they are leaving the churches to embrace Goddess worship, nature religions, and humanistic personal spirituality (Daly, Christ, Spretnak, Goldenberg, Stone). The revisionist/liberationist movements, on the other hand, call for the full participation of women in ministry and church government, a retranslation of the Scriptures that incorporates inclusive language and images, and the reinterpretation of problematic Scripture passages (Ruether, 1975; Fiorenza, 1983; Lardner-Carmody, 1982; Wilson-Kastner, 1983; Mollenkott, 1977; Scanzoni and Hardesty, 1974). While these two approaches vary in their radicalness, both have provided women with permission to seek and use female-formulated images of womanhood and power. Both have provided a process of identifying strong female models in Scripture, mythology, history, and personal lives by asking, "What were women doing when . . . ?"

Another major feminist contribution to theological reflection lies in the focus on the process and context of theological reflection rather than on the content. This enables men and women to move from the law-and-rule-abiding approach of childhood religion to a more self-reflective spirituality, one that considers the broader spiritual significance of events and beliefs in terms of personal connection to and participation in the world. All feminist theologians promote women's quest for identity, equality, personal improvement, and empowerment in the world. Some also consider the impact of these changes on men.

2. Contributions to Larger Society. One important political implication of the feminist challenge to dualisms, especially the us/other dualism, is that women can no longer be seen as "other." If women are no longer seen as "other," the logic and threat of the "other" declines and with it the justification for war, racism, sexism, and exploitation of the environment.

It is not possible to correct the past imbalances of a male-dominated society without theological reformation, since religion has provided legitimacy to male power. Feminist theology strives to reduce the dichotomization of gender roles and the deification of the "masculine" type. A primary approach to these concerns has been an insistence on inclusive (nonsexist) language in Scripture, theology, and ritual—a crucial insistence because language determines thought and sets behavioral limits. Critics of feminist theology have argued that the words *man* and *mankind* are generic terms that include both women and men. Recent studies in linguistics, dreams, and imagery, however, have shown that the unconscious is extremely literal in its interpretation of language, despite conscious rationalizations otherwise.

3. Religion and Women's Identity. Feminist theologians have recognized the formative role of religion in creating and complicating the problems of identity for women in a society modeled after a patriarchal religious worldview. They seek total transformation of society and not merely the assimilation of a few "token" women. Yet it is in this call for transformation that feminists meet some of their most challenging critics. Many agree that the predominant male language and imagery of traditional religion has hurt and stifled women, and yet they question the relevance of consciously self-generated alternative religious images and symbols. Some critics suggest that feminist theologians only want to replace male images with female ones and thereby change the balance of power. Perhaps balance does demand a swing from one extreme to the other. Some women are developing alternative images through reexploration of goddess myths and remnants of cave paintings. Others are searching history for women's contributions that have been overlooked. But the issue is not really one of determining the authenticity of the images—distinguishing "natural" religious images from the "arbitrary" images of culture, for instance. All images are products of culture to some degree; the role of culture cannot be eliminated. Rather, the issue is how women can determine their loyalties to particular images when all images, as "arbitrary" expressions of culture, are in question.

4. Implications for Pastoral Care. Feminist theologians raise issues that are emotionally charged for both men and women. They challenge tradition and thus threaten change. The lines of support are not drawn between men and women but across the gender line. The discussion of concerns is heated and often angry because of women's experience of inequality on one hand, and men's fears and insecurities on the other. Women and men both fear abandonment and abuse.

Individual and collective struggles with these issues follow a grief process of denial, anger, bargaining, depression, acceptance, and hope. The loss grieved for is the loss of naïveté and the security of knowing what to expect, even though the expected has not been working. This process of challenge and change has profound implications for pastoral care. Each stage needs to be accepted and facilitated without judgment. Women may deny that a problem exists, or that their depression comes from repression of urges to be who they are, rather than from their personal failing to be what someone expects. They may feel angry at having sold themselves short or at having been denied equality. As women begin to ask for what they want, bargaining results in little increments because they do not feel worthy of more. Depression sets in with the realization that things will never be as they once were and with women's fear that they may be inadequate to the quest for self-acceptance. The acceptance in the process comes with accepting God's love, and realizing the internal and external beauty of women's will and contribution to the world. The process ends with hope for a world of equality and full valuation of both sexes.

5. Suggestions for Pastoral Caregivers. To incorporate practically the insights of feminist theology in pastoral care, the caregiver should: (1) consider that women undergoing identity re-formation best profit by seeing a woman caregiver who has worked through these issues; (2) use inclusive language unless referring to a gender-specific situation; (3) set the goal of facilitating women's sense of self and empowerment rather than a sense of coping and adjustment; (4) encourage women to identify models of strong women through suggested reading, wise-woman imagery, and women's support or consciousness-raising groups; (5) validate the exploration of alternative images of divinity, including the wise woman or goddess; (6) facilitate the development of a new and stronger self-concept based on trust of personal and community experience; (7) explore and use reinterpretations of problematic scriptural passages; (8) reread and reinterpret Bible myths in such a way as to give women their rightful place in history; (9) be careful not to project male experience onto female experience without checking out its appropriateness; (10) encourage experimentation with new behaviors; (11) work through any discomfort raised by these issues with a peer or supervisor; and (12) see women as beautiful daughters of God regardless of the forms of their struggle.

The pastoral caregiver should encourage men to: (1) work on their own fears and angers that arise as a loved one explores her concerns; (2) understand the grief process for both men and women; (3) experiment with new behaviors; and (4) incorporate the feminine within themselves. Together men and women should learn to tell the truth without fear or judgment and to contract for new behaviors in a way that encourages frequent reevaluations.

Bibliography. C. Christ, *Diving Deep and Surfacing* (1980). C. Christ and J. Plaskow, eds., *Womanspirit Rising* (1979). S. Collins, *A Different Heaven and Earth* (1974). M. Daly, *Beyond God the Father*, rev. ed. (1985); *The Church and the Second Sex* (1968); *Gyn/Ecology* (1978). E. Fiorenza, *In Memory of Her* (1983); N. Goldenberg, *Changing of the Gods* (1980). D. Lardner-Carmody, *Feminism and Christianity* (1982). V. Mollenkott, *Women, Men and the Bible* (1977). E. Pagels, "Christianity's Masculine Orientation," *New Oxford Review* (March 1979). R. Ruether, *New Woman, New Earth* (1975). L. Scanzoni and N. Hardesty, *All We're*

Meant to Be (1974). A. Schaef, *Women's Reality* (1981). C. Spretnak, *Politics of Women's Spirituality* (1982). M. Stone, *When God Was a Woman* (1976). P. Trible, *God and the Rhetoric of Sexuality* (1978). P. Wilson-Kastner, *Faith, Feminism and The Christian* (1983). P. Zulkosky, *The Wise Woman in Guided Imagery*, PhD dissertation, Claremont School of Theology (1984).

P. ZULKOSKY

GRIEF IN THE GAY AND LESBIAN COMMUNITY. Grief in the gay and lesbian communities goes underground. Grieving partners stay quiet because the relationships to which they have been committed are not recognized as legal by almost every state, respected by the majority of religious denominations, or honored as commitments. It also results from the fact that it is often not safe to talk about the loss of one's gay or lesbian partner since people's responses are unpredictable and there may be consequences for disclosing one's sexual orientation.

The consequence to silence, however, is that grief increases when discrimination becomes a part of it: when there is a double standard or judgment, when the grieving people are silenced or treated as if they are invisible, when the loss is not recognized. Grief is hard enough to live with when it is not silenced, but being made to feel invisible, to feel as if your loss wasn't a "real" loss, that your relationship wasn't a "real" relationship, or that your family wasn't a "real" family is devastating. It is as if the pain and loss didn't and don't exist. Partners are not offered the same opportunity or status as a partner from a mixed-sex relationship when his or her loved one has died, even in the use of the title of "widow" or "widower."

The grieving partner who stays quiet is denied both the opportunities to grieve as part of a community and to receive the comfort and support that a community can offer. And without that community connection, isolation and a sense of being all alone in the world with no one who understands can make the loss and its accompanying grief unbearable, disorienting, and at times life threatening. This is known as complicated grief.

Alongside the emotional experience of the loss of a partner is the process of the settlement of the estate. Unlike male/female spouses, gay and lesbian partners are forced to pay taxes for a jointly owned home, property, or vehicle and are denied the deceased partner's Social Security benefits. If there are children involved, there may be custody battles with

101

genetic family members where the surviving partner is not seen as the children's parent.

One Family's Story. In August 2000 we were married in the presence of the people who knew us and accepted us. My sons read readings and lit candles, and one played the violin. Two of our best friends co-officiated the service and we celebrated what we anticipated would be a full life ahead of us. But exactly two months later my partner was diagnosed with stage-4 breast cancer. Three weeks later, on my eldest son's eleventh birthday, she had a mastectomy. Two months later she had a second surgery for what we had been warned would probably be ovarian cancer.

While she was in surgery I paced the hallways, not knowing what the future held. I wandered down into the chapel, hoping for some quiet and privacy. Across from the chapel was the office of pastoral care, the place where the chaplains worked. I was grateful at first that I had found their office in case I needed their help if the surgery went wrong or the news was bad. It was a comfort to know that I was not alone if I needed help. But my sense of safety and comfort didn't last long. As I sat in the chapel I heard the clear sound of three voices, all talking about patients with whom they had visited, who they were certain and quite pleased, it seemed, would go to hell. "They deserve it," said one. "Disgusting perverts," said another. And then I heard one voice say, "Those damn gays should all be dead." There I sat, my partner in surgery, feeling afraid and unsure of the outcome, and the chaplains of the hospital, the people who were supposed to be the comforters and the godly ones, were damning us and our amazing circle of friends to death, banishing us to their "hell." For what seemed like a lifetime, I don't think I even breathed. I was overwhelmed by a myriad of conflicting emotions. Mostly, though, I knew that we were not safe here and that most certainly I was alone if anything went wrong. So I left the chapel and fumbled down the hallway to friends who had arrived to wait with me. And as I told them tearfully what had happened, I searched my pockets for the power of attorney, medical power of attorney, and living will documents that I had brought along. I knew that in order for me to be able to see her or advocate that her wishes be followed if necessary, I needed these documents on my person at all times. In this facility I did not have the rights that a husband or wife would have for each other. Instead, as the rotations of ICU nurses stated hours later, I was her "sister," "such a good friend," or her "mother." I was not seen as her partner or her spouse but rather as just some nice woman who came to visit this unfortunate soul. Luckily for us, the surgeon was not only a skilled physician but a welcoming, nonjudgmental, and warm man. He allowed me access to the ICU at any time. "You know how to do this," he told me and respected that I was her partner.

Since my partner never wanted to hear the results of tests and clearly told her physicians to tell me instead, I had learned to keep the paperwork close by for every appointment, every surgery, and every treatment. I never knew when I would be challenged or denied access. I was warned that I might need them. The proper legal paperwork is lifeblood in the gay and lesbian community during the illness process. It is the best chance we have at rights in our relationships, rights that mixed-sex couples assume in their wedding vows and marriage licenses, rights that same-sex couples are denied in almost every state in the country.

At Christmas we traveled to our families' homes and to our favorite beach. I knew it was her last Christmas. And all the while, I traveled with the directions to the closest cancer center right next to the legal documents, and kept the oncologist's phone number hidden in my pocket. We returned home on January 2, 2003, and nineteen days later she died in my arms. I had promised her that if and when the time came, I would hold her and talk her through it until she was at peace. I was graced with keeping that promise.

Her obituary listed me as her "companion." I had been her companion, partner, roommate, friend, caregiver, listener, protector, confidante, lover, cook, housecleaner, bather, wound dresser, medication provider, launderer, social planner, appointment planner, comforter, chauffeur, workbag packer, paper editor, organizer, and so on. I was not her companion; I was her partner. I did what partners and spouses do for each other. I lived out my part of "for better or worse, in sickness and in health, until death do us part." But around me, our relationship was not identified, validated, or honored. I could not claim to be a widow. Both my sons could not talk and receive support from friends or teachers. They could not say that their stepmother had died without receiving lots of stares, ignorant comments, or consequences. We were denied the status of a grieving family.

Gratefully, we were not silenced at church but rather had the embracing arms of the members around us. And we were surrounded by loving and supportive friends. It is what helped us through. But not every same-sex couple or family has the same experience. In fact, most do not.

S. E. VOLLMER

LIBERATION THEOLOGY AND PASTORAL CARE. The mutually critical intersection of a particular (esp. Latin American) theology and a particular (esp. North American) therapy, each of which draws in different ways on the secular disciplines of sociology and psychology as well as from Scriptures and church tradition.

1. Liberation Theology. *a. Development and response.* The critique of domination presented by Latin American Catholic bishops at their meeting in Medellin, Colombia, in 1968 set the stage for what has come to be known as liberation theology. The meeting outlined three fundamental pastoral directions for the church in Latin America, which have come to constitute the core of liberation theology: (1) forming basic communities comprising persons from all walks of life for Bible study and worship, (2) becoming a church for the poor, and (3) collaborating with Protestants in the pursuit of justice and freedom for all people. The bishops based these directives on the conviction that the salvific work of Jesus Christ is inextricably bound to the emancipation of the poor and oppressed from the sociopolitical structures of domination, and that God calls Christians to stand in solidarity with all victims of oppression.

Given its revolutionary implications, theology of liberation disturbs those who consider it a threat to ecclesiastical orthodoxy and democratic capitalism. These critics maintain that the gospel is not to be politicized along lines drawn by socioeconomic and class distinctions. Furthermore, liberation theologians express a strong affinity with the Marxist critique of capitalism, a fact often adduced as evidence of their subversive communist-socialist intentions and religious blasphemy. Such charges against liberation theology are simplistic, however. One cannot reduce the emancipatory objectives of liberation theology to an argument between capitalism and communism.

b. Emancipatory praxis. Aristotle's definition of praxis as action governed by intrinsically valuable ends, such as justice and freedom, provides a useful point of departure for explicating the relationship of theory and praxis in liberation theology. Theology as an authentic praxis must be critically informed by the emancipatory ends of its tradition. This means that theology must be committed to interdisciplinary collaboration and must, furthermore, be critical of itself. Its task is to "acutely experience the contradictions—not complementarity—between past and present theories, on the one hand, and the imperatives of authentically transformative praxis on the other" (Lamb 1982, 84).

Liberation theology understands itself as critical reflection and action upon the vocation of ministry set forth in the gospel. It reaffirms the gospel's liberation of the poor and the oppressed, it argues that poverty must be examined as a systemic condition involving power relationships, and it asserts that theology must be interpreted in the context of the total society in which the gospel is preached. Succinctly stated, authentic, gospel-centered self-transformation necessitates the transformation of power relationships. Accordingly, liberation theology incorporates a Marxian critique of domination as a method of social analysis.

Following Marx's critique of religion as "the opiate of the people," theologians of liberation have attempted to bring to consciousness the class interests and social domination underlying theological discourse. They challenge any theology that supports any form of oppression to come to terms with the imperatives of freedom and justice. Consequently, liberation theology must necessarily hold together critique (drawing on critical social theory) and crisis (a turning point eventuating from contradictions inherent in a system or situation). Thus, the theoretical project of liberation theology, including critique of domination, relates directly to concrete action—the emancipatory praxis of social transformation. Whether such transformation assumes a specifically Marxist-socialist form of government or democratic socialism is secondary to the goals of justice and freedom. Critique takes precedence over orthodoxy, and theory is not divorced from praxis but is the reflective dimension of praxis.

Without elaborating on the constitutive elements of Marxian analysis of class structure and capitalist production, it is sufficient to point out two aspects of Marxian anthropology relevant to pastoral care: first, the belief that persons create themselves and society through their work; and, second, the claim that the historical material forces of production and the social fabric of human relationships change and are changed by each other over time. These claims help Marx demythologize all forms of transcendence, which distort the truth that the human condition is the product of material life. He aims to ensure emancipation from all forms of domination and subordination, thereby eventuating in a classless society.

Marx's critique of capitalism is attractive to theologians of liberation who witness the pathological dependence of the poor on the power elite in Latin America and the economic injustice fostered by capitalist-industrialist nations upon the "developing nations." His polemic against individualism resonates with efforts on the part of theologians of liberation to cultivate "basic communities," in which corporate responsibility for social action takes hold at a grass roots level in persons from all walks of life. These "basic communities" are an appropriate location for putting into practice the emancipatory objectives of pastoral care and theology of liberation.

2. Pastoral Care as Emancipatory Praxis. From a liberationist's perspective one should conceive of pastoral care fundamentally as the care of society itself. That is, one should understand the needs and hurts of individuals in their primary relationships—the primary focus of pastoral care and counseling—in terms of the macrosocial power relationships of domination and exploitation. For these larger relationships structure selfhood, personal experience, and individual behavior in fundamental, if usually unrecognized, ways. Thus pastoral care must always engage in a mutually critical conversation with theological and social scientific methods informed by an emancipatory praxis.

The therapeutic objectives of pastoral care as ordinarily conceived and practiced span a wide spectrum, including personal adjustment, self-realization, self-acceptance, and emancipation from the quasi-causal power of the unconscious. Especially with respect to the latter objective, Jürgen Habermas's interpretation of psychoanalytic therapy as "an emancipatory science of communicative interaction" (Lamb, 1982, 85) offers a bridge between pastoral care and liberation theology. J. Habermas argues that psychoanalysis is praxis oriented by virtue of its commitment to the elimination of ideological distortion and instrumental rationalism. Although pastoral care is not psychoanalysis, Habermas's point suggests that pastoral care, like critical social theory, and liberation theology, may have the goal of identifying "possibilities for radical change towards a society in which human beings exercise fully their capacity for self-conscious control over social processes" (Keat, 1981, 3). To this extent, pastoral care needs to be informed by critical social theory.

Serious difficulties preclude accepting Habermas's critical social theory in its entirety, however. The theory targets no group for application—no congregation as the locus of communicative praxis. Thus, the imperatives of social justice and undistorted communication, though commendable, remain sterile insofar as passion is divorced from reason, tradition is perceived as an inevitable bearer of distorted communication, and humanity and nature are treated as though ontologically separate. Most important, Habermas has no feeling for the nuanced mysteries of theology; hence his project in social transformation lacks any appreciation for divine transcendence, while transcendence is the cornerstone of pastoral care and the theology of liberation.

Liberation theology thus brings to pastoral care the same concerns offered by critical social theory but mediates these concerns theologically through the church, as it struggles to ensure the fullness of life. "Basic communities" express concretely the concern that the political realm is the most comprehensive and decisive arena of praxis (Sölle, 1974, 69). Here the emancipatory goals of pastoral care thrust beyond the contours of individual life history and into "the broadest horizon within which human life unfolds and develops" (Fierro, 1977, 28).

3. Conclusion. The basic premise that liberation theology is guided by faith in the transcendent means that it carries a "surplus of meaning" extending beyond the emancipatory praxis of any particular person or group. This is the same basic premise of pastoral care. In a mutually critical dialogue the theology of liberation challenges pastoral care to resist elevating *techne* (i.e., clinical mastery) over praxis and divorcing the private interior self from public life. On the other hand, pastoral care challenges the theology of liberation to resist being transformed into dogma or identified simply as the manifesto of a particular political party.

Bibliography. R. S. Chopp and D. F. Parker, *Liberation Theology and Pastoral Theology* (1990). C. Davis, *Theology and Political Society* (1980). A. Fierro, *The Militant Gospel* (1977). G. Gutierrez, *A Theology of Liberation* (1973). J. Habermas, *Knowledge and Human Interests* (1971). E. B. Holifield, *A History of Pastoral Care in America* (1983). R. Keat, *The Politics of Social Theory* (1981). R. Kinast, "The Pastoral Care of Society as Liberation," *J. of Pastoral Care* 34 (1980), 125–30. M. Lamb, *Solidarity with Victims* (1982). S. Pattison, *Pastoral Care and Liberation Theology* (1994). D. Sölle, *Political Theology* (1974). S. Torres and J. Eagleson, eds., *The Challenge of Basic Communities* (1981). D. Tracy, *The Analogical Imagination* (1981).

R. M. MOSELEY

NATIVE AMERICANS, PASTORAL CARE OF. The great majority of counseling techniques and therapeutic methods used with Native Americans have proved sympathetic but ineffective. Much of the problem lies in a lack of cross-cultural understanding, coupled with a predominance of mass stereotyping, media-created images, and romantic projection. Having experienced two hundred years of a government's unconscious and, at times, conscious attempts at political genocide,

Indian people's historical and ongoing resistance to be accommodated, healed, and acculturated by a more pervasive, sophisticated social system is a testament to their remarkable status as unique survivors. In 1900 the U.S. Department of the Census estimated Indian peoples to number fewer than 200,000. In 1980 the figure stood at 1,400,000. The current birthrate of this one-time "vanishing race" is double that of the national average. Reminding us of our own history, and the blemished, often brutal effects of national policy, they refuse to disappear. An encounter with groups or individuals of Native American descent warrants sensitivity, caution, and the deepest respect.

1. Questions of Identity. Indian people represent some 516 federally recognized tribes in the United States. They find themselves in any one or a combination of the following groupings, each one, in turn carrying distinct characteristics: (a) Reservation, (b) Urban, (c) Traditional, (d) Assimilated, and (e) Militant.

Reservation and rural populations make up approximately 48 percent of Native Americans. Two hundred six reservations were historically established by treaty agreements and currently are coordinated by and work in cooperation with the Bureau of Indian Affairs, an office of the Department of the Interior with the U.S. government. Due to complex historical factors, tribal governments are often riddled with conflict. The sporadic and inconsistent support of treaty rights by federal agencies has frequently contributed to the violence and cyclical poverty so reflective of much reservation life.

Urban Indian people live in metropolitan areas, usually in clusters or neighborhoods; they tend to be mobile, and often constellate around urban Indian centers. *Traditional* native people, living on and off reservations, carry certain long-cherished values that include a political conservatism rooted to the concept of consensus, a respect for diversity, noncompetitiveness, and a relative understanding of the importance of material wealth. *Assimilated* Indian people, although in many instances still committed to traditional roots, are those who have identified and adapted to the dominant culture in terms of goals and expectations, many of them having reached positions of social power and influence. *Militant* native groups, typified by the American Indian Movement (AIM), are media conscious, politically organized, and popular among the press.

Each of the above-mentioned groups reflects differing expectations and experiences, which need to be respected. The terms "Native American" or "Indian" are interchangeable among most Indian people, with the exception of the Eskimo, who are very determined in distinguishing themselves from other land-based tribes. A clue in approaching groups and individuals is how they choose to identify themselves. In dealing with native people, it is wise to make as few assumptions as possible.

2. Contrasting Values. Working with Native Americans often entails an encounter with a subtle but intricately defined value system that is frequently troublesome and frustrating for the therapist or counselor. Several of these values warrant special mention.

a. Time. Attitudes toward time among Native American subcultures frequently pose a marked contrast to more dominant and pervasive understandings. Appointments, meetings, and organizational concerns find their significance in light of basic tribal understandings of what is important. From the outside this may appear as a casual disregard for more normative time structures. From the inside, it is simply a deeper respect for the seasonal and more natural unfolding of events and situations.

b. Materialism. Material goods, including money, carry a relative sense of value among most native communities. There is an emphasis on sharing, not saving. What may appear to be a disrespect for material things is frequently a more community-oriented, utilitarian understanding of possessions. Gift giving remains a strong tradition among many native cultures and holds a central place in the psychological language, the lingua franca of tribal peoples.

c. Respect for diversity. Respect for another person's philosophy or opinion is a characteristic inherent in most Native American belief systems. Embracing apparently contradictory ideas and experiences is common among Indian people. One uses "what works" with an emphasis on the experiential rather than the dogmatic.

d. Family. Loyalty to family and clan is held in high regard by native people and in a counseling situation should be sensitively explored and honored. Many Indian people have been reared by members of extended families, and so it is common to hear individuals refer to grandmother or sister to designate any one of several persons. Children and animals are traditionally understood to carry special power. At most meetings, and frequently in therapeutic situations, it is not unusual for Indian people to bring their children with them. This may prove to be disruptive or uncomfortable for the pastoral counselor and needs to be dealt with in a sensitive and affirming manner.

3. Therapeutic Relationship and Intervention. In initiating relationships and responding to Native American persons, it may prove helpful to consider the following suggestions. (1) When Indian people become nervous, they frequently become quiet. In similar situations non-Indians generally talk more. This reflects an underlying commitment to noninterference that is characteristic of many native groups and individuals.

(2) Confrontation is usually not helpful. Indian people carry a strong sense of an inner world and will withdraw and appear passive to the outside observer. It is, has been, and will continue to be a part of cultural survival. To enter another's inner world, one must be invited; one does not break in. This is a difficult but important concept for all who share a part of reinforcing more dominant aggressive social norms.

(3) There is often an unspoken understanding that patience and nature will heal. Pacing with an Indian client is extremely important. There is a seasonal quality to any pastoral interaction that Native American people are often more in touch with and which they implicitly express through behavior and patterns of communication.

(4) The intuitive edge of native peoples has been traditionally more nurtured in the development of their communities. This is a kind of "trump card" in relationships between Indian and non-Indian persons that needs to be given appropriate consideration. It can also prove helpful in distinguishing what is a specifically native problem dealing with culture and identity, and what may be identified as a more transcultural issue regarding interpersonal relationship or psychodynamic concern.

To enter into a pastoral relationship with Native American peoples is a great gift, as it is with any people, but in the Indian world it is also an invitation into a rich but dark history of institutional racism, community violence, and deep personal wounds. It is a journey of shadows, of mystery, courage, and soul. It is a good place to test one's own identity and begin to examine the ambivalence that have so threatened the Indian people and defined non-Indians on this continent as a dominant people of conquest and power.

Bibliography. M. Craven, *I Heard the Owl Call My Name* (1973). V. Deloria Jr., *Custer Died for Your Sins* (1969). R. Mazur-Bullis, "Pastoral Care in a Native-American Context," *J. of Pastoral Care* 38:4 (1984), 306–9. D. McNickle, *Native American Tribalism* (1973). M. Momaday, *The Way to Rainy Mountain* (1969).

J. W. MAGNUSON

PASTORAL CARE IN THE AIDS CRISIS: FOR AN AFRICAN PERSPECTIVE

1. The Impact of HIV and AIDS in Africa. In 2007, it was estimated that 32 percent of the world's infection of HIV and AIDS was found in sub-Saharan Africa. Also, in 2007 more than three-quarters (75%) of all AIDS deaths worldwide occurred in sub-Saharan Africa. Africa is a continent that has been hit most and affected by HIV and AIDS compared with other continents (unaids.org, 2008). The pandemic has caused many deaths, poverty, illnesses, and many other problems. Africa has been facing economic, social, religious, and political problems. Bad governance and social and economic injustices have contributed to the challenges that have been brought by HIV and AIDS.

Tanzania is one of those countries in sub-Saharan Africa. With a population of about 38 million, the prevalence for HIV and AIDS in 2007/8 was estimated to be 6.5 percent. The primary transmission of the disease occurred through unprotected heterosexual intercourse, which constituted about 80 percent of all new infections; the rest were through blood transfusions, unsafe injections, or traditional practices such as circumcision and genital cutting. It is estimated that there were 1,400,000 people living with HIV in 2007. It is also estimated that Tanzania in 2007 had 1,100,000 orphans and vulnerable children (OVC); by the end of 2010 there will be 1,044,096 OVC in Tanzania (unaids.org, 2008).

2. An African Perspective. One of the popular sayings in the African context, especially for Swahili people, is the proverb *maisha ni duara* or *maisha ni mzunguko*, which means that life is a cycle. If we want to understand the life of a person in the African context, we need to understand the mind-set of the people, and their values, philosophy, customs, and traditions.

In the case of HIV and AIDS one needs to understand the whole issue of illness and health. The life of a person in the African context must be understood in a holistic way. People in Africa do not separate life between what is secular and sacred, physical and spiritual, body and spirit, heaven and earth. All of life is in one circle and all people are one and they all belong to one circle.

Illness is the result of an imbalanced life in the circle and when one suffers, the whole family, kinship, or society suffers. When illness happens in the society one thing is obvious—that there must be a disconnection somewhere in the relationship of a circle. Illnesses are a suffering or a disease that needs to be dealt with by looking at where the circle has been broken or weakened.

Health, contrary to illness, is a balanced life, the life that is holistic and whole in its relationship. Physical and spiritual life must seek the balanced life that will ultimately bring about health and wholeness. A person with *utu* is a person who is mature and healthy who knows to balance his or her life in a manner that is acceptable in the society.

3. The Challenges of HIV and AIDS. The late father of the nation of Tanzania, President Mwalimu Julius Kambarage Nyerere once said *"Mfichaficha maradhi kilio kitamuumbua,"* which means that a person who hides her or his illnesses will be revealed in death.

HIV and AIDS have brought many challenges to African societies in all sectors of life but also to the African church. AIDS is a disease that has caused fear, guilt, and shame in the lives of many people. People are afraid of death because AIDS is incurable. They are also afraid of being cursed or being excommunicated from the church or society. AIDS is also associated with sexual immorality, where many people feel shy and sinful. Therefore people in these circumstances prefer to remain silent to avoid the guilt, judgment, and stigma, brought about in part because the African church is very sensitive to sins related to sex (Eide et al., 2008, 137). Openness and transparency in Africa are scarce because of society's mind-set on such issues of sexuality, in particular, but also because of the relationship that has existed in the African mind between sin and sickness.

HIV and AIDS have stagnated the economy of Africa because many young people are dying who are the backbone of the nation. Poverty is increasing in every corner of the sub-Saharan continent. The consequences of death have also resulted in the increase of orphans and street children in our society. All of these challenges and others should be looked at and responded to in accordance to the African perspective in relation to God's word in the Bible and in accordance to African Christian theology, which actually speaks about *utu* of a person, which is only gained through God's extravagant grace.

4. Pastoral Care. Most of the African proverbs and sayings point to the humanness of a person. This humanness of a person is known in Kiswahili as *utu* or *Ubuntu* in Zulu. *Utu* is something that a person must have in order to gain his or her respect and dignity. A person is a human being who is not an animal or any other creature; a person is someone who has been created in the image and likeness of God. The HIV and AIDS crisis needs to be understood and responded to in the sense of *utu* in order to provide effective pastoral care in an African context. That means the church should treat a person according to who he or she is in the sight of God the Creator and not by what she or he has become.

If we want to make a ministry that works, we must implore the African perspective on dealing with crises and broken lives of people. Pastoral care in the African perspective must be integrated with the cultural values of the people and their spirituality. Pastoral care in the African context must seek the integrated approach without putting more emphasis on the Western therapies or approaches. The goal of the integrated approach is to find the wholeness in the life of a person who has been broken (Waruta, 1995, 21). The African perspective in the whole issue of HIV and AIDS must therefore be responded to with humanness and hospitality (i.e., *utu*), which is the real core of a person.

In Kiswahili we have a proverb, *mficha uchi hazai,* which means the one who hides his or her private parts will not be able to bear children. Pastoral care invites people to be open and transparent to the challenge of issues they are facing everyday in life. Silence must be broken by inviting people to talk freely and share their narrative stories about life. These life stories can be theologically analyzed to bring about healing and wholeness in the life of a person in the midst of HIV and AIDS (cf. Healey and Sybertz, 2005, 324).

The word of love and grace is the primary foundation and function of pastoral care. It is the pastoral care that understands the person as a human being with *utu* and not as an object or a thing. HIV and AIDS have brought negative stories that need to be translated to bring about stories that are healing, empowering, and sustaining. Instead of stigmatization, judgmental attitude, condemnation, evil myths, and silence, pastoral care in the African context needs to open up conversation that will bring about the stories that will change negative attitudes. Pastoral care is called upon to bring care, compassion, and *utu* to persons in need and to all who have broken lives.

Bibliography. O. M. Eide et al., *Restoring Life in Christ: Dialogues of Care in Christian Communities: An African Perspective* (2008). J. Healey and D. Sybertz, *Towards an African Narrative Theology* (2005). The Joint United Nations Programme on HIV/AIDS (UNAIDS) Report on the Global AIDS Epidemic, www.unaids.org (2008). J. Mbiti, *African Religion and Philosophy* (1969). Tanzania Commission for AIDS (TACAIDS) UNGASS Country Progress Report: Tanzania Mainland, www.tacaids.co.tz (2008). The United Nations Children's Fund (UNICEF), www.unicef.org (2008). D. W. Waruta, ed., *Caring and Sharing: Pastoral Counseling in the African Perspective* (1995).

T. A. MWENISONGOLE

POOR PERSONS. (Lat.—*pauper*; Heb.—*anaveem*; Gk.—*Ptochos*; Span.—*Los Pobres*). A class of people of any age and in any country, designated as living below a certain set of visible and spiritual standards. Historically, there have always been persons who were destitute and considered part of the "underclass" (D. Moynihan), including slaves, indentured servants, the uneducated, beggars, the unemployed, the racial and ethnic minorities, the unmotivated, the dependent, the helpless, the indigent, the handicapped, the elderly, and those who need financial assistance from others such as the state or federal government to survive. The poor are not confined by geography, race, or sex. Poverty cuts across and transcends all lines of definition. There are the collective poor, the situational poor, and the individual poor.

Collective poor are those considered to be of a certain group with certain common traits such as the black poor, the Appalachian poor, the unemployed, the migrant workers. Anyone who lives below a defined economic level and whose lifestyle limits him or her from moving away from the group can be viewed as part of the collective poor. For example, in the United States there are twenty million persons who are termed "functionally illiterate," which means their future is bleak and their hopes are limited. They are confined within the framework of poverty.

Situational poor are those who become poor at a certain time and because of situations over which they have or had little control. For example, the worldwide depression caused significant poverty, the results of which were reflected in the lives of certain individuals. Other situational poor would include substance abuse victims, the chronically mentally ill, the criminal offender, dependent children, and other persons who have experienced semipermanent hardships, resulting in the loss of income and the loss of hope.

Individual poor are those persons who lack the ability to obtain the basic necessities for survival at any given time or place. An individual who is poor becomes poor whenever earnings are not regular or substantial enough to purchase food, clothing, and shelter.

While being poor has long been a common experience of human beings, in a wealthy society the state of being poor is a contradiction.

Poverty is a degrading and harsh event for those who are caught in its vise. One of the problems in examining the poor is that it is difficult to know how many poor people there are in any area at any time. Statistics are not absolute because someone is being born into a poor condition daily.

The poor in the United States may be seen as having some general formula. A person runs the risk of being poor if he or she: (1) is non-white, (2) belongs to a family of nonearners, (3) belongs to a female-headed household, (4) belongs to a family of more than four persons, (5) is between fourteen and twenty-five or over sixty, (6) lives in a populous urban area or a deprived rural area, or (7) has minimal education.

The poor live in specific geographic areas. In a 1968 survey 15 percent of the poor lived on farms and 25 percent lived in inner cities. The rest of the poor—60 percent—live in rural nonfarm areas and in the outlying areas of large cities.

Pastoral care and counseling with the poor is a call for a special challenge and opportunity. Jesus announced in the Gospel of Luke that he was anointed to "preach good news to the poor" (Lk. 4:18). This statement and the ones that follow in Lk. 4:16-21 are an adaptation of Isaiah 61. There is a theological concern for the poor getting out of their condition both from the OT's point of view and from that of the NT. This concern was continued into the early church when a dispute was settled between the Jewish Christian leaders (Peter, James, and others) and the Apostle Paul and his followers, who were evangelizing the Gentiles. In Gal. 2:9-10, it is recorded that the two opposing camps agreed to "remember the poor."

Preaching the gospel to the poor suggests that pastors and pastoral counselors think through their own attitudes and feelings toward the poor. If the gospel is "good news" and preaching and pastoral care are functions of the ministry, then pastoral care and preaching may need to take on the form of liberation theology, a theology that seeks to free the poor from their bondage and to release them from their "stigmata" of helplessness, dependency, and hopelessness.

The traditional European-American style of counseling may or may not serve to help liberate the poor. If tradition means, as is often suggested, acceptance of the situation as it is, then other methodologies should be considered. Such methods of counseling as behavioral therapy, motivational therapy, educational counseling, Gestalt therapy, and action-directed counseling may be more helpful and may get the poor actualized and energized for goal-directed and hope-oriented plans to alleviate their suffering.

Pastoral counselors and pastoral caregivers may need to see themselves as educator/mentor counselors to the poor. It should be clear to the pastoral counselor that poverty, or "being poor," is not an acceptable way of life, except as a chosen religious vocation. The goal of pastoral counseling with the poor is to empower the poor with changed attitudes about God, about themselves as people of God, and about their circumstances.

Poor people have the same dreams as other people. However, these dreams get repressed, denied, and deferred. Pastoral care and counseling should take on the form of dream resurrection, dream nurturance, and dream fulfillment. For example, in a tenement housing development in St. Louis, Missouri, pastoral care took on the form of Gestalt counseling. A group of concerned persons transformed the blighted area. After ten years, the *U.S. News and World Report* (August 4, 1986) reported that "the secret of the Cochran Public Housing Project is re-education—we changed people's attitudes."

Appalachia has its share of the poor, primarily "poor whites." The U.S. government spent $5 billion within twenty years in an effort to change the poverty situation. The geographic, economic, and cultural isolation spans thirteen states and suffers all the indignities listed in the studies as bondage factors: economic hardships, hopelessness, and helplessness. A poor resident is reported to have said, "We don't have an easy time here. I don't like this place . . . but I guess I'll be here till I die." The mountain areas of Appalachia have a 50 percent high school dropout rate and one-third of the people are functionally illiterate—a mark of poverty. Teenagers account for one out of five pregnancies in Kentucky and in 1983 Kentucky had the highest rate of births to white teenagers in the country. Poverty cuts across racial and cultural lines. Poverty is no respecter of persons. Children born into mountain poverty find it as different to escape as do children born into an inner-city environment.

In working as a counselor with the poor, one should expect hesitation and resistance (C. F. Kemp, 1972). The reasons for this resistance are: (1) distrust of the helping persons, (2) lack of patience, (3) need for immediate gratification, (4) poor educational background, (5) pessimism about the future, and (6) disvaluation of goal-directed plans. The poor have varying degrees of motivation and may have difficulty using traditional structures of counseling. The pastoral caregiver needs to be aware of these dynamics and work within the framework of the poor person's worldview.

Traditional counseling modalities are generally seen as "middle-class," primarily of an unreachable value system, and offered to those who can pay a consistent and long-term fee for the service of "talking." Pastors who serve inner-city parishes may discover that "methods and goals of pastoral counseling are usually ineffective with people suffering from the pains of poverty" (Clinebell, 1970).

The pastoral counselor or pastoral caregiver will need to make some alterations and some modifications in counseling procedures, including time, fees, process, and methods. Pastoral presence is acutely important to the poor. It becomes a part of "incarnational theology" associated with liberation theology—a theology of action and location. The praxis of pastoral care and counseling should not be confined to a designated office space. It should be flexible, mobile, and need-focused. It takes a dedicated caregiver with a willingness to reach out and go "the second mile" in order to work creatively, meaningfully, and relevantly with the class of people in our societies classified as "the poor."

Bibliography. H. J. Clinebell, *Community Mental Health: The Role of the Church and Temple* (1970). P. Couture, *Blessed Are the Poor?* (1991). P. Freire, *Pedagogy of the Oppressed* (1970). M. Harrington, *The Other America: Poverty in the United States* (1962). C. F. Kemp, *Pastoral Care with the Poor* (1972). R. L. Kinast, "The Pastoral Care of Society as Liberation," *J. of Pastoral Care* (1980). G. Seldes, *The Great Quotations* (1967). A. Simon, *Faces of Poverty* (1968). H. Thurman, *Jesus and the Disinherited* (1959). E. P. Wimberly and A. S. Wimberly, *Liberation and Human Wholeness* (1986).

G. POLK

POWER. The ability to act or to be acted upon. A psychologically, socially, philosophically, and morally necessary part of our personal and social experiences, it is also open to great abuse.

Awareness of the fact of power has existed since ancient times. Anthropologists sometimes named it "Mana" (Melanesia), but it has more generally been referred to as *magic* (Malinowski, 1954). Almost all religions impute power to the gods, to priests, events, and social relationships (Schmidt, 1972 [1931]).

The Greeks, especially Aristotle, both contributed to and spawned a long and rich tradition of political thinkers, foremost among them Locke,

Hobbes, Rousseau, Hume, and the amazingly clear and pragmatic approach to power by Machiavelli in *The Prince*.

A more variegated understanding of power has emerged in recent social science, particularly with Comte, Spencer, Sumner, Ward, and especially Gumplowics through his idea of *domination*. Political scientists focused mainly on power in the process of government (the distribution of power), while sociology was concerned with interpersonal and institutional power, and psychology has focused on subjective feelings and dynamics (McClelland, 1975; Winter, 1973).

Institutional settings such as politics (McClelland, 1975) are one area in which power is particularly prominent. Among ideological systems, Marx's is premised on classes and power domination. "The proletarians have nothing to lose but their chains. They have a world to win" (*Communist Manifesto*). Another powerful system is Freudian psychoanalysis, which projects societal power in the form of the superego over the "normal" expression of the self (Brown, 1959). Other systems, such as Buddhism, emphasize the renunciation of desire, which includes the desire for power.

1. Definition of Power. (1) *Physical power* (might) is the ability of one agent to act upon another object, or the ability to be acted upon (Aristotle, *Metaphysics*, viii. ix. I). (2) The *psychological* definition of power almost always slips into discussions of "Social Power" (Raven, 1974). D. C. McClelland (1975) states that the psychological function of power is "to feel stronger" either by "strengthening myself" (Stage I), or being strengthened by others (Stage II). Stages III and IV are actually sociological power that have as their object the influence of others.

(3) The generally accepted *sociological* definition is "Power (*Macht*) is the probability that one actor within a social relationship will be in a position to carry out his own will despite resistance, regardless of the basis on which the probability rests" (Weber, 1947, 152). This definition has been shortened to "the determination of the behavior of others in accordance with one's own ends."

The sociological approaches to power have included *magnitude* (how much?), *scope* (how broad is the power?), the *domain* (in which areas does the person have power?), *distribution* (who has power?), and the *permanence* of power (how long does the person retain power?).

2. Bases of Power. The controller has power when he or she (1) has information needed by the controllee (information power), (2) can punish the controllee if he or she does not respond positively (coercion), (3) can provide rewards that the controllee desires (reward), (4) has the *right* to demand responses (this right derives from political, religious, economic, or other type of institutional status [Weber's legal and traditional types of authority]); (5) is able to move others by virtue of personality or psychological factors (charisma); and (6) can expose or otherwise embarrass the controllee so that the social costs of noncompliance are too great (blackmail).

Institutionalized class power derives from group or class membership. An illustration would be the poor and impoverished in Latin America. The impersonality of this kind of power, also exemplified in the modern corporation and state, makes the question of justice and ethics of power very complex (Tillich, 1967, vol. 3). Some ethicists in fact claim that organizations cannot act morally (Ladd, 1979). This perspective helps explain how individuals in institutional or political structures (e.g., Nazi Germany) are able to use power in the most brutal ways with seeming impunity.

3. Forms of Power. (1) *Coercion* is compliance achieved by physical means, either potential (threats to hurt, shoot, maim, etc.) or kinetic, actually carrying out the threats. However, there is power on both sides, because the recipient of coercion has the power to resist being acted upon (Aristotle, 1908).

(2) *Manipulation* is achieving the conscious or unconscious compliance of the controllee through forces that do not involve physical means (or threats).

(3) *Influence* and *domination* are forms where the controllees are in varying degrees able and willing to be influenced or dominated. Influence by advertising is an example.

(4) *Authority* is power that is recognized as legitimate by the controllee(s) and can involve voluntary or eager compliance (cf. Tolstoy's account of the French armies under Napoleon in *War and Peace*).

4. The Motivation for Power. The drive to power has been assumed to be universal (Adler, 1927; Tillich, 1967, vol. 3), and many philosophers have built systems on the desire for power (Machiavelli, Nietzsche, Carlyle, Bismarck, Marx, etc.). Newborn babies and the handicapped and weak usually have power in societies that have developed a "humane" moral system.

Psychologically, the drive for power has developed numerous theories—compensatory theories, frustration theories, fear of weakness, deprivation theories, neurotic needs, and others. Obtaining power has normally been assumed to result in desired status, but self-denial of power and giving of self to others (altruistic love) has helped confound these theories (Sorokin, 1950).

Most theories of psychological power drives basically transform into sociological motivation theories where power is a means of achieving some form of advantage or status with significant others. But basic forms of power motivations are institutionalized value systems that place highest prestige on certain forms of domination through wealth, property rights, status allocations, political position, and so forth.

5. Theories of the Consequences of Power. One of the most abiding sociological concerns has been the relative or absolute powerlessness of societal classes. Numerous scholars have stated that anomie results from powerlessness—not having the power to influence or direct one's own life in any sense (Marx; Mills, 1959; Moore, 1978).

a. Psychological. "Power asymmetry" has produced a number of theories. In Freudian psychoanalytic thought, the individual is caught in an irreconcilable conflict between his or her instincts and social restrictions, especially sex inhibitions, but above all the power of death (Brown, 1959, 81). Neo-Freudians of various persuasions have focused on the neuroses and psychoses resulting from the frustration of drives, dynamics, needs, urges, and so forth (Sullivan, 1953; Maslow, 1954; Erikson, 1964). Maslow's "self-actualization" theory, for example, is an attempt to bypass this power vacuum.

Psychological therapy systems themselves assume a lack of power to achieve the "reality principle" (Freud, 1938). To work through or around guilt, repression, or self-defeating neuroses and psychoses demands outside assistance: the therapist. Psychotherapy, in its various forms, is a culturally defined way to assist individuals (and groups) to achieve inner states that they lack the power to achieve by themselves (Brown, 1959, 246).

b. Social power. Psychologists have realized that individual neuroses and psychoses are often socially and culturally determined (May, 1972; Fromm, 1941). Social scientists have long assumed that power in society is asymmetrical—some individuals are vested with more power than others. This asymmetry is presumed to reflect the evolutionary process of developing statuses with rights and obligations—which is a central element or factor in social order without which a society could not exist (Maduro, 1982; Marx; Moore, 1978).

Asymmetry of power is a necessary fact of social life. But when a challenge to the distribution of power emerges, social structure is changed. For example, women's power has been asymmetrical in most cultures (Pescatello, 1976). In relatively recent times, women are demanding and achieving more power. To be equal, or to be considered a fellow human being, demands the source of that equality and humanness, which *includes* power. To be human and social means possession and exercise of power by *everyone* (Tillich, 1967). The really interesting question is why power asymmetries have developed, become accepted, and why they have not been challenged. Sociology, especially, has been evasive of this fact, and both Marxist and critical sociology have alerted us to this reality.

One final locus of asymmetry involves the domination and subordination of ethnic groups, cultures, and nation-states. Liberation from oppression is a modern password for the desire of small groups and weak nations to achieve freedom from oppression and to develop their own autonomy (Moore, 1978).

Cultural asymmetry refers to the way in which some cultural systems overpower others ("cultural determinism," Malinowski, 1945a).

6. The Ethics of Power. Most systems of power analysis do not address the central moral and ethical issue: "How and when is power used correctly?" But it is the moral-ethical dimensions of power that seem to have the best potential for solving personal, interpersonal, institutional, and political problems of power. Thus the discussion of power remains largely academic, which is probably why society(ies) have not been able to solve issues such as the threat of nuclear arms; ethnic, political, and religious conflicts; terrorist attacks; and wars between nations—all of which threaten humanity with cataclysmic misuse of power. (This personal analysis of the ethics of power derives from a Christian value-and-moral system, and more specifically an Anabaptist-Mennonite one.)

a. Personal misuse of power. Persons can misuse power by suppressing legitimate urges and desires; they can also demand more of themselves than they are able to achieve. The former is expressed in unnecessary guilt or self-condemnation for one's own acts and desires, the latter in self-denigration for failure to achieve goals or objectives. More obvious misuses of power include obsessive actions toward self-enhancement and self-service that, when expressed in an overt manner, conflict with social norms and become social misuse of power (Erikson, 1964).

One dimension that has not been fully developed in psychotherapy is the misuse of the power *not to be acted upon.* The contemporary scientific paradigms that focus on causality may be downgrading the other side of power (Aristotle, 1908)—"other directed" in distinction to "inner direction" (e.g., Riesman, 1950). The Christian religion, however, refers to this as "resisting the devil," "temptation," or "not letting the world squeeze one into its mold." Christianity has maintained the idea of the "responsible individual" who is in charge of his or her life, and who has a "free will." Psychology, along with psychotherapy, has tended to deny that humans have the power to be in charge of their actions, and has rather assumed that behavior is caused by forces outside a person. This has had the profound consequence of encouraging people to *believe* that they are powerless victims of their environments. But if power is by definition two-faced—on the one side, the ability to exert force, and on the other, the ability to resist force—then individuals are never powerless. "We are suspicious of the very word 'instinct'; it suggests an unalterable biological datum, and therefore seems to deny man the power to alter himself" (Brown, 1959, 77). According to Christian belief, what a person is emotionally, sexually, and so on, is to a degree within his or her own power to decide.

b. The social misuse of power. The misuse of social power is ultimately based on a moral or value system that stipulates what is correct social behavior. In the case of a society dominated by Christian values, the misuse of power can thus be squarely defined as all those expressions of power that: (1) cause the controllee to act against his or her own will; (2) limit the freedom of the controllee to act as an autonomous individual; (3) diminish or destroy the controllee's humanness, which means the freedoms to enjoy life in all its aspects; (4) use other people for the controller's own benefit without their express and free desire; (5) refuse the controllee the chance to reciprocate by using *his* or *her* power on the controller; and (6) exploit other people's power, that is, when a weaker person, a handicapped person, or a neurotic person in a dependency relationship evokes sympathy power, this can become a form of *coercion*.

c. Institutional misuse of power. All institutions exert tremendous power, be they religious, economic, political, familial, and so on. It is through institutional power that individuals are most often dehumanized. The institutional misuse of power becomes an almost impossible phenomenon to evaluate from a moral/ethical point of view, because it is so difficult, if not impossible, to ascribe moral aspects of power to individuals.

Removing moral/ethical responsibility from individuals and positing it in the organizational structure then makes power become a "systems process." This may be what the apostle Paul meant by "principalities and powers" and "spiritual wickedness," and thus he could say, "None of the rulers of this age understood this [hidden wisdom of God]; for if they had, they would not have crucified the Lord of glory" (1 Cor. 2:8). A flurry of theological writings in the 1970s articulated a new appreciation of the "principalities and powers" (Berkhof, 1977; Miguez Bonino, 1975; Gutierrez, 1973, etc.).

From psychological, sociological, philosophical, and moral standpoints therefore, power is a given, necessary for human life. *How* it is applied is the crucial issue, and health and harmony depend upon its moral application. Most societies may have solved the use of power much better than our contemporary Western society. Could one assume that it is the *misapplication* of Christian faith that has resulted in such a tragic misuse of power? Some writings suggest that biblical teachings, especially those of Jesus (Phil. 2:5-8), state that the end of power is to "give it away" by empowering others (Tillich, 1967, vol. 3, 388; Redekop, 1976), whereas liberation theology proposes "action in the present, in favor of the oppressed" (Miguez Bonino, 1975, 77; Gutierrez, 1973). The *misuse*, not the use, of power may be the most serious issue in human existence.

Bibliography. A. Adler, *Understanding Human Nature* (1927). Aristotle, *Metaphysics*, W. D. Ross, trans. (1908). H. Berkhof, *Christ and the Powers* (1977). R. Bierstedt, "An Analysis of Social Power," *American Sociological Review* (1950), 730–38. P. M. Blau, *Exchange and Power in Social Life* (1964). J. Miguez Bonino, *Doing Theology in a Revolutionary Situation* (1975). N. O. Brown, *Life against Death* (1959). D. Cartwright, "Influence, Leadership and Control," in J. G. March, ed., *Handbook of Organizations* (1965). C. Doehring, *Taking Care: Monitoring Power Dynamics and Relational Boundaries in Pastoral Care and Counseling* (1995). E. Erikson, *Childhood and Society* (1964). S. Freud, *Basic Writings of Sigmund Freud* (1938). E. Fromm, *Escape from Freedom* (1941). G. Gutierrez, *A Theology of Liberation: History, Politics and Salvation* (1973). F. Hunter, *Community Power Structure* (1963). J. Ladd, "Morality and the Ideal of Rationality in Formal Organizations," in Donaldson and Werhane, eds., *Ethical Issues in Business* (1979). J. Locke, "Of Power," in *Essay Concerning Human Understanding* (1952). N. Machiavelli, *The Prince* (1952). O. Maduro, *Religion and Social Conflicts* (1982). B. Malinowski, *The Dynamics of Culture Change* (1945a); *Magic, Science and*

Religion (1945b). K. Mannheim, *Systematic Sociology* (1957). K. Marx and F. Engels, *Basic Writings on Politics and Philosophy* (1959). A. Maslow, *Motivation and Personality* (1954). R. May, *Power and Innocence* (1972). D. C. McClelland, *Power in the Inner Experience* (1975). C. W. Mills, *The Power Elite* (1959). B. Moore Jr., *Injustice: The Social Base of Obedience and Revolt* (1978). A. M. Pescatello, *Power and Pawn* (1976). J. N. Poling, *The Abuse of Power: A Theological Problem* (1991). B. H. Raven, "The Comparative Analysis of Power and Power Preferences," in J. T. Tedeschi, ed., *Perspectives on Social Power* (1974). C. Redekop, "Institutions, Power and the Gospel," in J. R. Burkholder and C. Redekop, eds., *Kingdom, Cross, and Community* (1976). D. Riesman, *The Lonely Crowd* (1950). W. Schmidt, *The Origin and Growth of Religion* (1972 [1931]). P. A. Sorokin, *Altruistic Love* (1950). H. S. Sullivan, *The Interpersonal Theory of Psychiatry* (1953). J. T. Tedeschi, ed., *Perspectives on Social Power* (1974). P. Tillich, *Systematic Theology* (1967). J. Veroff and J. B. Veroff, "Reconsideration of a Measure of Power Motivation," in *Psychological Bulletin* 78 (1972), 279–91. M. Weber, *The Theory of Social and Economic Organization* (1947). D. G. Winter, *The Power Motive* (1973). B. B. Wolman, "Power and Acceptance as Determinants of Social Relations," *International J. of Group Tensions* (1974), 151–83. E. M. Woodward, "The Uses of Power in Community," *Human Development* 4:2 (1983), 24–32.

C. REDEKOP

RACISM. The term "racism" is not easily defined. The most common (and commonsense) definition—racism as a scheme of oppressive social classification based on physical features, mainly skin pigmentation—suggests that its roots are in the biological realm, where classifications based upon physical distinctiveness can be made. There is a history of scientific attempts to define races on the basis of such distinctions. Related to this is the history of defining races on the basis of blood, or at least along certain "blood lines." Literature, as well as popular language, is filled with references to this notion. Kings and queens have "royal blood" and aristocrats are said to possess "blue blood." In the United States, laws have been passed to ensure against the mixing of bloods. For many years an accepted definition of a black person was anyone who had a "quantum of Negro blood." The effects of this law still linger on in some parishes. The key here is the contention that certain hereditary characteristics are

124

transmitted through the blood (Haller, 1971). The actual definition or meaning of racism, however, is far more differentiated and complex.

1. Meanings of Racism. ***a. Relation to nationalism.*** Racism is also related to certain theories of nationalism. Here the definition often shares certain pseudoscientific opinions about racial characteristics or potentials with theories about the role or calling of particular people. Here racism functions as part of an ideology, and seen in this light has been most fully developed by Western societies. When it functions as part of a political system, racism becomes a significant part of the ideology of white supremacy. As such it developed as part of a colonialist rationale in the mid-eighteenth century (Arendt, 1968).

The theory that some races are inherently inferior to others was deemed a necessary support for colonial exploitation on the part of European powers. As an ideology, racism functions as an official position by which certain groups and their governments arrange their societies and policies to further their self-image and vested interests. When combined with religion, the ideology of white supremacy becomes a powerful civil religion in which God, or the gods, is said to be the source and protector of such a system. Logically, such a system, so conceived, could not be opposed. The most blatant expressions of this nationalist ideology in the past eighty years are Nazism in Germany and the government policy of apartheid in South Africa. Both systems share the same view of nationhood: a theory of ancestry based upon blood, reinforced with religion. These views are buttressed by or interpreted through the application of selected Scripture references that seem to offer divine sanction for racialist practices.

b. Relation to white supremacy. It is important to distinguish between racism and white supremacy. The latter has become official doctrine in some countries, whereas it is possible for a person to be a racist without having developed a systematic supremacist rationale. Racism, at a popular level, is rarely subjected to the rigors of rationality. This attitude, often unconscious and always undisciplined by reference to facts, is based upon erroneous assumptions about others. Walter Lippman referred to them as "pictures in our heads." These mental attitudes can easily be translated into forms of discrimination. Nevertheless, some form of official sanction for racialist attitudes is necessary if personal hostility toward others based upon racial characteristics is to become institutionalized. The most recognizable forms by which racism expresses itself are patterns of segregation, attitudes of stereotyping, and ordinances of discrimination.

c. Racism as attitudes and values. Racism can be defined in terms of the attitudes and actions of persons or institutions toward others based upon color or ethnic origin with a view to depriving them of access to the rights and privileges of those holding this view. Central to this definition is the issue of power. In order to maintain a racialist position over others, the racist must have some access to power. Or if lacking power, must manipulate the system so as to give the oppressed the impression that such power is possessed. To be successful in either case, a racist must be able to manipulate the image-building apparatus of a society. "Reality" must be carefully managed by those in power.

Thus education, politics, the arts and sciences, and even religion constitute the multiple ways in which a given culture expresses its fundamental values, serving as channels for its reigning ideology. It has been demonstrated, for instance, that the dictionary can be used to reinforce the values of the dominant group, or conversely, to reinforce the dominant group's negative images of the subgroup. References to "black" or "blackness" are associated with negative qualities, whereas "white" or "whiteness" are associated with characteristics of a more positive nature. By this means language serves as the chief conveyor of a nation's cultural values.

These values (held as early as the sixteenth century by some Europeans), when wedded to Scripture that seems to identify whiteness with salvation and cleansing (e.g., Isa. 1:18), became the basis for racial discrimination anchored in Holy Writ and the divine will. Later, an elaborate theology developed that sought to base discrimination and segregation on God's "curse" upon Ham. This theology, though long discredited by both science and responsible exegesis, still persists among supremacists in the Christian community (Buswell, 1964).

2. Effects of Racism on Persons. Minorities within racist societies, to the extent they are exposed to the majority culture, are systematically exposed to negative images of themselves, which become internalized. Such exposure is the chief source of various forms of self-abnegation on the part of minorities. Self-doubt, self-hatred, and "compensatory grandiose behavior" are only several ways in which negative self-image is internalized and acted out in minority behaviors.

The effects of racism in any society are too numerous to mention, but it is important to appreciate the ways in which persons have come to terms with this reality in the society. For many of the victims of racism in American society (who are usually people of color), it is all too easy to internalize the definitions, explanations, and expectations of the majority. Their hard work in school or the workplace often yields disproportionate benefits compared to the efforts of their white counterparts (Loehlin et al., 1975). It is all too easy, when confronted by daily reminders that one's efforts are not good enough for even a modicum of success, to assume that the fault lies within oneself. This is often followed by harder work, and if this proves unfruitful, the resultant despair often leads to alcoholism, violence toward loved ones, or various forms of dropout.

For others, adaptation takes the form of accommodation, the acceptance of the values, styles, and behaviors of the dominant culture. The price of such an accommodation has often been a form of ethnic schizophrenia, or at least a struggle for an identity that could no longer be defined internally or in terms of one's cultural heritage. W. E. B. DuBois referred to this as the black person's attempt to mediate between "is-ness" and "two-ness," what one knows oneself to be as a black person and the definition of identity pressed upon one by the oppressing culture, a wrenching split that produces rage and violence in the victim. Violence is the consequence of this prolonged loss of well-being in powerless persons. Thus violence is not an expression of power, but of powerlessness. Its source is in frustration, impotence, and an inability to assert oneself in human relations.

It is important to keep in mind, however, that power in the service of racialist attitudes is not merely personal and private in its expression. It is also institutional (Knowles and Prewitt, 1969). It is in its institutional forms that the minority person is most likely to encounter repeated denial aimed at his or her personhood. The schoolroom, the courtroom, the factory, and the corner store can exhibit attitudes that tend to reinforce majority attitudes of superiority and power. Hence in the riots that shook American cities in the late 1960s, neighborhood mom-and-pop stores were set on fire because they were perceived as perpetuating powerlessness in those neighborhoods. Churches have also contributed to the climate of racism in the society by remaining segregated, often by the simple device of moving when people of color occupied the same neighborhoods. Thus is communicated to the community that Christianity is incapable of relieving racialist attitudes. The aim of the civil rights movement was not revolution, let alone secession. It was integration.

3. Coping with the Power of the Oppressor. The issue in the conflict between victim and oppressor is power. Oppressed persons are typically powerless. They lack the ability to say no or yes to their oppressors. Power, as Rollo May has reminded us, is derived from the Latin *posse,* meaning "to be able," and connotes the ability to effect change in one's life or in the lives of others. It is crucially related to a sense of being, and it is the legacy of racism that its victims are denied the right to be.

The oppressor is also oppressed by the power he or she assumes. This is not always perceived by the oppressed. There is something illusory about power also. It promises more than it can deliver to those who possess it. It can be likened to a prison-house syndrome: those who keep others imprisoned are themselves incarcerated. Thus the genius of the civil rights struggle was Dr. King's realization that the oppressor will also be set free if the oppressed are liberated (see Roberts, 1971; King, 1958).

a. Separatism. Many victims of discrimination have found recourse in various forms of separatism. For some, this has taken the form of self-imposed segregation, for example, the refusal to have any more social intercourse with the majority than is necessary, and the refusal to cooperate in any political options such as holding political office. This is a form of self-determination and in its most extreme expression was championed by the former Black Muslims in the 1960s, when demands of land grants were made to further secure a status of independence from the oppressor.

b. Integration. Another attempt at coping with racism on the part of its victims has been integration. The strategy carries with it certain assumptions about the goodwill of the oppressor and confidence in the oppressor's willingness to abide by the laws of the land, where those laws seem to provide equal protection for all its citizens. Experience has shown, however, that people who have power over others rarely live up to their stated values unless it can be shown that it is clearly in their best interests to do so. For this reason integrationists have taken care not to appear too aggressive in the pursuit of equality while pressing claim to the benefits of the legal system. The civil rights movement changed even this strategy in the main when nonviolent confrontation forced the issue of power and vested interests to the fore, and the white majority was made to see that its interests were clearly in jeopardy if they refused to live up to their laws.

Integration, as an experience, has proved to be illusory for many. At best it holds out the prospect of resolving racial conflicts in the most radical way—by getting the victims and victimizers together, or at least within proximity. Attempts have been made to integrate neighborhoods, schools, and workplaces. Pressure has been applied to effect changes in the image-making industries such as those responsible for writing text-books and television commercials. But after years of legislation, busing of children, and multicolored images on TV screens, integration has achieved only a modest success.

Integration is limited in its ability to effect the necessary resolutions between antagonists. The chief shortcoming is that integration requires that the victims make most of the adjustments. When this is resisted by minorities, the majority has only to recall its goodwill. Or when the majority feels it has gone as far as it can, it suspends the arrangement. It simply walks off or changes the rules of the game. This can be done legally by outvoting or outspending the minority. These are expressions of majority power.

It may be true, as Fred Harris, former senator from Oklahoma, has claimed, that racism is America's number one mental health problem. Many victims of racism in our society would agree. Such a mentality, if unchecked, would have profound influence in all our domestic relations, especially in urban life, and in foreign affairs as well.

4. Pastoral Care and Counseling of Racists. Racism is, more often than not, irrational. It is based upon images in the mind. But these images, given enough time, can become reality. As a first step in helping the person afflicted by these images, it is important to help him or her trace the origins of these images. In a pastoral conversation with the author, a professional football player, upon hearing the OT story of the tower of Babel, recalled another story, "something about a curse" on "somebody." I recalled the story of Noah's "curse" of Canaan. I could tell he was trying to find a connection between that dimly recalled story and race relations on the team. "Where did I hear that story?" he asked. I inquired where he was from, and he mentioned a southern state. When I asked him if he had ever attended church, he replied that he had gone to Sunday school as a boy. It became clear as we talked that his earliest recollection of teaching about the supposed inferiority of black people came from his religious teachings in Sunday school.

Related to these mental images about others is fear, and help is needed to identify these fears. Often they are grounded in the person's own sense of guilt for past failures in human relations. "I know how I'd behave toward people who have done me wrong if I had the chance" (the chance, of course, to get even). Such a person needs to realize that not everyone who has been wronged as a result of racist actions or policies wants to get even. Black Americans, for instance, have generally not sought to get even but to catch up in the arena of opportunity. But then, that may be another fear—that if given opportunity, "they" will take over. This needs careful analysis, for this fear may mask the real issue, that of a pervasive sense of powerlessness in the racist. The issue may never have been racial in nature, but embedded in deep personal, family, and social inequities. A classic illustration is the emergence of the doctrine of apartheid in South Africa. When the budding Afrikaner nation severed itself from Holland in 1806, the issue was not racialist hostility toward the neighboring Xhosa people to the east. Rather it was an understandable reaction to an alien British administration bent on Anglicizing them. This was the beginning of an intense struggle for self-definition on a national scale. Only later did a native *herrenvolk* nationalism develop into an official ideology of apartheid aimed at native Africans. The origin of the ideology was fear and a deep-seated sense of national insecurity.

Racialism of the right and left seems related to the need to be in control, especially when social circumstances suggest that others, unlike themselves, threaten to supplant or marginalize their social position. Here it is important to assist racists to see that by surrendering stereotypes and relinquishing the need to dominate others, they are acting in their own best interest. This suggests that, finally, the best way to deal with racism is to expose racists to their victims. If part of the problem is ignorance—"being down on what you're not up on"—and social isolation, then ways must be structured to expose people who fear others to those very people whom they fear. Assistance must be given to assure that "the enemy" has a face, a name, an identity. One way to do this is to identify a task or problem that affects a plurality of people, the solution to which is not possible except in a cooperative effort. United by such a problem-solving venture, people often discover that past feelings of animosity and stereotypical thinking do not hold up under the dynamics of cooperation.

Bibliography. H. Arendt, *Imperialism, Part Two: The Origins of Totalitarianism* (1968). J. O. Buswell, *Slavery, Segregation, and Scripture* (1964). J. S. Haller, *Outcasts from Evolution: Scientific Attitudes of Racial Inferiority 1859–1900* (1971). M. L. King Jr., *Stride toward Freedom* (1958). L. L. Knowles and K. Prewitt, *Institutional Racism in America* (1969). J. C. Loehlin, *Race Differences in Intelligence* (1975). R. May, *Power and Innocence: A Search for the Sources of Violence* (1972, 1981). J. D. Roberts, *Liberation and Reconciliation: A Black Theology* (1971).

W. PANNELL

SEXISM. Refers to the belief or attitude that one gender or sex is inferior to, less competent, or less valuable than the other. Sexism is also attitudes, conditions, or behaviors that promote stereotyping of social roles based on gender.

Although generally used pejoratively, the term "sexism" is the expression of attitudes about the relationship between genders that many people deem legitimate or right; for example, "women are naturally more emotional than men," or "men are better leaders." Those who hold such views would generally regard them not as "sexist" but as valid statements of fact or truth. General usage, however, both in common parlance and in dictionary definitions, asserts that all beliefs and practices that confine one gender to particular spheres or denigrate their status in relation to others are discriminatory, arbitrary, prejudicial, restrictive, exploitative, and therefore sexist.

1. Origins of Sexism. Scholarship in feminist anthropology, archaeology, and theology affords convincing evidence that sexism and its underlying misogyny (hatred of women) and gynephobia (fear of women) are of relatively recent advent in human history. Data, both tangible and mythological, from Paleolithic and Neolithic times, document the existence of cultures that were both egalitarian and biophilic. In the high civilization of the Keph (Minoan) people of ancient Crete, and at Çatal Hüyük in Anatolia, for example, no evidence of weapons or violence can be found. The earliest deity all over the world was female, the great Earth Mother, at first undifferentiated, later the One Goddess of Many Names. No evidence exists of domination of one sex by the other. There is clear evidence of respect for women, often awe of their life-giving powers. Excavations and artifacts from late Paleolithic and early Neolithic sites in many parts of the world suggest many-faceted cultural characteristics shared in an endless variety of ways between women and men. It is increasingly clear that women played an active role in the evolution of human civilization, not only in domestic arenas, but also in public ones. The invention of agriculture by women is well documented. Also, because the first deity was female, the earliest priests were female.

It is still unclear, however, whether the concept of male superiority grew as a result of a growing human awareness that men had a part in reproduction, or whether spreading populations began competing for resources and war was invented; nevertheless, with these developments came the devaluing and denigration of women. Mythologically, the creation story underwent several transformations from a world created solely by a goddess, to the world created by the goddess and her consort, to the world created from the body of a goddess by a male god, to the world created by a male god without benefit of female. Nearly every culture carries a story of the takeover of power by men, who wrest the secrets of life from women by violence or trickery. Most such stories, which accompany the rise of male deity, are comparatively recent in evolutionary time—within the last five thousand years.

Thus in Semitic tradition, Yahweh replaces Iahu as creator and life-giver. Yahweh at first cocreates Lilith and Adam. Lilith (in Babylonian tradition the earth aspect of the great goddess Ishtar) refuses to be dominated by Adam; when God supports Adam's appeal, Lilith flies away, unwilling to submit. In Jewish tradition she becomes an evil spirit. In Christian tradition she is scarcely heard of and a new myth arises: Adam is created first and Eve second, taken from man's side and named by him. Man is responsible to God and woman to man. Woman is the first to sin; therefore, man will rule over her.

This second myth is incorporated into the OT and the myth of feminine evil is codified. In spite of the obvious biological fact of birth as woman's process, and even today in spite of current knowledge that the embryo is female for the first six weeks after conception, a male God as Father Creator prevails. Man has become the normative human, woman is "other." As the myth is sanctioned socially and politically and transformed into divine revelation by a father god, dominance of the male is assured; woman becomes property.

With the rise and spread of Christianity, woman is increasingly defined by her sexuality. Her worth is determined by her role as birth medium; she is dutiful daughter, faithful wife, devoted mother, or she is seductress and whore. Virginity and its loss are determined by the male. Woman is inferior to man. She becomes the embodiment of those qualities that man himself wishes to deny: carnality, vulnerability, emotionality, mortality. What becomes encoded as woman's "innate natural physiological and intellectual inferiority" and mythical responsibility for evil are used to justify misogyny and gynephobia not only in Jewish and Christian tradition but also in cultural and religious traditions all over the world. These are manifested in a variety of atrocities against women throughout patriarchal times: torture and burning of witches, genital mutilation, foot binding, suttee (widow burning), rape, battering, incest, and sexual slavery.

Debate over what, if any, gender distinctions are innate and what are learned is far from resolution. Although some things are understood about biological difference, little is understood about the effects of bio-logical difference on other human characteristics. There is no conclusive research data to suggest that there are innate differences in intelligence or emotional and psychological characteristics. No behavioral traits or role assignments have been found to be common to all known cultures. There is more evidence that points to a wider spectrum of difference within sexes than between them.

2. Effects of Sexism. Beyond the simple and arbitrary divisions of sex roles, a pervasive sexual identity affects every aspect of women's and men's lives. Women are objectified and victimized psychically, physi-cally, and socially. Men are cut off from those qualities they have assigned to women—nurturance, vulnerability, emotionality, attachment. As R. Ruether (1984) points out, although women are more victimized by patri-archal culture, men are more dehumanized.

Since power continues to reside with men, women are overtly victim-ized in many ways: (1) discrimination on the basis of sex is not explicitly prohibited by the U.S. Constitution; (2) in spite of their advancing edu-cational level, women hold few elite and powerful positions in governing bodies; in business and industry; or in educational, health, and social service institutions; (3) the pauperization of women continues to accel-erate. Seventy-five percent of the country's poor are women and children. Two-thirds of the adult poor are women. Eighty-four percent of fathers fail to pay court-ordered child support; (4) women earn sixty-eight cents to every dollar earned by men overall; the figure is even lower among the less affluent. A female college graduate can expect to earn less in her life-time than a male high school dropout; (5) violence against women con-tinues to be overtly and covertly sanctioned. One in three women will experience attempted or completed violent sexual assault at least once in her lifetime (this figure takes into account the fact that between 20 and 50 percent of such crimes go unreported). Six of ten women in marriage or cohabitation will be battered while in the relationship. One in three girls will be a victim of incest before she is eighteen (and minority women are disproportionately represented) (see U.S. Department of Justice entries in bibliography; also Bagelow, 1984); (6) women still must fight to control their own bodies. Choice to bear or not bear children is not controlled by the woman herself. Unnecessary surgery, drug experimen-tation, victimization by prescribed drugs, and major responsibility for birth control all affect women predominantly; (7) woman as sexual object, as victim, and as servant continues to dominate media images;

(8) language continues to exclude and subsume woman. She bears her father's and her husband's names. The man remains the norm for both the universal human and the individual male. Father and Son continue to be the prevailing images of deity.

3. Sexism and Racism. These are inextricably linked in complicated ways. Both are founded on the institutionalized belief in the superior humanity of the white male. In white Western culture all who can be defined as "other"—women, all people of color, and often those of non-European ethnic origin or non-Christian heritage—are exploited or oppressed. White woman's racism stems from her identification with and loyalty to white males. The woman of color lives in double jeopardy. Racism and sexism combine to make her social and political struggle unique. Women of color and women of no color are often set against each other by conflicting loyalties and patriarchal policies that keep women emotionally identified with "their men" rather than with each other. A. Davis (1983) points out that "racism nourishes sexism," causing white women to be indirectly victimized by the special oppression of their sisters of color. Sexual oppression and violence also link sexism and racism. Rape of the women belonging to "the other," for example, in slavery and its continuing aftermath in this country and with regard to the relationship between Vietnamese women and American soldiers, are legitimized both by sexism, which makes woman "other," and by racism, which makes all who are different "the other."

Sexism and racism are also economically related. While the overwhelming percentage of the poor are women, the overwhelming percentage of poor women are women of color.

4. Sexism and Homophobia. These are closely allied and reinforce each other. Homophobia (*homo:* same, *phobia:* fear) is also a word reflecting the emergence of homosexual and lesbian identity as vital human expressions. The heterosexual bias of the culture is closely linked to sexism. A. Rich (1980) raises the issue of heterosexuality as a political institution. Male dominance requires the heterosexual control of women, either benevolently or violently. The lesbian who chooses to relate emotionally and sexually to women (and to a lesser extent the male homosexual) are a profound threat to male power and dominance. Rape, battering, incest, pornography, economic dependence of women, all are partly manifestations of compulsory heterosexuality. The violence, both psychic and physical, with which male dominance and heterosexuality is often enforced suggests an attempt to control something fearful and potentially powerful.

5. Reverse Sexism. This is the cry often heard in response to affirmative action programs directed toward improving opportunities for women in education and employment, and as women begin to assert their rights across the political and social scene. J. Cone sees black or reverse racism as a myth created by whites to ease their guilt feelings; the facts do not support the charge. Likewise, reverse *sexism* is a deception. Indeed, when women and men compete on equal terms, some men will have to wait longer to achieve their goals as women move into equal participation in the culture. However, this cannot be equated with the sexist assertion that women are inferior and therefore men have the right to dominate. The insistence of women on equal participation in society does not suggest that women wish to dominate men or to discriminate against them.

R. Ruether (1984) asserts that sexism is primarily a male problem that men have imposed on women. The attempt of women to right that wrong is not reverse sexism, but the inevitable struggle of an oppressed group to gain equal access to all that society has to offer. Assertions of male superiority and institutionalized dominance are attempts to prevent women from having equal participation in decision making and to deny full humanity to women. Women's assertion of their rights is an affirmation of the full humanity of women rather than an attempt to assert female superiority or to deny the humanity of males.

6. Relevance for Pastoral Care. All that has been said about sexism in the culture as a whole is reflected in the church, both as institution and as theological environment. In churches, as in other institutions, the largest percentage of authorities are men, and the largest percentage of participants are women. Ministers and pastoral counselors, therefore, must be aware both of their own sexist biases and of the ways in which the church or pastoral counseling setting perpetuates the dominance of men and the denial of women's humanity.

Bibliography. M. D. Bagelow, *Family Violence* (1984). R. Bleier, *Science and Gender: A Critique of Biology and Its Theories on Women* (1984). J. Cone, *Black Theology and Black Power* (1969). M. Daly, *Beyond God the Father* (1973); *Gyn/Ecology* (1978). A. Davis, *Women, Race and Class* (1983). V. Gornick and B. Moran, eds., *Women in Sexist Society* (1971). G. Lerner, *The Creation of Patriarchy* (1986). A. Rich, "Compulsory Heterosexuality and Lesbian Experience," *Signs* 5 (1980): 631–60. R. Ruether, *Sexism and God Talk: Toward a Feminist Theology* (1984). P. Sanday, *Female Power and Male Dominance: On the Origins of Sexual Inequality* (1981). For government crime statistics see Bureau of Justice

Statistics, U.S. Department of Justice, Sourcebook of Criminal Justice Statistics (1986); Federal Bureau of Investigation, Uniform Crime Reports (1986).

C. ELLEN

SOCIAL JUSTICE ISSUES IN PASTORAL CARE. The concept of justice is the fundamental normative principle for evaluating and harmonizing conflicting claims of rights, duties, and responsibilities. Social justice issues come to focus most clearly with respect to *distributive* justice, the impartial taxing and distribution of values, so as to achieve the common good. (Social justice may also be concerned with equal treatment in three other forms of justice: commutative justice, which adjudicates conflicts between parties within the state; retributive justice, which is imposed by the state; and remedial justice, which requires the present redress of past injustice.)

Social justice advocacy and pastoral care may be perceived as in four possible relationships with one another: (1) autonomous; (2) competing; (3) complementary, that is, common parts of a whole ministry; or (4) supplementary, that is, mutually corrective and enabling.

1. Autonomous. Social justice claims autonomous authority when it claims one of the following three bases: (1) civil law, (2) natural law, and (3) utilitarianism.

   a. Justice as conformity to the law. Civil law is a conception of great moral and social importance, for the rule of law is a major achievement in human history, creating justice by mitigating the arbitrary and exploitive exercise of power by those with political and economic advantage. Yet the law's claim to autonomous authority must be challenged by the recognition that the codification of law and its interpretation remain subject to political and other power. Theologically speaking, even as law limits human sinfulness, it also reflects human sinfulness. Law tries to adjust for this by systems of checks and balances and by respect for due process. But it still must rely for justice on factors outside of law, including the commitment to justice of individuals who create and implement law.

   b. Justice as the harmonization of values. One basis for appeal beyond civil law is to the natural law concept of the harmonization of values; the primary categories of this concept are merit (to be contrasted below with need) as the just basis for what is due, and the impartiality of rational judgments in terms of fairness and proportionality. However, limits on this natural law remain; since there are competing claims even among the values of a good creation, and since there are competing interpretations of the principles of harmonization, social justice issues remain even after the appeal to this natural law basis.

   c. Justice as the maximization of values. This utilitarian definition of justice circumvents the distributional issue by adopting the market metaphor of capitalism. Since freedom ensures the right to determine one's own values, and to pursue them without restraint, values are privatized and public issues are reducible to supposedly value-free, technical determinations of the productivity of means. This technical, quantitative definition of justice has been widely espoused in Western capitalistic countries where economic productivity has been great and the advantages of maximizing values through this process are clearly evident. This conception of justice, based on an ever-expanding pie of resources and values, has not, however, always created justice; great inequities have developed. It is a conception that requires correction, as from other views of justice, and from the regard of more human, less technical perspectives.

   (A fourth basis for justice, grounded in the righteousness of God, will be discussed below.)

   These legal and technical bases, then, leave issues of social justice still subject to essentially political struggles. Different groups appeal to the same concepts of law and justice to legitimate their own demands. Groups and individuals must be relied on for commitment to justice and to the meeting of essential human needs, along with their more restricted self-interest. In this sense, social justice advocacy is not independent of the concerns of pastoral care (see below).

   At the same time, it is equally limited to suppose that pastoral care's promotion of personal empowerment and wholeness can be effective in the absence of socially just distribution of resources.

2. Competing. Social justice advocacy and pastoral care are commonly perceived as competing, in at least these aspects: (1) In practice, each is supremely demanding of time, energy, and commitment; it is difficult for a person or group to expend the requisite resources on more than one such demanding enterprise. (This itself becomes an issue of distribution of resources—a social justice issue—and an issue of role conflict and identity diffusion—a pastoral care issue.)

   (2) Social justice advocacy is traditionally addressed to social structures and institutions, pastoral care to individuals and primary relationships. The inherent and classically recognized conflict to interest

between individual and collective welfare, then, generates some inevitable conflict between the practice of social justice advocacy and of pastoral care.

(3) Social justice advocacy typically focuses on human sinfulness and is more often perceived as an activity of law and judgment; pastoral care focuses on resources and is more often perceived as an activity of grace.

(4) Social justice advocacy is more often directed toward the disruption or transformation of established patterns, pastoral care more toward the reestablishment of what is ruptured or the conservation of what is precarious. Pastoral care may be a silent supporter of an unjust status quo; social justice advocacy may be the active disrupter of social systems on which individuals have come to rely as supports of identity.

3. Complementary. Social justice advocacy and pastoral care can be described in language that makes them analogous or closely complementary parts of the same ministry. Both individual health and the social health of justice can be understood as grounded in the righteousness of God—an alternative basis for justice to those cited above. The Judeo-Christian heritage points ultimately to a righteous God whose justice is redemptive, liberating, and remedial. God's righteousness empowers the powerless and justifies those who are without merit, on the basis of need. Pastoral care and social justice advocacy are similarly engaged in this enterprise of empowerment and of liberation from the oppression of need. Both aspire to empower the powerless and to loosen the grip of existing powers. Both aspire to a wholeness (whether of individual or of society) that emphasizes interdependence and mutuality. Both attack the limited idolatries and addictions to which people cling and by which they define their lives, and both encourage more "faith"-ful, adventurous, vulnerable, even sacrificial postures.

4. Supplementary. Even given statements more limited than the general common goals just expressed about the aims of social justice advocacy (to promote equitable distribution of resources and values) and of pastoral care (to promote the wholeness of individuals and their relationships with others), it is possible to identify ways in which the work and the perspective of social justice and the work and perspective of pastoral care become indispensable to each other. Both are value-laden, value-driven enterprises that need the corrective of the other's values.

(1) The wholeness of individuals, to which pastoral care aspires, depends greatly on the satisfaction of elemental human needs by the fair availability of economic and other resources, that is, on social justice. In

particular, the interpretation of particular pastoral care situations may benefit from the kind of assessment of social realities that consideration of social justice requires; for example, the effects of social location or social role, the oppressiveness of some social conditions, the destructiveness of the withholding of some social resources.

(2) Wholeness of individuals is incomplete without a consciousness raised and tuned to issues of justice and injustice, without a capacity to relate even to remote others with compassionate identification.

(3) The processes of social justice—such as the just implementation of law, the awareness of the need to transcend and transform law, the capacity to make impartial judgments in adjudicating and harmonizing value conflicts, the readiness to recognize the special claims of need and the needy—require the participation of moral actors who are as whole as possible, relatively free of prejudices, defensiveness, fears (especially fears triggered by social differences), and other such characteristics that are impediments both to close personal relationships and to participation in social justice.

(4) The tactics and structures for the delivery of pastoral care, themselves part of social structures, may participate in and support unjust characteristics of their parent institution as, for example, in the selective attention to individuals, or in providing merely palliative support to victims of injustice. The enterprise of pastoral care itself needs a corrective from the perspective of social justice.

(5) The tactics and structures of social justice advocacy may be carelessly destructive of individual wholeness, as, for example, in reckless use of guilt-inducing tactics, or in paternalistic manipulation, and themselves need a corrective from the perspective of pastoral care.

Bibliography. T. Aquinas, *Summa Theologica*, vols. I–II, q. 90, 91, and 93–95 (1952). J. Bennett, *The Radical Imperative* (1975), ch. 5. P. D. Couture and R. J. Hunter, *Pastoral Care and Social Conflict* (1995). P. DeVos, "Justice," in C. Henry, ed., *Baker's Dictionary of Christian Ethics* (1973). C. V. Gerkin, *Prophetic Pastoral Practice* (1991). J. Macquarrie, "Justice," *Dictionary of Christian Ethics* (1967). R. Niebuhr, *The Nature and Destiny of Man*, vol. 2 (1941), ch. 9. Plato, *The Republic*, F. Cornford, trans., (1945). P. Ramsey, *Basic Christian Ethics* (1950), 1–24. J. Rawls, *A Theory of Justice* (1971), par. 1–4, 11–17, 20–30. P. Tillich, *Love, Power, and Justice* (1954).

D. RHOADES

4

INTERFAITH ISSUES AND METHODS

During the production of the original version of the *Dictionary of Pastoral Care and Counseling* (1990), there was a brief discussion among the editors about whether to title the volume *Dictionary of* Religious *and Pastoral Care and Counseling* instead of simply *Dictionary of* Pastoral Care *and Counseling.* This was due to the fact that the volume sought to expand the understanding of care in religious traditions beyond the Christian faith, as seen in the collection of articles below. However, because the original *DPCC* was primarily and intentionally centered in the Western Christian tradition, it was decided to keep only the term "pastoral" in the title. Nevertheless, the postmodern world demands all the more that pastors, chaplains, and pastoral counselors have an interfaith understanding in their work in order to provide religious, spiritual, and pastoral care in the most sensitive and effective way possible.

AFRICAN TRADITIONAL RELIGION, PERSONAL CARE IN. Research done in recent years has brought to light complex patterns of psychosocial and medical systems existing in African traditional societies. Diviners, herbalists, therapeutic groups, and a variety of healers specialize in the diagnosis and treatment of illnesses, including mental disorders and deviant behaviors.

1. Cosmology. African cosmology is perceived and lived as one composed of seen and unseen spirit-beings. They constitute life forces that constantly interact with, and thus influence, the course of human life for good or for bad (Mbiti, 1970). The departed ancestors are part of this constellation of living spirits. By virtue of being part of the extended family and living in the proximity of God, the Creator, the ancestors are endowed with special powers. Therefore, they enable the birth of children and protect the living family members from attack by malevolent spirits. As those who sanction the moral life of both individuals and community, the ancestors punish, exonerate, or reward. Thus, the health of the living depends to a great extent on their relationships within the extended family and with their ancestors who mostly communicate their wishes through dreams (Pobee, 1979). Evil divinities coexist with other spirits. The Vusugu of Kenya believe that an evil divinity uses witches and sorcerers to bring about misfortune and illness and to cause the death of human beings (Mbiti, 1970).

Thus, traditional African cosmology is dynamic. It recognizes and integrates the duality of mind and body, magic and rationality, order and disorder, negative and positive powers, and individual and communal consciousness. The maintenance of personal and social equilibrium in the midst of this apparent dualism becomes the major role of traditional diagnosis, psychotherapy, and medical systems.

Beliefs in witchcraft and sorcery form the most important cosmological and medical etiological category of the traditional African systems studied thus far. E. E. Evans-Pritchard (1937) demonstrated that the Azande used witchcraft and sorcery as symbolic interpretations of misfortune, illness, and death. C. Kluckhohn (1944) views these beliefs as functional in that they are used as a channel through which people deal with feelings of hatred, hostility, frustration, jealousy, guilt, and sexual fantasies, the expression of which is culturally discouraged. These beliefs therefore engender abreactions that prevent the formation of severe neurosis. They perform the psychological function of dealing constructively with ambivalent feelings aroused by the ambiguity of both the cosmological and social orders.

2. Health and Illness. A large quantity of literature exists describing the traditional etiological and diagnostic system. Organic factors such as bad diet, heredity, stress, anger, hostility, rivalry, anxiety, fear, fatigue, ambivalence, and identity crisis can bring on illness. Such psychological factors, however, are almost always perceived as having a precipitating function in individuals whose vulnerability has been exploited by the possessive power of malevolent forces (P'Bitek, 1971; Dawson, 1974).

Etiology and diagnosis in the context of traditional African thought pose the following basic question: "Who is the cause of my illness? Is it I, or is it someone else?" In this context, organically manifested symptoms are always the result of some aggression and are thus not just physically induced. What is essentially sought in every illness, either somatic or emotional, is the significance of such disease.

3. Diagnosis. Diagnosis is always synthetic: it searches for and announces the cause of illness by providing its sociopsychological and spiritual significance. The consequences of such an illness for the individual and the community are also indicated. This approach obviously differs from the classification method characteristic of Western psychiatry. In African thinking, mental disorder is perceived to be persecution of, or more precisely, aggression against the individual self by other sociocultural and spiritual selves. Thus, the ancestral spirits participate in the therapeutic process primarily by solving relationships arising from the violation of traditional norms. The healer, on the other hand, orchestrates significant events capable of reconciling broken relationships. Thus, diagnosis aims at clarifying the type, the nature, and the significance of each conflict that is supposed to be the basic cause of illness. There are as many types of mental disorder as there are possible conflicting relationships.

4. Healing and Care. The restoration of broken relationships, the reestablishment of social equilibrium, and the revitalization of individual identity within the context of the renewed community are the major means and dynamic ends underlying traditional therapies and healing processes in traditional African societies. Care for the troubled person is a process involving many steps, usually beginning with a tentative consensus reached by the family members. The kin diagnostic group, that is, a therapeutic palaver, led by the extended family's elders, brings together the clan in order to fathom the meaning of the patient's illness (Janzen, 1978). In certain places, for example, in the Congo of central Africa, the elders perform therapeutic rites in which members of the matriclan and the patriclan of the patient discuss the case and then terminate the session with a rite of reconciliation.

A second consensus is sometimes sought by the healer through meeting with the wider community. Here, the symptoms yield their symbolic significance. The patient becomes the visible sign of the underlying dynamics within the group and of its value. The socialization of guilt and of the individual, as well as the communal confessions, provide a catharsis. Public acknowledgment of the fault brings about reconciliation of the patient with others. Symbolic psychodrama, exorcism, and rites to effect reconciliation with the ancestors and good spirits are traditional therapeutic devices that help the community and the individual bring into consciousness and reenact symptoms and myths that are part of traditional African systems of illness and of health.

Bibliography. G. Bibeau et al., *Traditional Medicine in Zaire* (1980). J. Dawson, "Urbanization and Mental Health in a West African Community," in A. Kiev, ed., *Magic, Health and Healing* (1974). E. E. Evans-Pritchard, *Witchcraft, Oracles and Magic among the Azanda* (1937). J. M. Janzen, *The Quest for Therapy in Lower Zaire* (1978). C. Kluckhohn, *Navaho Witchcraft* (1944). J. S. Mbiti, *Concepts of God in Africa* (1970). Masamba ma Mpolo, "Kindoki as Diagnosis and Therapy," *Social Science and Medicine* 15–B (1981), 405–13. O. P'Bitek, *Religion of the Central Luo* (1971). J. S. Pobee, *Toward an African Theology* (1979).

M. MA MPOLO

BLACK MUSLIM CARE AND COUNSELING. "Black Muslims" is a pseudonym for the Nation of Islam organization, headed by the Honorable Elijah Muhammad ("the Messenger of Allah to the Black Man in America") until his death in 1975. Under the leadership of his son Imam Warith Deen Muhammad, the doctrinally new organization was most recently known as the American Muslim Mission. Dissolved in 1985, the former *masajid* (Arabic plural of *masjid*, mosque) became administratively independent; the former Chicago headquarters is known as Masjid Elijah Muhammad. Despite some similarities, this article does not concern the present Nation of Islam, also called the Black Muslims, led by Minister Louis Farrakhan.

Counseling in the Nation and its successor organizations was based on the premise that African Americans ("Bilalians," "Afro Americans," or "black Americans") are in need of religious and social rehabilitation. During the time of Elijah Muhammad, the rehabilitation program began with the formal "acceptance of Islam," that is, conversion to his heterodoxy. His weekly sermon, radio broadcast, and column in the Nation's organ *Muhammad Speaks* were concerned with solutions to the psychological and social conditions of African Americans.

Adult males became members of the Fruit of Islam (FOI). They were taught the dietary laws of Islam, physical fitness and defense, personal hygiene, proper dress, and behavior. They were encouraged to be self-respecting, industrious, supportive of their families, and law-abiding citizens. Indulgence in drugs, smoking, gambling, fornication, adultery, and criminal activities was proscribed. A member who was known to have such proclivities was given special attention in a private or group session. He was encouraged to sever unnecessary associations with females and nonmembers of the Nation. If he violated the behavior code, he was subject to a "trial" before the membership; if found guilty, he was reprimanded severely, suspended for a period, or both.

Adult females became members of the Muslim Girls Training and General Civilization Class (MGT and GCC) and received guidance similar to that of the males. They learned home economics and were taught to be respectful and obedient to their fathers and husbands, within the framework of the Islamic code of conduct. They were required to cover their heads, bosoms, arms, and legs in public, including the workplace.

Young students received care and counseling in the Universities of Islam, the Nation's primary and secondary schools, now called Sister Clara Muhammad Schools.

Under Warith Muhammad, Muslims were urged to seek guidance from the Qur'an (Koran), Hadith (sayings of the Prophet Muhammad), and *khutbas* ("sermons") of Imam Muhammad himself and other imams. Members received guidance from the group's weekly newspaper, *Muslim Journal*, which contained the following regular columns: "Imam W. Deen Muhammad of Masjid Elijah Muhammad," "A Message of Concern to the American People," "Observations," "Science and Health," "Family Life," "The Holy Qur'an," "Hadith," "Mind Matters," "Your Health from a Dental Point of View," and "Small Business." Also, a growing number of books and audio recordings on religious, theological, psychological, marital, and social matters were available for purchase. Muslim prisoners had access to Muslim chaplains, as well as to printed materials. All members could address queries to the editor of the *Muslim Journal*.

A. MUHAMMAD

HASIDIC CARE AND COUNSELING. Hasidism is a popular, charismatic Jewish movement originating in southern Poland in 1734. A Hasid (literally, pious) is one who has accepted a *rebbe* as a guide and spiritual director and has allied himself with a Hasidic congregation. Israel ben Eliezer founded the movement. Born in about 1700 in the Ukraine, he came to be known as the Baal Shem Tov (Master of the Good Name). The movement spread rapidly among Eastern European Jews and continues to occupy an important place in the Jewish community.

1. Origin. During the seventeenth and eighteenth centuries, the life of the ordinary Jew in Eastern Europe was characterized by political and social oppression, persecution, and ostracism. Efforts among the poor and uneducated to gain or regain their dignity as persons and as a community and to assuage a deep yearning for greater contact with Jewish life were generally unsuccessful. Among the rabbis and the leisured, a retreat to the world of the spirit was possible through a study of Jewish literature and the Talmud. But the anguish of the masses who sought to escape the inferior position in which they were held and to participate in a religion they could understand was largely unacknowledged.

It was into this void that the Baal Shem Tov stepped. Firmly grounded in the Jewish Mystical Tradition (Kabbala) and possessed of unusual gifts of speech and imagination, he insisted that the primary duty to seek God and to find one's place in his purpose required neither great learning nor long prayers. God is to be found all about us and the path to him is not despair and gloom but the awareness of his presence in joy and lightness of heart and in acts of love and mercy.

Initially, Baal Shem Tov ministered to the religious and emotional needs of his neighbors from his position as a teacher of children. However, as his reputation grew, persons traveled great distances to seek his benediction and his advice on relations with God and each other. His ideas were presented simply, usually embellished and illustrated with examples and stories from daily life. His followers, known as Hasidim, included any number of important religious leaders, many of whom became *rebbes* themselves and established congregations. Baal Shem Tov came to be regarded as having direct contact with God, serving as an intermediary and as a defender of the Jewish people before the Almighty. Stories of miracles were associated with his name and although he left no writings, his words were transmitted orally by his followers and he became a legendary figure. More scholarly successors, like Magged of Meseritch, sought to undergird his teaching with traditional Jewish learning and the writings of the mystics. They also began to train *rebbes* to carry on the movement.

During the course of these developments, Hasidism experienced considerable opposition. The Hasidim's emphasis on prayer as opposed to study and on emotion rather than intellect caused their opponents (Mitnaggedim, i.e., Orthodox Jews) to accuse them of attempting to destroy learning, dignity, and the Jewish Tradition. Finally, the Hasidim were excommunicated and a period of persecution and animosity continued until the appearance of a common enemy, the eighteenth-century Enlightenment, which caused the various factions within Judaism to unite. Even in the midst of this conflict, Hasidism continued to expand, and to provide examples of saintliness, wisdom, and spirituality in Jewish life.

The price the Hasidim paid for their acceptance as a legitimate expression of Jewish life was to see once-spontaneous practices become institutionalized. S. Schachter (1983) suggests that this resulted in a suppression of their more exuberant and emotional expressions and a surrender of some aspects of their work, for example, meditative techniques. Following the bloodlines of the original leaders, Hasidic dynasties emerged all over Europe, some faithful to the original intent, while others took on regal characteristics and removed themselves from the people. The ideal that a religious leader ought to be expert in the Tradition and in Jewish Law came to characterize the Hasidic *rebbe*. But the commitment that he not neglect or be aloof from the people and from his primary task of bringing all Jews closer to God receded.

2. Care and Counseling. What the Baal Shem Tov brought to a dispirited people was the hope of a life unified in all its parts, personal, interpersonal, and metaphysical. He captured their alienation and personal and social ostracism with his characterization of life as exile. By utilizing classical mystical concepts, he insisted that the separations they experienced between good and evil, rich and poor, male and female, mercy and judgment, all their inner and outer contradictions contained holy sparks that were separated from their true source in God. The entire cosmos possesses immense and largely unacknowledged possibilities, so that all that exists is to some degree estranged from the source of its life.

The task of the Hasidic master, or *rebbe*, then, was to gather up these fallen sparks everywhere. They sought to provide a path to unification and vital relatedness to God for those unable, either through want of learning or leisure or because of the pressing distractions of life, to pursue the traditional way of study and debate of the Torah. The uneducated needed a guide. They needed to be reminded by instruction and example that no situation in life should be neglected. The divine sparks are always present, and the inner exaltation of raising these sparks to their source follows from devoted attention to the vicissitudes and activities of daily life. Thus whatever one does, whether prayer, work, family life, or play, becomes an occasion for participation in the unification and fulfillment of the universe. Despair, self-pity, and sadness are marks of distance from

147

God; ecstasy, physical liveliness in song and dance, and devotion and service reflect a life bound to God.

These *rebbes* or *zaddikim* (righteous ones) were the key to the Hasidic communities. They were known as Teachers of the Way. Their participation with the people enabled them to serve as examples, so that the task of the Hasidim was to emulate the *rebbe* in works of charity, justice, prayer, song, and ecstasy. As intermediaries their lives were understood to be a reflection of the unification of earth and heaven, body and soul, male and female, and so forth. By simply observing their daily activities, the Hasidim could learn about wholeness. As J. S. Woocher says, "The Hasidic communal ideal rested on a faith in the power of simplicity, joy, and the encounter with a counselor and healer, who himself embodied wholeness and intimacy with people and God, to effect a unification embracing all the dimensions of human life" (1978, 30).

At the heart of the *rebbe's* relation to the Hasidic community was the *yehidut*. The *yehidut* (literally, "oneing") involved a private meeting with one's *rebbe* that at its best reflected a sacred encounter among the *rebbe*, the Hasid, and God. Generally, a Hasid met with his *rebbe* annually and at all the major turning points of his life, for example, at bar mitzvah, with the decision about the choice of a partner. At times of crisis the Hasid was also expected to consult with his *rebbe*. The sessions were formal and private. The Hasid prepared ritually and spiritually for the event and gave thought to the issues/dilemmas he wished to present. Moreover, simply by appearing for the *yehidut*, the Hasid agreed to abide by the *rebbe's* advice and instruction and to offer a gift to help support him.

The bond between Hasid and *rebbe*, then, required a lifetime commitment. Each stage and place in life offered opportunities to gather the sparks, to observe the injunctions of the Torah, to perform good deeds (*mitzvot*), and to do *teshuvah* (repent or return and ascend to one's divine source of origin). The *rebbes* were astute in their efforts to uncover and to understand the Hasid's inner life and situation. As the movement grew, specialization occurred among the *rebbes*, and referral to another master or to a *mashpiyim* (influencer) was possible. Only after this effort to understand did *rebbes* offer prescriptions for action, prescriptions that might include meditative techniques, acts of charity, healings, and miracles. They saw the depressed, the financially distressed, the barren, the abandoned, those with family conflict, and the politically oppressed, always seeking ways to encourage relatedness to God in the midst of life. And at the conclusion of the *yehidut*, they offered their blessing, frequently a whispered word cherished as a mutual pact among Hasid and *rebbe* and God.

This relation to the *rebbe*, as reflected in the *yehidut*, formed the basis for communal life among the Hasidim. More often than not, the Hasid would emerge from his meeting with his master to celebrate in song and dance the blessing that was his. For the meeting was understood to transcend simple personal distress and to link persons to one another and, finally, to the purposes of God in the unification of his creation. Thus the substance of the *yehidut* became the stuff of daily interchange among the Hasidim, linking them to each other and to the Almighty.

3. Present State. A renewal of interest in the Hasidic tradition reflects both the psychological and the theological wisdom and insight it contains. Martin Buber (1947) and Elie Wiesel (1982) have each acknowledged their indebtedness to the tradition. In Buber's case, his formulation of the I-Thou relationship owes much to the encounter in the *yehidut* between *rebbe* and Hasid. In the psychological sphere, Woocher demonstrates the possible dialogue of Hasidic thought with neo-Freudian, Jungian, humanistic, and even behaviorist theories. He also notes that Hasidic attempts to "embody growth" and "wholeness" resemble the work of Rogers, Maslow, Fromm, and Frankl. Any number of scholars have also demonstrated the affinities of the *yehidut* to some contemporary work in psychotherapy. Schachter (1983) especially has delineated these affinities. But each of these writers is also careful to point out that the transcendent dimension of Hasidic thought, expressed in myth, mystery, and religious symbolism, moves beyond the personal and social aspects of contemporary psychology. Finally, Hasidic psychological insight was an expression of Torah.

Within the Hasidic community there appears to be no acknowledged relation between their thought and contemporary psychology. Indeed, within Judaism generally, there seems to be a certain tension between its Reformed and Conservative expressions and the Hasidim, and one dimension of this tension is the differing attitude among these groups toward secular knowledge. Hasidic orientation and training are more closely akin to the Orthodox tradition as this is modified by their allegiance to their particular dynasties.

Bibliography. M. Buber, *Tales of the Hasidim* (1947). S. Grayzel, *A History of the Jews* (1947). E. Hoffman, *The Way of Splendor* (1981). J. C. Safier, "Hasidim, Faith and Therapeutic Paradox," *J. of Judaism and Psychology* 3:1 (1978), 38–47. S. Schachter and E. Hoffman, *Sparks of*

Light: Counseling in the Hasidic Tradition (1983). M. H. Spero, "Discussion: On the Nature of the Therapeutic Encounter Between Hasid and Master," *J. of Judaism and Psychology* 3:1 (1978), 48–59. E. Wiesel, *Souls on Fire: Portraits and Legends of Hasidic Masters* (1982). J. S. Woocher, "The Kabbalah, Hasidim and the Life of Unification," *J. of Judaism and Psychology* 3:1 (1978), 22–37.

L. O. MILLS

ISLAMIC CARE AND COUNSELING. Pastoral dimensions of Islam derive from its sacred scriptures, from the evolution of fundamental institutions, notably the mosque, and from a history of syncretic adaption to a variety of societies and cultures. Strictly speaking, Islam rejects the notion of a clergy. Therefore it lacks the formally defined role and conceptually discrete functions of the pastor as found in most Christian traditions. The guidance of the community of believers and the care for individuals beset with difficulties of faith, moral dilemmas, or life crises occur within the framework of an all-encompassing law. However, more recently spiritual reactions have exposed the limits of jurisprudence, and diverse currents of socioreligious reform have shaped responses to modern challenges.

1. Classical Foundations. According to the teaching of Sunni Islam, which accounts for the vast majority of the world's Muslims, the fullness of creation consists in obedience to the divine will as expressed in the Sharia (literally, "path"). This is a corpus of variegated texts that together make up Islamic law. Its primary sources are the sacred book of the Quran and the Sunna, that is, the words and deeds of the Prophet Muhammad (570–632), along with the normative precedent of Islam's generations. The Shia tradition adds a reverence for Ali, the husband of Muhammad's daughter. Shiites believe that Ali inherited his father-in-law's spiritual charisma, which was then transmitted to his descendants, the last of whom has disappeared but is expected to return in millennial fashion.

Matters of doctrine, worship, personal hygiene, family life, commercial affairs, and government are all treated in the Sharia. It lays out a totalistic scheme for living as well as the elements of a religion. In principle, therefore, believers who conform to its dictates both achieve merit in eternity and remove obstacles to their prosperity in this world. Within such a system pastoral care is embedded in the prescribed duties incumbent upon all Muslims. However, special responsibilities are defined for those who hold positions of greater influence.

In theory, this single law regulates both personal and public affairs, but in practice the domain of civil enforcement has diverged from specifically religious institutions. Thus a distinctively pastoral authority has emerged that largely coincides with a recognition of superior knowledge in the law. In effect, the exercise of pastoral care has come to be concentrated in a variety of specialists who differ sociologically, according to a broad range of perceptions as to what determines preeminence or learning in the Sharia. Normally, it is the prerogative of these scholars, known classically as the ulema, to preside at rituals and to preach, while at a practical level they also frequently admonish, issue opinions, give advice, and respond to cases of perplexity or distress.

Islam lacks an explicit theology of sacraments. But it does view such devotions as prayer, fasting, pilgrimage, and almsgiving with a significance that points toward inner transformation and efficacy. The Quran's counsel that "prayer preserves from impurity and evil" (29:44) thus suggests the special symbolic quality of the mosque, the privileged place of prayer. As the scene of regular collective worship, the mosque is a center for the performance of spiritual works, and those who serve there are witnesses to the mercy of God present and active amid human efforts.

2. Sufi Developments. Sufism has its origins in a pious and ascetic reaction against the legalism and materialism that accompanied the consolidation of the Islamic empire. Among its key concepts is "trust in God," which has been variously elaborated into doctrines of pure love and disciplines for attaining inner knowledge and ultimately mystical union. Sufism also encourages a deep attachment to the person of Muhammad as an intercessor and an example of holiness based on the Quranic declaration: "You have in the Apostle of God an excellent model" (33:12). Sufis see their quest as an imitation of the Prophet who enjoyed direct and vivid experiences of God.

Almost from its beginnings a definite pastoral concern has also marked Sufism. What started as devotees gathering around a master later developed into diverse patterns of discipleship, both solitary and communal, eventually involving widespread and sophisticated organizations with pronounced hierarchies. Throughout, however, an interpersonal relationship was considered indispensable. The great medieval theologian al-Ghazali (d. 1111) wrote: "The disciple must of necessity have recourse to a director to guide him aright. For the way of faith is obscure, but the devil's ways are many and patent, and he who has no Shaykh to guide him will be led by the devil into his ways."

Sufism has been an important vehicle for the spread of Islam beyond the Middle East to the Indian subcontinent, Central Asia, sub-Saharan Africa, and Indonesia. As a result, aspects of Sufism have fused with many indigenous methods and structures to provide care and counseling. Also, in many cases, the cohesion established through affiliation with Sufi fraternities has helped balance unequal power relations and reinforce moral bonds among members of a tribe, a village, a guild, or a military unit. The pastoral component of Sufism also includes a rich ceremonial life, notably, abundant forms of expressive spiritual exercises called Dhikr (literally, "remembrance"). These gatherings often make use of special garments, song, dance, dramatic recitations, and even shamanistic displays.

Although the practice is disparaged by many Muslims, an extensive cult of saints reflects a popular outgrowth of Sufism with clear pastoral features. Tombs and shrines dedicated to holy men or women attract especially the simple people who visit them to perform rituals or to seek favors or guidance. Frequently, persons related in some way to the saint reside near such sites, where they may reconcile adversaries or give instruction, advice, or blessings.

Historically parallel to Sufism and matching many of its concerns in a worldly perspective is a movement associated with the concept of Adab (literally, "culture" or "social graces"). Broadly speaking, this repository of teachings deals with character training, the cultivation of virtue, and the pursuit of happiness in a philosophical and ethical context. A sizable literature in many languages and genres presents these ideals of refinement and applies them to particular roles such as rulers, judges, preachers, and teachers.

3. Modern Trends. The encroachment of Western colonialism during the nineteenth century, followed by the rapid penetration of advanced technologies and growing global interdependency, have deeply affected the patterns of society and consciousness in the Muslim world. As a consequence, religious attitudes and institutions are changing under internal and external pressures and tend to reflect conflicting conservative and progressive directions.

Overall, the tendency has been to formalize pastoral care within the context of a nation-state that regards social welfare and the supervision of religion as its official responsibility. Hence bureaucracies, seminaries, and mosque community centers of many types have been established or subsidized. Initiatives have been taken to improve the quality of preaching and generally to professionalize the corps of those identified as representatives of Islam. In many instances, direct or indirect control of mosques and preachers involves their enlistment in campaigns of social reform or political mobilization. The intensity or the ideological orientation of such programs varies depending on differences in motives and available resources.

A strong puritanical strain also characterizes much contemporary Islamic thought. Both modernizers and traditionalists have sought to rid popular piety of practices that diverge from an acceptable range of orthodoxy. The former, which has been more of an elite approach, includes many who are open to Western ideas and are prepared to reexamine classical interpretations. The latter group has resisted intellectual accommodation, although they do embrace many achievements of science that benefit their ministry, such as electronic communication techniques and the study of psychology.

Another prominent current in many Muslim lands appears in movements that oppose the secular state's management of religion. For example, the Jamaat-i-Islami in Pakistan and the Muslim Brothers in Egypt and elsewhere, although they may also contain a political agenda, have their primary impact in the organization of local independent socioreligious societies. Leaders of such associations usually have a modern rather than a traditional educational background. They are nonetheless active in mosques as well as schools and assorted self-help cooperative ventures where the care and counseling of individual members is a priority.

The phenomenon recently described as the "Islamic resurgence" or "revival" epitomized by the revolution in Iran and the resulting Islamic Republic signals a shift in pastoral care as well as politics. Based on the denial of a dichotomy between sacred and secular power, those sharing this militant spirit advocate replacing present-day civil and criminal codes with the Sharia. This implies that religious specialists who are held to be experts in this law become themselves administrators of state authority, thereby conjoining civil and pastoral operations. The unity of these two spheres does correspond to an Islamic ideal. Yet many also argue that the best way to realize it in today's world is to maintain a functional distinction between the mosque and the seat of government.

Bibliography. T. W. Arnold, *The Preaching of Islam* (1913). K. Cragg, *The Call of the Minaret* 2nd ed. (1985). H. A. R. Gibb, *Mohammedanism: An Historical Survey*, 2nd ed. (1957). M. Hamidullah, *Introduction to Islam*, 4th ed. (1974). N. Keddie, ed., *Scholars, Saints, and Sufis: Muslim Religious*

Institutions in the Middle East Since 1500 (1972). B. D. Metcalf, ed., *Moral Conduct and Authority: The Place of Adab in South Asian Islam* (1984). F. Rahman, *Islam* (1966). J. Schacht, *An Introduction to Islamic Law* (1964). E. Sivan, *Radical Islam: Medieval Theology and Modern Politics* (1985). W. C. Smith, *Islam in Modern History* (1959). S. J. Trimingham, *The Sufi Orders of Islam* (1971).

P. D. GAFFNEY

JEWISH CARE AND COUNSELING (History, Traditions, and Contemporary Issues). According to Jewish tradition, the family is the germinal cell from whence come the spiritual and ethical values to shape the Jewish character. This attitude is expressed even in the language, for the Hebrew word for "parents" is *horim*, which comes from the same root as *moreh*, "teachers." The parent, by exemplary deeds, is the primary teacher. The Jewish home is regarded as the *Mikdash Me'at* (miniature sanctuary), where the husband and wife are priest and priestess. This kindred solidarity constitutes the basis of Jewish life and increases in cohesiveness when confronted with adversity and discrimination.

The reciprocal relationship between home and religion is seen in the practice of Judaism. Many of the important religious rituals are home-centered. These rituals are marked not only by extended family visiting but also by the use of distinctly Jewish foods associated with a particular holy day. Home religious observance requires the recitation of blessings at mealtime and frequently throughout the day. Festivals such as Passover involve extensive participation by family groups in their homes. A family celebration is the climax of the Jewish confirmation ceremony, the Bar or Bat Mitzvah, which takes place in the synagogue when a boy or girl reaches the age of thirteen. Some psychiatrists have noted that Jews, more than members of any other religious group, have reported experiencing their highest religious feelings in a family setting.

Since the first two decades of the twentieth century, there has been a marked alteration or abbreviation of home ritual ceremonies on the part of most American Jewish families. However, it is not the content of these ceremonies that is of concern but their function as a binding influence on the family.

Within the Jewish family setting, healthy attitudes toward sex, education, death, and other aspects of life had helped the family in the past withstand many of the disruptive influences of modern life. By preserving these attitudes and the accompanying religious practices, the Jewish fam-

ily preserved itself against some of the disorganization that was so currently widespread in other family lives.

1. A Healthy Attitude toward Sex. "It is well for a man not to touch a
woman," Paul wrote in the NT (1 Cor. 7:1), expressing his fundamental
conviction concerning sex. Recognizing immediately that these words
were far from the meditations in most hearts, he began to make conces-
sions. "Because of the temptation to immorality," he added, "each man
should have his own wife and each woman her own husband" (1 Cor.
7:2). Wistfully, Paul then wished that all could be as he was, unmarried
and with sexuality thoroughly bridled. Nevertheless, he granted that if
the "unmarried and the widows...cannot exercise self-control, they
should marry. For it is better to marry than to be aflame with passion"
(1 Cor. 7:8-9).

Judaism is not identified with the Pauline concept of sex. Even the sexual aspect of Freud's doctrines, which so alarmed the Christian world, was
in harmony with the Jewish viewpoint. Judaism maintains that if people
deny themselves the physical enjoyments of love, they also deny the spiritual potential within them. The sexual love relationship is a high adven-
ture of the human spirit, an opportunity for husband and wife to make a
oneness of the separateness. In Judaism one does not thwart the body, but
rather sanctifies it through love. Voluntary abstinence from sexual relations in marriage is a triple sin—against the health of the body, the fulfillment of the soul, and the welfare of society.

The Jewish view is neither hedonism nor prudery. Judaism asserts that
there is a middle ground between these two. Jewish proscriptions generally are not against the use of bodily appetites but rather against the
excessive indulgence of such desires.

In the United States, while it is true that Jews tend to have relatively
few illegitimate children, the explanation lies partly in the widespread
acceptance by Jews of birth control measures. For example, Alfred Kinsey
found that American Jews have more marital intercourse than non-Jews
at all age levels except the youngest. Even more significantly, Kinsey and
his associates reported that Jews talk more freely about sex than their
Christian neighbors. Mental health experts are generally agreed that the
subject of sex is too seldom discussed by parents and church or synagogue.
Consequently, many young people have distorted ideas and information
on sex. By allowing a fuller discussion on this vital subject, Jewish parents
realize their responsibility to help children obtain more correct information so that their youngsters may develop healthy attitudes toward sex in

their youth. They begin to build a way of thinking about marriage that will help them in establishing Jewish homes.

Judaic counseling considers the starting point in the sexual relationship to be the recognition of God as Creator and sovereign Ruler of the universe and all that is in it. In the first chapter of Genesis it says: "So God created man in his own image...; male and female he created them. And God blessed them, and God said to them, 'Be fruitful and multiply, and fill the earth'" (Gen. 1:27a-28a). Jewish tradition maintains that sex is good, not bad, because it is one of God's endowments. Procreation is one of God's commands. Sex is not nasty, but holy; not sordid, but sacred. However, Judaism acknowledges that people can misuse and pervert that which God meant for good, and teaches that sex should not be divested of its dignity and meaning.

The Jew is taught that the sex act has more than biological meaning; a real marriage is a combination of physical attraction plus companionate love. A person's masculinity or femininity makes one look for a person of the opposite sex, but a person's loneliness makes one look for a friend to relieve one's solitariness. When God said, "It is not good that the man should be alone" (Gen. 2:18), this indicated that God's plan for man and woman was not only for propagation of the race but also for their mutual welfare, for the well-being of society, and the strengthening of family ties. This Jewish concept of the sexual function is considered by some mental health experts to be less likely to lead to neuroses caused by sexual conflicts than the Pauline concept.

2. Judaism: A This-Worldly Faith. Judaism is more than a creed; it is a way of life. One of the distinctive values of the Jewish subculture is that of "life's pleasures" or "nonasceticism"—the belief that "better is one day of happiness and good deeds in *this* world than all the life in the *world-to-come*." Since Jews do not consider their bodily appetites as sinful, their behavior in matters of sex, drink, and food is affected accordingly. The practical, realistic approach of the Jewish concept helps promote more stable reality testing.

In the view of normative Judaism, the way to God is not through flight from the world or through self-mortification. Holiness, *Kedusha*, while representing a unique category of the spirit, is realizable in one's earthly life. The physical, far from being antithetical to the spiritual, may serve as its vehicle. *Kedusha* is attained through molding the human into the patterns of the divine. *Kedusha* is not in the extirpation of natural instincts and desires, but in their refinement, discipline, and direction toward godliness and social as well as personal welfare.

"And God saw everything that he had made, and behold, it was very good" (Gen. 1:31a). So almost with its first words, Scripture states a thesis that echoes and reechoes down the centuries; life is good, and should be treasured and affirmed as a gift from God.

The purpose of this life is the wise, good, and creative enjoyment of the material, intellectual, moral, and spiritual blessings provided for humanity by the Creator. Judaism regards as sinful both *rejection* of the pleasures of life, which is in effect the denial of the wisdom and loving-kindness of a beneficent Provider, and *indulgence* in exclusively material satisfactions that desensitize us and make us unconscious of our intellectual or moral-spiritual-aesthetic needs. Each of us is body, mind, and spirit. Denial of any aspect of the self, or failure to satisfy its legitimate needs, rules out maximum self-fulfillment.

Judaism holds that when we are born we are not enchained by original sin. We are inherently good and endowed with a moral conscience that is reinforced by freedom of will. The great Rabbi Akiba said that although everything is foreseen by God, God has given us free will. Maimonides, the medieval philosopher, stated that everyone by free will may be as righteous as Moses or as sinful as Jeroboam, wise or foolish, kind or cruel. Sin exists, and temptation is always with us. But by our own strength we can overcome them. At the very beginning of the Bible story, Cain is told that "sin is couching at the door; its desire is for you, but you must master it" (Gen. 4:7). We are not doomed to will the good and yet do evil. With goodness, we can and must be the architects of our own lives.

3. Well-Defined Pattern for Meeting Death. While Judaism's major emphasis is thus on life, there are theological beliefs concerning death. Jews understand that the individual is a dying being who, at the same time, must declare: "One world at a time is enough." Judaism does not ignore the mystery of death but is more concerned with the miracle of life. While other religions are, in general, otherworldly, Judaism's concepts of a hereafter are not completely harmonized and integrated.

Although Jewish beliefs about death do not totally center on concepts of a hereafter, Judaic tradition demonstrates a concern for the survivors' reactions to a death. Indeed, the Jewish faith surrounds death with rites that later play a vital role in the healing work of grief. The bereaved must of necessity realize that a loved one has died and must therefore gradually fill the void in a constructive way. They must not suppress memories or even disturbing, often guilt-producing, recollections that are an inevitable part of all human relationships. The spiritual confusions of shock and grief are structured through definite and solemn procedures.

From the moment that one learns of the death of a dear one, Judaism offers specific religious rituals to be followed, which help order one's life. Formal mourning periods of diminishing intensity follow death. The Jewish funeral is the rite of separation. The bad dream is real. The presence of the casket actualizes the experience, transforming the process of denial to the acceptance of reality.

In the ritual of bereavement, Jews could well feel that even though they should have done more for the deceased, these ceremonials can be done right. Here they know in clear-cut, unmistakable terms what is expected of them. Perhaps by carrying out the ceremonial, they will regain the love they have lost, the love of their own conscience, which could personify the highest internal ideals.

The first seven-day period following a death is *Shivah*, which tides the mourners over the first dazing shock. The survivors remain at home, receiving a continual stream of condolence calls. Difficult as this may be, it helps in keeping their minds active and their attentions engaged. Also, it is important because it lends the comfort of the loving concern of family and friends.

Sigmund Freud called *Shivah* the "ties of dissolution." Friends help review with the bereaved their experiences with the deceased. As each emotion is reconsidered, a pang of pain is felt that the experience will never be repeated. As the pain is experienced, the bereaved are able to dissolve their emotional ties with the deceased and thus establish new relationships by which they must take an active place in the company of the living.

After this comes the *Shloshim*, covering the following thirty-day period. The mourners resume normal activity, although avoiding places of entertainment and continuing to observe certain forms and prayers. At the end of the thirty days, ritualistic mourning is over except for the reciting of the *Kaddish*, the Jewish prayer for the deceased, daily for an entire year. Through the ancient, hallowed tradition of *Minyan* (daily worship), Jews perpetuate the memory of their loved one. Each time they recite the *Kaddish*, they reinforce both the reality of death and the affirmation of life. They publicly display their own concern and profound feeling of being a good child, parent, sibling, or spouse.

By participating with others who are also suffering the emotional trauma of bereavement, the mourning Jew belongs to the largest company in the world—the company of those who have known suffering and death. This great, universal sense of sorrow helps unite all human hearts and dissolve all other feelings into those of common sympathy and understanding. Such communal religious rituals create a sense of solidarity, with all the comfort, gratification, pride, and even pain that such a sense brings.

The Jewish ceremonials of *Shivah, Shloshim,* and reciting *Kaddish* communicate the concepts of faith, love, and finality. The event of death is placed in a context greater than that of each individual life. The observance of the Jewish laws and customs of mourning helps one face reality, give honor to the deceased, and guide the bereaved in the reaffirmation of life.

Judaism is strict in limiting mourning to the given periods and the customary observances. Excessive grief is taken as want of trust in God. The faith holds it as natural and desirable that with time the havoc wrought by death should repair itself. Though no one is ever the same after a bereavement as before, one is expected, when mourning is over, to take up existence, suppressing for the sake of life itself the remnants of grief. The garment that the pious mourner rends can be sewn and worn again. The mark is there, but life resumes its course.

4. Exalted Position of Learning. For the Jew, education is one of the most effective compensatory dynamisms to meet the inner conflicts of life. Historically, the respect for learning is one of the cornerstones of Judaism. Judaism is the religion of *Torah,* not alone of the *Chumash* (the five books of Moses) or the written law, nor even of the oral tradition, but of the progressive growth of all religious knowledge and culture. Knowledge is stressed as one of the chief duties that Jews owe not only to themselves but to their God. *The Ethics of the Fathers* (teachings of the rabbis of the Mishnaic period) states: "*Torah* is the first of the three pillars which support the Jewish world as well as the inspiration and vitality of the other two supports, worship and benevolence." The Hebrew term *Bet Hamidrash* and the Judeo-German *Schul,* which both mean school and learning, are commonly used as a synonym for synagogue.

The ideal of learning kept the Jewish people on a high plane of cultural and intellectual, as well as religious, enterprise. It further provided an ideal occupation and interest for people who were forced to look inward and find a symbolic status gratification. The Jew may attempt to surmount a "handicap," as in the legendary case of Demosthenes, who overcame his stuttering and became a famous orator. Feeling that Jews may suffer a handicap, Jewish people often urge their children to study and work harder than their Christian competitors in order to run the unequal race. To be successful, they may point out, a Jew must be better prepared, must have higher academic records, and more experience than the non-Jew. Freud once stated that the one thing that distinguishes the Jews is brainpower, for traditionally they had directed their psychic energies not to athletics but mental gymnastics.

With some other peoples, learning was an afterthought, a by-product of normal living or an entertainment for leisure hours. Historically, for the Jew it was a precondition for a sound mind. Education was revered and respected in that it aided the Jew in looking inward to a life of contemplative content away from the myriad forms of oppression and suggested a belief in the omnipotence of thought.

The importance given to learning and knowledge finds expression among contemporary Jewry in many ways. Students have often been given a higher status in Jewish community life. Settlement workers in immigrant quarters have always noticed the exceptional value that Jewish parents placed on schooling for their children, and this is manifest both in the high figures for Jewish attendance at colleges and universities, and in the grades of Jewish students. In addition, Jews are generously represented in highly esteemed professions, which require the most advanced educational training and intellectual discipline.

5. High Concept of Social Justice. In a graphic statement, Erich Fromm asserts in *The Art of Loving* (1974):

Man is gifted with reason; he is life being aware of itself; he has awareness of himself, of his fellow man, of his past, and of the possibilities of his future. This awareness of himself as a separate entity, the awareness of his own short span of life, of the fact that without his will he is born, and against his will he dies, that he will die before those whom he loves, or they before him, the awareness of his aloneness and separateness, of his helplessness before the forces of nature and of society, all of this makes his separate, disunited existence an unbearable prison. He would become insane could he not liberate himself from this prison and reach out, unite himself in some form or other with other men, with the world outside.

The experience of separateness causes the feeling of anxiety. For Jews, the feeling of separateness may be great. They often feel like marginal beings or, in Sigmund Freud's words, "prescribed from the compact majority." Kurt Lewin likened the lot of the Jew to the condition of adolescents who are never quite certain whether they will be admitted to the dominant adult world. The Jew lives on two levels: as a member of the general community and as "a child of the covenant."

The psychological problem for Jews is to find the relation between their interests and needs and the world in which they exist. These needs, such as the need to love and to be loved, can for a time remain ungratified without disturbing psychological health, but over a longer period of time they create mental distress and may lead to mental disease. Well-being is also disturbed when love is unrequited, curiosity unrelieved, and sympathy unexpressed. And many feel such distress "mentally" even though no bodily ill is noted. Freud, Jung, Adler, and Horney agree that there can be no health for the individual without appreciative and cooperative interaction.

One of the most important Jewish values is *Zedekah*, the Hebrew word for appreciative charity and cooperative social justice. In explaining the continuing solidarity of the Jewish people, Albert Einstein placed the Jewish respect for *Zedekah* above everything else. Although he may have stated the proposition too strongly, there is a partial truth in his claim that "the bond that has united the Jews for thousands of years and unites them today is above all the democratic ideal of social justice, coupled with the ideal of mutual aid and tolerance among all people" (Schmidt, 1959, 240).

The strong feeling on the part of the Jewish family created a social consciousness that transcended the solitary demands of the individual. In addition, there were the Jeremiahs, Isaiahs, and Amoses who were not only the teachers of ritualistic religion but were forerunners in the promulgation of a monotheism that was ethical in content. Social legislation was vast and revolutionary, dealing with relief of the poor; protection of the laborer, women, and children; filial duty; charity; hospitality; and relation with one's neighbors. These laws were mandatory because they were the will of God: "Ye shall therefore be holy, for I [the Lord, your God] am holy" (Lev. 11:45b KJV)

The history of the Jewish religion is essentially that of the emergence of ethical ideas and ideals out of a background of purely ceremonial and ritual observance, and the creation of a moral law that declared that God was to be served by means of right conduct. There is the statement of God declaring: "Would that you forsake me but keep my commandments." Today, the Jewish outlook prods Jews constantly to strive for a better world, to be prominently involved in movements for social reform. Even many Jewish radicals who may ignore their Jewishness are the product of this messianic fervor.

There are many reasons that form the basis for Jewish liberalism. Lewis Browne has forcefully stated the proposition that Jews are radicals in politics because they are an urban people. In addition, Jews realize that their security is inextricably interwoven with progressive governments. For example, in Czarist Russia anti-Semitism was the direct result of the interplay of the reactionary regime with a burgeoning liberal movement of the people. When reactionary governments triumphed, the Jew was often the scapegoat in Europe.

The minority-conscious Jews may direct their hostility against the dominant group or the more vulnerable low-status races (projection). But being victims themselves, they often display sympathy rather than aggression for the underdog. These two diametrically opposed reactions may be evident in the same person at different times. Jews are often among the most vigorous workers for liberal causes.

Social justice through the fight against prejudice is a way of sublimation for the Jews and a means for mental health. *Zedekah* is forged as a result of the frustrating outer world and deflected in favor of the cathexis of its substitute, but still showing some of the qualities of the original impulse. Jews are often active in leading protest meetings, raising funds, attempting to persuade friends among the dominant groups to aid in many liberal crusades. When the neighbor lends support to the Jew, the Jew is not only helped in terms of additional aid for the other minority groups but is given added ego reinforcement by the non-Jew's concurrence. For while Jews have often achieved a higher economic status, they still find themselves excluded from certain private clubs, organizations, and from high administrative posts in many corporations dominated by non-Jews. Because of this exclusion, Jews have not always developed a true sense of solidarity with the American economic elite and have reacted against the political values of the dominant group.

Jews may throw themselves into the struggle for equality with tremendous vigor, since for every injustice corrected, they experience deeply the satisfaction of a personal wrong redressed. They have stiven to handle their own suffering without inflicting suffering in return, and have been instrumental in helping others less fortunate. They have sought to overcome their separateness and leave the prison of their aloneness.

6. Positive Approach to Medicine. Judaism derives its optimistic view not from shutting its eyes to evil in all its forms but rather from the conviction that it can be overcome. As a co-laborer with God in the creative task of bringing order out of chaos and of endowing existence with meaning and with value, it is humankind's objective to harness their intelligence, skill, and adventuresome spirit to remove the obstacles that block the road to their physical and mental health and to their full self-realization as moral and spiritual beings.

Judaism is not a system of medicine but a *torat haadam*—a law for the whole person. While the religion has certain therapeutic value for the sick and suffering, it is not confined to healing. The concern is with the enrichment and sanctification of life and with the establishment of society upon the foundations of righteousness. Judaism is not an art of healing but an art of living for the sound and healthy as well as for the ailing. Judaism is the agency of personal and social morality, of care and counseling.

Some have attributed the Jew's relative acceptance of psychology to the fact that theology and doctrines play a lesser role in Judaism than in Christianity. Emphasis in Judaism is not placed upon creed but deed: reason is of primacy. Medieval Jewish philosophers stressed the idea that all knowledge is vital; it is the pillar of our very being. Faith without reason is mute. Thus a balance is sought and wrought in striving for a synthesis of faith and health, of religion and psychiatry.

7. The Present. Roles within the Jewish family are dramatically shifting within the Orthodox, Conservative, and Reform communities. For Jews—as indeed for all Americans—there is the slow but perceptible change to the nonnuclear family. One out of two Jews who married in the 1980s divorced by 1990. One out of every three children born to a Jewish mother or Jewish father will have a non-Jewish parent. One out of every two Jewish college students who married in the 1980s married out of the Jewish faith. Increasing divorce and general dislocation are the emerging facts of Jewish life.

In the past, rabbis were reluctant to enter the area of pastoral counseling. Indeed, in the major Jewish seminaries, the emphasis upon understanding the psychological needs of the congregation was minimal at best.

The needs of the changing Jewish family are no longer being neglected. Efforts are made to sensitize and educate congregational leadership, rabbis, and educators. Within the religious school curriculum, there are developing courses on marriage and the family, sexuality, divorce, and family dislocation. Discussions are held as to who chants the *Kiddish* on Sabbath eve (usually the father) when there is no daddy at home. At the Bar or Bat Mitzvah ceremony, questions are raised as to who brings the youth to the pulpit, who reads, and who blesses (and with the parents, even who pays). At the wedding, who walks down the aisle; who stands under the *chupah* (marital canopy); and who sits in the front row. Rabbis are now better prepared when to counsel, advise, and make a referral and how to reach out to the separated, divorced, and widowed families.

The question is how once again to create a *Mikdash Me'at* (miniature sanctuary) with a healthier attitude toward sex, a this-worldly faith, an establishment of a well-defined pattern for meeting life and death, an exalted position of learning, a higher concept of social justice, and a positive approach to medicine, as well as knowledge of how to regain the peculiar and special quality of Jewish family life. There is a reexamination of attitudes, traditions, rituals, and habits. Changing families require changing congregations.

Though many suggestions have been offered, there is one thread that unites all Jews. The agreement is that family life is the cornerstone of Judaism's survival kit. The thrust for Jewish continuity and affirmation still remains strong. Jews are challenged as never before to forge new combinations of community that continue to provide for the enlarged development of Jewish identity and care, for a *torat laadam*, a law for the whole person.

Bibliography. E. Fromm, *The Art of Loving* (1974). N. S. Goldman, "The Unconscious in Pastoral Psychology: A Rabbinic Perspective," *J. of Pastoral Psychology* 34 (1968): 193–203. R. L. Katz, *Pastoral Care and the Jewish Tradition* (1984). C. G. Montefiore and H. Loewe, eds., *A Rabbinic Anthology* (1939). H. Schmidt, *Judaism* 8 (1959), 240.

E. A. GROLLMAN

NATIVE AMERICAN TRADITIONAL RELIGION, PERSONAL CARE IN. Early Western observers reported that American Indians lived their lives within cultural contexts formed by sacred powers that transcended the human world. These powers appeared in their dreams and visions as luminous human, animal, or plant beings. Special relations with transcendent powers were established and maintained through the activities of persons who occupied specific social roles. Interpreters referred to such persons as shamans or medicine men or women. In this context a more general term will be applied: persons of medicine power. Furthermore, the term "medicine" should be understood in the general sense of *sacred*.

Persons of medicine power often served both as "doctors" and as "priests." An examination of their role shows how they performed some functions that may be compared with certain dimensions of practice within contemporary pastoral care.

1. Health and Healing. Aboriginal peoples on the North American continent were divided into hundreds of tribal groups exhibiting great linguistic and cultural diversity. For this reason it is difficult to generalize about their relations with transcendent powers. Perhaps the clearest case, however, appears in tribal views of health and healing. These views embody diagnoses of disease that required spiritual as well as physical therapy. Persons of medicine power functioned at both of these levels.

Some tribes believed disease arose as a consequence of sorcery or witchcraft. Others attributed disease to a lapse in behavior that offended transcendent powers. Still others believed disease arose because a foreign object or spirit intruded into a person's body. And some tribes understood disease to be caused by the theft of an individual's soul or personality by a malevolent spirit or power. Among other tribes, notably those of Iroquoian ancestry, unfulfilled dreams or desires were understood to cause physical or psychological disorders.

2. Ritual and Life Crises. Persons of medicine power engaged in symbolic action believed to be appropriate to crises in individual or tribal life. If the cause was sorcery, then a ritual of power might be directed against the offending being; if difficulties arose because taboos had been violated, then appropriate restitution was accompanied by special ritual processes; if an object or spirit had entered the person's body, then specific acts, such as sucking and other manipulations, along with appropriate rituals, were necessary. In other cases, such as on the Plains, the opening of a bundle, containing various sacred objects, might be at the center of the ritual process. Sometimes these techniques were combined with herbal remedies drawn from the stock of folk tradition.

Disorders of the personality, such as soul loss, were addressed by persons of medicine power in a variety of ways. Among the Eskimos, for example, the medicine person would enter the spirit world, there to seek for the lost soul, often doing combat with powers that held it in bondage. When the ailment was caused by unfulfilled dreams or desires, as in the Iroquoian case, then both the medicine person and the community may have been involved. In addition to rituals of healing led by the person of medicine power, the patient may have been treated to communal feasts, dances, and gifts.

3. Other Functions. Persons of medicine power related to tribal life in a more general manner as well. Such persons were repositories of ritual knowledge, keepers of sacred objects, and often occupied priestly roles in tribal societies. In such roles, these persons surrounded critical events, such as birth, death, marriage, and puberty, with important ritual processes. In addition, persons of medicine power had a central place in tribal rituals of social and world renewal.

In their more general role, medicine persons in Indian societies served broad therapeutic purposes within religious contexts. As compared with contemporary pastoral care, the role of medicine persons was certainly broader. But whether the issue was physical illness, delirium consequent upon soul loss, or important individual and tribal life crises, the role of the medicine person was central. It is also clear that success or failure was dependent not only upon appropriate rituals but also upon confidence in the medicine person and sharing his or her religious worldview. These features indicate some general kinship between modern pastoral care and the wisdom of aboriginal tribal peoples.

Bibliography. J. Brown, *The Sacred Pipe* (1953). M. Eliade, *Shamanism: Archaic Techniques of Ecstasy* (1964). J. H. Howard, *Oklahoma Seminoles: Medicines, Magic, and Religion* (1984). D. Sandner, *Navaho Symbols of Healing* (1979). J. Vogel, *American Indian Medicine* (1970).

H. L. HARROD

WEST INDIAN TRADITIONAL RELIGION, PASTORAL CARE IN. The West Indian soul personality is complex because it is drawn from many cultures and is still in the process of formation. The dilemma might best be illustrated by a simple grammatical question. Do we write the West Indies *is* or the West Indies *are?* It is this dilemma that creates a difficulty for pastoral care.

The diversity of cultures is basically drawn from the residual Amerindian bases, the overlay of Western Europeanism (Christianity) in its several forms (Spanish, French, English, Danish, and Dutch), later the overlay of African traditional religions, and in more recent times the newer Christian sects from the United States.

This religious potpourri also includes Hinduism and Islam in the larger English-speaking Caribbean area. At times of crisis there are many human and religio-cultural responses within the larger traditionally orthodox Christian environment.

Traditional (folk) religion is based upon West African sources. Voodoo (Haiti), Obeah (Jamaica), Shango (Trinidad), and Santeria (Cuba) each display the dual role of remedy for societal dysfunction as well as personal healing and comfort in times of distress. All derive their strength from a belief in a total unity of all things (not to be confused with pantheism) in which all the world is invested with a spiritual life force. This invisible power (life force) might be used for good or for evil since by its very nature it is neutral. This bifocal nature may be seen in the practice of Obeah and Myal in the Jamaican context, in which it might be interpreted in traditional Western European terminology as black and white magic. In fact, each is a tapping of the life force for specific purposes. So that Obeah is used in healing, to seek certain benefits, and also to produce death, while Myal tends wholly toward healing and counteracts the nonbeneficial elements in Obeah. The rituals resemble each other so that it is only the trained eye that can discern the differences (Morrish, 1982).

It has recently been suggested that Myalism formed an alliance with orthodox Christianity, particularly the Baptists, during the 1840s, and elements of African traditional religion are very much a part of pastoral care even within the mass-orientated Caribbean church membership (Schuler, 1980). Examples of this might be seen in the development of revivalism, Pocomania, and even Rastafarianism at the extreme end of the spectrum (Barrett, 1976). Revivalism (Zion Revival, 1861) took its rise from the Moravian revival in 1860 and has a distinct Christian orientation, while Pocomania (whose origins are more deeply Africa-rooted) uses Christian rituals such as hymns and certain prayers. Obeah and Myal rely upon an expert knowledge of the use of herbal medicine and are not so deeply rooted in Christian faith.

Shango (Trinidad) has definite affinities with Yoruba religious practices. In *Religious Cults in the Caribbean*, G. E. Simpson has documented and commented on its belief system and its influence. For the devotees it serves the same need as Xango (Brazil) in its syncretistic tendencies, blending elements of Yoruba traditional religion with Roman Catholicism and the Baptist faith, as it was derived from the Great

Awakening in the United States and brought to Trinidad by the freed slaves. Like Obeah and Myal it serves both a psychological and a social function but is more elaborate in its organization. Its emphasis upon spirit possession and healing resembles the characteristics of revivalism.

The *Spiritual Baptists* are perhaps closest to other Afro-Christian groups. They bear similarities to the black churches of the United States. They maintain (1) the inerrancy of the Bible, (2) the Virgin Birth, (3) the supernatural atonement, (4) the physical resurrection, and (5) the reality of the miracles of Jesus. At the same time, symbolic writing, as may be seen in voodoo, is present. The baptismal ceremony is a departure from the power of Satan and the defeat of the powers of evil through dance and other baptismal preparations.

West Indian traditional religion deals with the elemental events of life, the rites of passage. Birth is celebrated by blessings, baptisms, namings, and horoscopes, depending on the island culture. Marriage, puberty, and menopause each finds its place in religious celebration. Sometimes the influences are those of Western Christianity in its several forms. At other times influences are African or Indian oriented and in some instances bear an Islamic stamp as, for example, the Jordanites of Guyana. Death is celebrated also in all these forms, as the markings on the shrines or tombs of the departed in each territory illustrate. The ceremonies surrounding death, the mourning, the anointing, the wake, the "nine night," the forty-day, the memorial service, the direction of the funeral procession, and the libations each have a part to play.

Soul care, then, is not an individualistic exercise in the first place but the healing, reorganization, and arranging of a new society. It is holistic in its approach and method. At the same time, chosen individuals play important roles, and in them both the corporate and individual are integrated. Thus the priest, the politician (recently), and the doctor complement one another in the healing of the society. And in this regard the sex, social status, and background of the individual are not of greatest significance. Rather it is whether they can tap the life force, the energy that controls life and death. And this is true both for West Indian (folk) traditional religion and for the more orthodox Christian churches.

Bibliography. L. E. Barrett, *The Sun and Drum: African Roots in Jamaican Folk Tradition* (1976). I. Morrish, *Obeah, Christ, and Rastaman: Jamaica and Its Religion* (1982). M. Schuler, *Alas, Alas, Kongo* (1980); "Religion and Spiritism," *Caribbean Quarterly* 24 (1978), 3–4. G. E. Simpson, *Religious Cults in the Caribbean* (1970).

H. O. RUSSELL

5

CLINICAL METHOD

In the limits of this volume, it is impossible to completely "cover the waterfront" of the clinical issues that pastors and pastoral counselors will face in their ministry. Missing from the following collection, for example, are discussions of general care of the sick and developmental theory. However, it is guaranteed that almost anyone involved in the ministry of pastoral care and counseling will encounter persons with HIV or AIDS; engage in marital, family, and premarital counseling; do crisis and suicide intervention; deal with the individual and systemic issues of alcohol and drug addiction; and find grief as an underlying dynamic in a majority of pastoral issues. In addition, Pamela Cooper-White's contemporary analysis of the use of the self in all of this work is a primary commentary for clinical method.

AIDS (Pastoral Issues). Acquired Immune Deficiency Syndrome (AIDS) is a disease that cripples the body's defenses against infection. The Human Immunodeficiency Virus (HIV) immobilizes the key blood cells that in healthy people activate the immune system, leaving the body defenseless against certain cancers and opportunistic infections. HIV may also enter the central nervous system, leading to dementia and paralysis. Many individuals live for years without symptoms of HIV infection. However, by the mid-1980s the mortality rate for persons experiencing full manifestation of AIDS was 80 percent at twenty-four months and approaching 100 percent at four years. More recent advances in medical treatment and the development of new drugs have increased the life expectancy of persons with AIDS (PWAs), particularly when treatment is begun before the onset of symptoms.

When people become seriously sick or disabled, they experience social isolation and a number of deep-seated fears: fear of infection and impairment, of uncertainty, of stigmatism and ostracism, and of death. Regardless of its nature, a serious health crisis results in emotional stress associated with significant changes in outlook over a short period. In turn, this may involve adaptive changes in personality of a brief or long-term nature.

These factors are all present in the lives of PWAs. However, these features are exacerbated by deeper fears related to stigmatization and ostracism arising from the disease's association with its two main patient populations, homosexual males and intravenous drug users. Because AIDS is primarily a sexually transmitted disease, and because of societal attitudes related to homosexuality, prostitution, and drug abuse, patients in these population groups must confront such issues at a time when the diagnosis thrusts each into a confrontation with death. Those who have contracted the disease in other ways, for example, through heterosexual contact, blood transfusions (primarily until 1985, when blood began to be stringently screened), or as an unborn child in the infected mother's womb, suffer similar stigmatization and ostracism. In any event, PWAs have "fallen into death's realm of power." Just at the point when they are most in need of support and compassion, they are most vulnerable to the deepest pain and threat.

It is important for pastors and counselors to remember that the threats faced by PWAs are also confronted by parents and other family members, lovers, and friends. Like the patient, the family and friends struggle to come to terms with the disease and its often inevitable end in the context of societal attitudes toward AIDS and PWAs. This anguish is deepened for parents who learn that their son is gay at the same time they learn he has AIDS. Parents may learn that their son-in-law is bisexual or has been infected by a prostitute when they learn their daughter has AIDS. In many cases, denial and bewilderment will often be replaced by a sense of helpless rage.

Pastoral care of PWAs is a response to grief. Experience suggests that the most basic need is a climate in which grieving people may tell their stories of loss or threatened loss. This in turn must be shaped by an openness to the specific needs of the patient or family members. To the extent that PWAs have usually experienced rejection and derogation, they are searching for acceptance and affirmation. In particular, gay men seek understanding and acceptance of their being and lifestyle. The degree of hostility to both gay men and drug users indicates a need for advocacy of both their personal needs and their patient rights. In end-stage disease, advocacy may include representing the patient's wish to discontinue invasive therapies and to maintain comfort without life-prolonging intervention. Since many patients with AIDS face loss of mental faculties, the caring person may raise with the patient the matter of arranging power of attorney, should mental deterioration make it impossible for the patient to act on his or her own behalf.

People facing threat of imminent death look for some way to find meaning, both in their lives and in their deaths. It is inappropriate to "preach at" the patient or family members in such a setting. It goes without saying that this ministry is one that excludes the kind of empty moralizing that treats the other as an "it." One of the most creative attempts to analyze the caring role of the helping person is suggested by Alan Keith-Lucas (1972). He contends that effective help and support are offered only when composed of three elements: reality, empathy, and support. This concept is presented in summary form via three caring responses: Reality—"This is it"; Empathy—"I know it must hurt"; and Support—"I am here to help you if you want me and can use me," or, more succinctly, "You don't have to face this alone." Reality by itself is harsh and can be destructive. It is only reality by approaching with empathy and support that a ministry can truly be caring.

In addition to compassionate pastoral ministry to PWAs and to the circle of people immediately affected, it must also be remembered that neither the carer nor the patient and family functions in a vacuum; each is a member of a wider community. The pastor bears a unique opportunity and responsibility to minister not only to the people immediately affected but to the "worried well" in the wider societal groupings of which they are members. This may mean interceding at the patient's request with an employer, or assisting the patient to obtain legal assistance and other benefits. This issue raises a further matter, namely, the prophetic aspect of pastoral care, or the pastoral care of the "system" (Shelp and Sunderland, 1985). The pastoral function relates to the church's role as a mediating and reconciling agency in the community. This function is furthered by the provision of appropriate educational opportunities for the general public—a task for which the local congregation is well suited. The exploding effects of AIDS and the emotions of hurt and bewilderment it has stirred will only be alleviated through the efforts of people who meet the challenge with compassion, and, to the extent it is possible, that proper level of dispassionate response that encourages people to work and talk with one another to heal the wounds created by fear and grief.

Bibliography. J. Ablon, "Stigmatized Health Conditions," *J. of Social Science and Medicine*, 15B (1981), 31. A. Keith-Lucas, *Giving and Taking Help* (1972). R. J. Perelli, *Ministry to Persons with AIDS: A Family Systems Approach* (1991). K. Seybold and U. B. Mueller, *Sickness and Healing* (1981). E. E. Shelp and R. H. Sunderland, *AIDS and the Church* (1987, rev. and enlg., 1992); *The Pastor as Prophet* (1985). E. E. Shelp, R. H. Sunderland, and P. W. A. Mansell, eds., *AIDS: Personal Stories in Pastoral Perspective* (1986). R. H. Sunderland and E. E. Shelp, *AIDS: A Manual for Pastoral Care* (1987).

R. H. SUNDERLAND

ALCOHOL ABUSE, ADDICTION, AND THERAPY. A progressive compulsive-addictive illness, the primary characteristic of which is the continuing excessive use of alcoholic beverages in ways that damage one or more areas of a person's life—mental or physical health, family life and social relationships, job and economic viability, creativity, and spiritual wholeness. To say that an alcoholic's drinking is "compulsive" means that psychologically the desire is driven to some degree from an unconscious level and to that degree is beyond volitional control. "Addictive" refers to a physiological adaptation of the organism to the presence of alcohol so that acute distress (withdrawal symptoms) and craving are experienced when the person stops drinking. The term "progressive" refers to the fact that the illness usually develops through predictable stages and if not treated will eventually result in irreversible dysfunction and death. The illness conception of alcoholism, recognized today by the American Medical Association and the World Health Organization, does not eliminate the ethical aspects of the problem. It simply shifts the focus from holding alcoholics responsible (and blaming them) for their compulsive drinking (over which they have relatively little control), to emphasizing their responsibility to get help and learn how to live without alcohol.

Terms in this field often are used with varying meanings. "Problem drinking," "compulsive drinking," and "chemical dependency on alcohol" are approximate symptoms of alcoholism. However, "problem drinking" sometimes is used more broadly to include nonaddictive alcohol abuse such as driving an automobile after drinking. The term "chronic alcoholism" refers to the advanced stages of the illness during which severe medical and sometimes psychiatric complications occur.

Alcoholism is America's third-largest health problem (following heart disease and cancer). More people are addicted to alcohol than to all other chemicals combined (with the exception of nicotine and caffeine). It is estimated that nearly ten million persons are at some stage of this illness, and each person with alcoholism is surrounded by a circle of pain in the lives of others, resulting from the alcoholic's excessive drinking. In our society, many people develop multiple addictions—to alcohol plus a variety of prescribed or street drugs.

1. General Features of Alcoholism. Understanding the nature of the problem is essential preparation for counseling alcoholics effectively. Alcoholism is an incurable, potentially fatal, but highly treatable disease. For reasons not fully understood, a certain percentage of those who use alcohol develop the illness (approximately 7 percent in America). The essence of the problem is increasing dependence on alcohol and loss of control of the amount or the occasion of one's drinking. Increased dependence and loss of control usually occur gradually (often over the course of five to fifteen years). In a small minority of alcoholics, the addictive process occurs much more rapidly, often after a traumatic crisis or loss.

There are at least three major types of alcoholism. The most common type in America is the *steady-drinker-with-binges*, whose heavy daily drinking is punctuated by occasional binges of several days or longer. The second type is the *periodic alcoholic*, who usually is abstinent between binges. This type may suffer from pronounced manic-depressive mood swings. Third and most difficult to identify is the *plateau alcoholic*, who drinks more or less continually but seldom seeks maximum intoxication or goes on binges. Instead, such persons keep their blood-alcohol level at a fairly constant level much of the time, a level that permits them to continue functioning but in seriously impaired ways.

Most alcoholism (other than the plateau type) involves frequent drunkenness, but not all drunkenness is symptomatic of alcoholism. *Recreational drunkenness* is a common form of behavior in which groups of people use alcohol to release their "child" sides to play. *Social desperation drunkenness* refers to intoxication to anesthetize suffering from social discrimination and injustice (e.g., among Native Americans). Frequent intoxication, whatever its motivation, tends to produce increased addictive drinking on the part of some.

The terms "high bottom" and "low bottom" alcoholics refer to the degree of personal and social disintegration alcoholics must experience before they become open to outside help. "Low bottom" or skid row alcoholics are what most people picture when they hear *alcoholic*. Actually, such alcoholics probably constitute 5 percent or less of all alcoholics in America.

2. Causes and Predisposing Factors. *a. Physiological and psychological factors.* Alcoholism is a complex illness of the whole person. Extensive research over four decades has failed to discover a simple or single cause to explain why some "social drinkers" become addicted and others with similar drinking patterns over many years do not. Psychological, socio-cultural, physiological, pharmacological, and spiritual causative factors are involved in producing alcoholism in varying degrees from one person to another. The cliché "Alcoholism comes in people not in bottles" is accurate in the sense that more than 90 percent of Americans who drink do not become addicted. But as a report by the World Health Organization's Committee on Drugs Liable to Produce Addiction shows, the pharmacological properties of alcohol do play an appreciable role in the etiology of alcoholism, though other factors also must be present. It would be accurate to say that alcohol lends itself to persons who tend to form compulsive-addictive behavior patterns relatively easily.

The "soil of addiction," which makes some people receptive to the seeds of addiction, usually includes psychological problems present before the person began drinking. Alcohol is widely used in most cultures because of its anesthetic or pain-diminishing effects. It is particularly attractive to pre-alcoholics because it can temporarily deaden awareness of painful anxiety, guilt, inner conflict, loneliness, and low self-esteem. Personality disturbance underlying the addictive process may be severe (psychoneuroses, psychoses, or character disorders) or relatively mild. Some severely disturbed persons do become addicted, but one does not have to be a psychological cripple to become an alcoholic, particularly if one is in a heavy-drinking culture or group.

Alcoholics drink so much because they hurt so much, but their excessive drinking increases the painful feelings that made alcohol so attractive in the first place. Thus a vicious, self-feeding cycle of increased drinking to overcome the painful effects of previous excessive drinking is established.

Why do only certain persons become alcoholics among all those who have elevated levels of inner pain? A few researchers hold to the hypothesis that there is a metabolic peculiarity that predisposes certain persons to this addiction. Atypical metabolic patterns have been identified in the advanced stages of some alcoholics. But whether these are predisposing causes or consequences of damage to the organism from prolonged excessive drinking is not yet known. Biochemical changes may be involved in the irreversibility of loss of control in most alcoholics—that is, the fact that once persons cross from controlled to uncontrolled drinking they ordinarily cannot recover the ability to drink in controlled fashion.

b. Sociocultural factors. Learned social and cultural factors probably are primary determinants of why only certain psychologically vulnerable people become addicted. These factors are reflected in the high rates of alcoholism in some cultures (e.g., Ireland and France) and among some heavy-drinking groups in America, and the contrasting low rates in other cultures (e.g., Italy) and groups (e.g., Orthodox Jews). A World Health Organization study comparing attitudes toward drinking and drunkenness and rates of addiction in some twenty-five cultures discovered this principle: the more easily accessible alcohol is, and the more heavy drinking is regarded as "normal" behavior in particular cultures or subcultures, the less psychological pain is required in individuals to produce alcoholics. In all cultures, social disapproval of drunkenness is much stronger for women than for men. This probably accounts for the considerably lower rates of addiction among women.

Thus, alcoholism can be prevented on two interrelated levels—by rearing psychologically healthy children (with less anxiety) and by fostering more constructive attitudes toward, and thereby stronger social controls on, drunkenness in a society. The gradual increase, since the founding of Alcoholics Anonymous (AA), of the percentage of Americans who regard alcoholism as a disease that can be treated (79 percent in 1982) means that social attitudes are making it easier to seek help.

c. Spiritual causes. An understanding of the spiritual causes of alcoholism illuminates the unique role of ministers. There is a dynamic relationship between alcohol and alcoholism, on the one hand, and religious strivings, fear of death, and meaninglessness, on the other. Bill W., the cofounder of AA, said on one occasion, "Before AA we were trying to find God in a bottle." William James suggested in his Gifford Lectures that the sway of alcohol is due to its power to stimulate the mystical faculties in human beings, and that drunken consciousness is one form of mystical consciousness. The widespread use of alcohol in religious rites related to the mysteries of human existence (e.g., birth, marriage, death) is based on its power to symbolize the transcendent and the ecstatic. Clinical evidence suggests that for many alcoholics, alcohol is not a *symbol* of the transcendent dimension of life; it *is* their transcendent dimension. The abortive attempt to satisfy spiritual needs by nonreligious, chemical means is probably a significant cause of many addictions, including alcoholism. Addiction can be understood as a form of idolatry—that is, making a false absolute out of a substance that is not ultimate. Persons attempting to satisfy spiritual needs by alcohol eventually discover that their god betrays them, turning out to be a demon, which makes their spiritual alienation, emptiness, and longing all the worse. Full recovery must include developing healthy ways to satisfy the universal spiritual needs for trust, values, meaning, experiences of transcendence, forgiveness, and development of one's higher self or soul (see May, 1988, 1991).

3. Treatment Goals and Resources. a. Goals. Therapy with alcoholics has four goals: (1) motivating them to accept their need for help; (2) obtaining detoxification and medical treatment for problems resulting from withdrawal (e.g., agonizing hangover or delirium tremens) and prolonged malnutrition from "drinking their meals" (e.g., cirrhosis of the liver); (3) enabling them to interrupt the addictive cycle by learning to avoid taking the first drink; and (4) helping them rebuild their lives and relationships without alcohol; learning to satisfy in interpersonal and spiritual ways the needs that they had attempted to satisfy by means of alcohol. The mainstream view of most alcoholism counselors and treatment approaches (including AA) is that permanent abstinence is the only realistic and viable objective for alcoholics. (This view has been challenged by a small minority of scientists and therapists in the field; cf. Pattison et al., 1977.) Counseling, psychotherapy, and marriage and family counseling frequently are helpful in achieving this goal. Full recovery—the achievement of stable sobriety (abstinence) within a constructive lifestyle—often takes several years, with temporary "slips" occurring, particularly during early stages of the process. Because alcoholism is an illness involving whole family systems, it is important to involve the family in treatment.

b. Resources. Most alcoholics resist facing their need for help long after the need is obvious to those around them. Openness to help comes when they "hit bottom" or "surrender." This occurs when the fear and grief of terminating drinking is outweighed for a time by the fear of the painful consequences of continuing to drink and by the faint hope of finding something better. Alcoholics ordinarily do not hit bottom as long as persons close to them (e.g., spouse, parent, employer) protect them from the painful consequences of their excessive drinking. Vernon Johnson (1980) developed the intervention, an innovative way of motivating alcoholics to accept help using a planned and unified confrontation by their family and other significant persons.

Getting alcoholics to a physician or to a detoxification center may increase the possibility of their achieving permanent sobriety. But if treatment stops with medical help, it seldom results in full recovery because the person has not learned how to avoid reactivating the compulsive-addictive cycle. Regular, ongoing participation in AA is the most widely available and effective means by which alcoholics can interrupt this cycle and achieve stable sobriety. In a deeply caring group of persons who are living proof that it *is* possible to recover, the newcomer acquires hope again and learns how to avoid taking that first drink that, for alcoholics, usually leads to intoxication.

Rebuilding one's whole life and lifestyle without alcohol is a demanding and essential part of recovery. The twelve-step program found in Alcoholics Anonymous is an invaluable resource in this process for many alcoholics. In fact, more alcoholics recover in AA than in all other treatment approaches combined. But residential treatment centers using medical help, group therapy, intensive education about the nature of alcoholism and recovery, individual counseling (often by recovered alcoholics trained in counseling), and frequent AA meetings often are effective with those for whom AA alone is not enough. Whatever the treatment, alcoholics must learn that their uncontrolled drinking is their first and most urgent problem and must be given top priority.

Antabuse (a drug that provides a period of enforced sobriety by its biochemical incompatibility with alcohol) is a therapeutic adjunct that is helpful for some people who cannot break the addictive cycle by AA methods alone. In some cases a dynamic religious experience may also break the drinking cycle, as illustrated by the recovery of Bill W. (AA's cofounder) and by the alcoholism programs of the Salvation Army and the rescue mission.

4. The Role of the Church. Ministers and their congregations can fulfill five valuable roles in the treatment and prevention of alcoholism.

a. Encouraging help seeking. The first step is to help bring hidden alcoholics and their families out of hiding and to accept help. In spite of the availability of treatment resources, the majority of alcoholics still die untreated because their problem is hidden or they deny their need for help. In sermons and other public statements clergy can communicate enlightened understanding of alcoholism and the hope for recovery. A congregation's alcohol education program should acquaint people with the warning signs of early-stage addiction (e.g., increased dependence, memory loss after drinking) and give them opportunity to hear AA and Al-Anon speakers tell their inspiring recovery stories. Thus hidden and resisting alcoholics and their families can be encouraged to seek help sooner. In pastoral care and counseling, ministers should be alert to the signs that may indicate drinking problems—for example, evidence of drinking excessively or at inappropriate times, escalating marital conflict, or emotional disturbance in children.

b. Pastoral counseling with alcoholics. The counseling of alcoholics involves using the basic principles of educative counseling, which integrates relevant information (about alcoholism, the recovery process, AA, and other treatment resources) with counseling aimed first at helping alcoholics accept AA or other treatment. If pastors are able to combine caring and confrontation with communicating information, they can help alcoholics and their families get to potentially life-saving help. Alcoholics Anonymous can provide crucial help that a non-AA pastor cannot, and vice versa; therefore, it is essential to encourage alcoholic counselees to attend AA meetings regularly while receiving counseling. By using counseling skills, ministers can help AA members who request this help deepen their moral inventory. As facilitators of spiritual healing and growth, clergy can be of unique help to alcoholics and their families in working through spiritual conflicts and enriching the essential spiritual dimension of their recovery.

c. Pastoral counseling with families of alcoholics. Counseling for spouses, children, and parents of alcoholics is a major opportunity for clergy, occurring more frequently than opportunities to help alcoholics directly. Alcoholism is a family illness both in the sense that interaction in the family system often helps perpetuate the drinking, and in the sense that most members of the family are themselves deeply disturbed by the alcoholic's drinking behavior.

The key to counseling with spouses and parents of alcoholics is the Al-Anon principle of "release." This means letting go of their inappropriate sense of responsibility for getting or keeping the alcoholic sober, and of their obsessive, counterproductive attempts to control the alcoholic's drinking by alternating overprotective and punishing behavior. Release by family members also involves severing the alcoholic's control over them by deciding to do all they can to have more constructive, fulfilled lives, regardless of what the alcoholic does or does not do about his or her drinking. To the degree that release is accomplished by a spouse, the neurotic marital interaction that keeps the alcoholic from hitting bottom will tend to be interrupted. Referral of adult family members to Al-Anon and adolescents to Alateen groups will give them massive emotional support from persons who understand from the inside the agony of living with an alcoholic. These two groups encourage participants to use the Twelve Steps to heal and renew their own lives. Ministers trained in marriage counseling can provide important additional help to couples in rebuilding their marital and sexual relationship as a part of recovery.

d. Church initiatives in the community. A valuable outreach dimension of the ministry of congregations and clergy is support of community alcoholism resources. This may involve inviting AA and Al-Anon groups to use church facilities, supporting the local National Council on Alcoholism group, helping establish outpatient or inpatient treatment facilities, writing state legislators to support enlightened alcoholism bills, encouraging general hospitals to establish alcoholism programs, helping set up an alcoholism program in one's business (many companies have these), or simply attending open meetings of AA and Al-Anon to get acquainted with members, learn from them, and express one's affirmation of their programs. This last form of outreach can help deepen a minister's emotional understanding of alcoholism and help build relationships with persons who can be significant assets in making referrals. A church's lay pastoral care teams should include stable AA and Al-Anon members of each sex.

e. Prevention. Programs aimed at prevention constitute a key contribution of clergy and congregation and should occur on three levels: First, parent education and mutual support can help the pastor and congregation nurture the self-esteem and responsibility of children and youth, which are the best defenses against the misuse of alcohol and other consciousness-altering drugs. Second, alcohol education and counseling can help develop constructive social attitudes and controls on drinking and drunkenness. Third, by helping alcoholic parents recover, the probabilities of future addiction and other personality problems among their children will be lessened. (The incidence of alcoholism among adult children of alcoholics is approximately five times that of the general population, probably not because the illness is hereditary, but because of the emotional trauma of living with an alcoholic parent.)

5. The Special Needs of Alcoholic Women, Youth, and the Aged. These special populations of alcoholics have recently begun to receive needed attention and should be of concern to churches and ministers. The gap between rates of male and female alcoholism is narrowing in America. Alcoholism among women, often hidden and of the plateau type, is tremendously complicated by the institutional sexism that damages women's self-esteem in our society. Problems around sex role identity, marriage, children, and sexual adjustment seem to be more prominent causative factors in female than in male alcoholics. Fortunately, treatment programs designed to meet the special needs of alcoholic women, using women as counselors, are becoming available.

The major alcohol problem of adolescents is not addiction per se but drinking and driving. However, the excessive drinking that sets the stage for alcoholism (pre-alcoholism) is common among teenagers, and the number of youth and young adults in AA has increased dramatically in recent years. The identity-establishing task of youth often is complicated and delayed by using alcohol and drugs to cope rather than struggling to use and thereby develop personality potentialities. Clergy and laypersons who work with teens need to be knowledgeable regarding alcohol and alcoholism to help them make constructive decisions in this hazardous area of their lives.

There is a sizable and increasing alcohol and drug problem among the elderly. Some lifelong moderate drinkers become alcoholics after retirement. (Older people sometimes use alcohol and prescription drugs to self-medicate depression caused by forced retirement.) Long-time excessive drinkers often develop alcohol-related mental and physiological complications during their older years. Many elderly persons are members of congregations. Enabling them to develop satisfying lives and find mutual support can help them avoid the destructive misuse of alcohol and prescription drugs.

Bibliography. *Alcoholics Anonymous*, 3rd ed. (1976). Anonymous, *Living with an Alcoholic with the Help of Al-Anon*, rev. ed. (1980). H. Clinebell Jr., "Philosophical-Religious Factors in the Etiology and Treatment of Alcoholism," *Quarterly J. of Studies on Alcohol* 24 (September, 1968); *Understanding and Counseling the Alcoholic, through Religion and*

Psychology, rev. ed. (1968). V. E. Johnson, *I'll Quit Tomorrow*, rev. ed. (1980). G. G. May, *Addiction and Grace* (1988); *The Awakened Heart: Living beyond Addiction* (1991). E. M. Pattison et al., *Emerging Concepts of Alcohol Dependence* (1977). J. E. Royce, *Alcohol Problems and Alcoholism: A Comprehensive Survey* (1981). M. Sandmaier, *The Invisible Alcoholics: Women and Alcohol Abuse in America* (1980). G. E. Vaillant, *The Natural History of Alcoholism* (1983).

H. CLINEBELL

CRISIS INTERVENTION THEORY. A practical theory that can be implemented by sensitized laypersons or by professional clergy and mental health workers of any theoretical persuasion. Crisis intervention theory (CIT) involves five sequential steps.

1. Understanding Crisis as Homeostatic Upset. A crisis is an upset in homeostasis. Crisis intervention theory has as its basic proposition that each person develops a certain homeostasis in his or her life. This basic stance toward life may reflect a relatively high level of functioning or a low level of functioning. In CIT the level of functioning is less important than the homeostatic nature of the basic stance toward life. As long as the homeostasis is not disturbed, there will be no crisis (although there may be lifestyle dissatisfaction). Consequently, a person functioning at a high level of adaptive behaviors may have a crisis in his or her life; a person functioning at a low level of adaptive behaviors, for example, a chronic neurotic, may also have a crisis in his or her life.

2. Recognizing the Kind of Imbalance. In order to accomplish long-term stabilization it is necessary to identify both the kind of and the deeper source of the homeostatic imbalance. That there is a homeostatic imbalance will be evidenced by the onset or intensification of emotional distress (anxiety, depression, guilt, or anger) or disorientation. The crisis intervention counselor will find that the various kinds of emotional distress or disorientation have their source in one of four dimensions. (1) In the *intrapersonal* dimension the source is within the individual and arises from the individual's inability to cope with his or her own cognitive, emotional, or behavioral impulses. (2) In the *interpersonal* dimension the source is the individual's relationship(s) with others and arises from the individual's inability to enter into constructive problem solving with others or from communicative dysfunction within the relationship. (3) In the *physical* dimension the source is the individual's health and arises from the individual's inability to cope with life-threatening or chronic illness, or physical malfunction. (4) In the *spiritual* dimension the source is the individual's response to God or the religious community and arises from the individual's inability to respond to the redemptive message. It is important to note that while elements of all four dimensions generally are present, one dimension typically predominates, and that one would be identified as the principal source of the homeostatic imbalance and thus its basic kind or character.

3. Recognizing the Cause of the Crisis. In order to bring relief to the immediate crisis it is necessary to identify the immediate or precipitating cause of the homeostatic imbalance, which usually comes from one of three situations. (1) A *loss of support*, when the person experiences a real or imagined loss of someone or something with whom he or she has established very close emotional ties. While this would generally be a family member, it could be a pet or a national or religious leader. (2) A *loss of control*, when the person experiences a sense of helplessness and powerlessness in the face of what is perceived as an overwhelming threat or a set of impossible demands. (3) A *new or unique situation*, when the person is confronted with a situation that calls for adaptive behaviors that he or she has not yet had opportunity to develop. This category includes new situations, such as an occupational change, or previously experienced situations in a new environment, such as moving into a new home.

4. Achieving Short-Term Stabilization. According to CIT, by the time the crisis counselor has identified the kind and cause of the crisis, short-term stabilization has begun. This is accomplished through the development of a model to help the person understand the cause and cure of the current crisis. The model of understanding develops as the crisis counselor coaches or facilitates the person's understanding of his or her current situation and as, through understanding and support, the individual begins to develop a sense of regained control over his or her life. The model of understanding is then used as the beginning point to help the person generate a program for long-term stabilization that will seek to remedy the problems identified as the source and cause of the homeostatic imbalance.

5. Achieving Long-Term Stabilization. Long-term stabilization results as the crisis counselor supports the person through the program for long-term stabilization. This program may include legal, medical, psychological, or pastoral counseling and intervention.

Bibliography. R. Edwards, *The ABC Method of Crisis Intervention Counseling* (1973). A. Freedman, H. Kaplan, and B. Sadock,

Comprehensive Textbook of Psychiatry, 2nd ed. (1975). H. Parad, *Crisis Intervention: Selected Readings* (1965). R. Pavelsky, *Proposal for the Development of a Crisis Service at Circle City Hospital* (1979).

R. L. PAVELSKY

DRUG ABUSE, DEPENDENCE, AND TREATMENT. "Drug abuse" refers to the use of any chemical substance, licit or illicit, that endangers or harms the physical, mental, emotional, social, or spiritual health or well-being of the user or other people.

"Drug dependence" refers to the most serious form of drug abuse and is characterized by a compelling need or craving to use a drug, regardless of the consequences, due to (a) psychological dependence, where the drug's effects are considered essential for well-being; and/or (b) physical dependence, where the body has adjusted to and requires the presence of the drug in order to maintain homeostasis and to avoid withdrawal symptoms. However, because it is not always possible to make a clear distinction between the psychological and physiological aspects of dependence, drug dependence should be viewed as on a continuum ranging from mild to severe.

"Treatment" refers to the help given to drug-dependent persons, and others close to them, that interrupts the dependency process and initiates the process of recovery in which an individual learns constructive ways to live more fully without abusing drugs.

Throughout history, men and women have used and abused various drugs. In biblical times, alcohol and other drugs were used for health and ritual purposes, but the immoderate use of alcohol and the use of drugs in connection with sorcery and magic were clearly condemned (Barnette, 1971). Today the problems of drug abuse and dependence have become a global concern, reaching epidemic proportions in many countries. In the United States, drug abuse has spread throughout society and includes many kinds of mind- and mood-altering substances (Blum, 1984). Although alcohol is the most widely abused drug, Americans increasingly have become "polydrug" users who abuse and become dependent upon more than one drug.

Abuse of drugs may initially be a matter of choice, but for some people voluntary abuse can lead to dependence. The complex process by which a person progressively loses control over, and becomes compelled to continue, drug use despite adverse consequences is similar to the manner in which people become trapped in other compulsive, harmful patterns of behavior such as overeating, gambling, and sexual obsessions.

Without intervention, drug dependency is a progressive, destructive, and potentially fatal condition for which everyone in society pays a price. Fortunately, increasing numbers of people are overcoming the social stigma attached to drug problems and seeking help to break out of the trap of dependency. The pastor is likely to encounter many drug-dependent persons as well as family members in need of help and can play a unique and important role in their recovery and growth as whole persons and families.

1. Drug Dependence. *a. Causes and perpetuating influences.* Drug dependence is a complex problem that has no single or simple cause, but instead arises from and develops according to the interaction of many factors—pharmacological, biological, psychological, sociocultural, and spiritual. An understanding of these factors is important for those who wish to offer effective therapeutic or preventive help.

Regardless of their differences, all drugs of abuse have in common the ability to alter the user's physical, mental, or emotional state. The more immediate, potent, and desirable these changes, the greater their reinforcement value and the higher the probability of drug abuse and dependence. With many drugs the development of tolerance, where increasingly larger doses are needed to achieve the desired effect, and physical dependence also contribute to and perpetuate drug abuse and dependence. Drug abuse can be viewed as essentially a conditioned response resulting from continued drug use that has been reinforced by the pharmacological effects of the drug.

Pharmacological research and learning theories offer only a partial explanation for drug dependence; they do not explain initial drug use nor why some drug abusers, but not others, become dependent. Research points to the influence of social and cultural conditions, such as the widespread availability and acceptability of drugs, affluence, media exposure, peer group influence, and socioeconomic pressures that foster and perpetuate individual drug abuse and dependence.

Parental role models and family environment also exert a strong influence. Children whose parents abuse alcohol or other drugs are at high risk; "without intervention, forty to sixty percent of children of alcoholic parents become alcoholics themselves" (Ackerman, 1978). Many substance abusers come from backgrounds characterized by familial dysfunction such as broken homes, parental neglect or rejection, enmeshed relationships, and unresolved dependency/autonomy conflicts (Clinebell, 1968; Kaufman and Kaufmann, 1979; Platt and Labate, 1976).

Sociocultural factors do not account for individual differences within the same environment; not all persons from high-risk backgrounds become substance abusers nor do all substance abusers come from high-risk backgrounds. Biological and psychological factors may account for some of these differences. Scientists continue to search for a specific hereditary factor or preexisting biological condition that would account for vulnerability to drug dependency (Gottheil et al., 1983; Lettieri et al., 1980).

Personality traits have also been cited as predisposing factors. Although certain psychological characteristics (e.g., low frustration tolerance; impulsiveness; low self-esteem; ambivalence toward authority; heightened levels of stress, anxiety, guilt, and anger) frequently appear in substance abusers, there is no single "addictive personality type" that characterizes all substance abusers or predicts who will become one. In addition, some of these characteristics may actually be an effect, rather than a cause, of drug abuse and dependence.

Often overlooked in secular research, but of crucial significance, especially for the pastor, are the spiritual causes of drug dependency. In a world characterized by rapid social change and the erosion of traditional beliefs, practices, and institutions, drugs hold out the promise of instant pleasure or relief—at least temporarily—from feelings of emptiness, powerlessness, meaninglessness, and alienation from self, others, and God (see May, 1988, 1991).

Etiological theories raise significant pastoral issues and challenges. If drug abuse represents, at least to a large degree, a tragic response to the problems and unmet emotional and spiritual needs within individuals and society, the fact that so many people "turn to drugs and not the church for a sense of meaning, love, community, and transcendence is a clear, valid judgment on what the modern church has become" (Cassens, 1970). It is a judgment, certainly, but also a challenge for the church today to reach out in love. For pastors this often raises the ethical question of whether drug dependence is a sickness or a sin, the answer to which influences one's relationships and effectiveness with such individuals.

At one extreme, the "all-sin" view, which sees drug dependents as weak or immoral people who bear full responsibility for their problems, generally results in a moralistic, judgmental attitude that reinforces their feelings of inadequacy, rejection, and guilt and makes them less open to help. An "all-sickness" view, which sees dependents as helpless victims who bear little, if any, responsibility for their problems, often leads to a condescending or unconstructive approach, which does not help them honestly confront, admit, and take responsibility for changing their destructive patterns of behavior. A more constructive view would take into account both the many complex causal factors and the drug dependency process that limit a person's ability to be completely self-determining as well as the basic tendencies of human nature such as the abuse of personal freedom, egocentricity, and self-deification, which alienate us from God and keep us from a life of genuine fulfillment without drugs. Thus, a reinterpretation of this moral question from a combined understanding of the complex etiology of drug dependence and a Christian theology that accepts drug dependents as individuals who share humanity's basic problems, needs, and weaknesses is more likely to lead to a compassionate and constructive approach. Such a view is compatible with the position of the American Medical Association and many helping professionals: that alcoholics and other drug dependents suffer from a diagnosable, primary, progressive, chronic "disease" from which, with help and an acceptance of responsibility for change, they can and do successfully recover.

b. Development and consequences. Etiological theories suggest causative and perpetuating influences in dependence but do not predict who will become drug dependent. Stages of development and their consequences, however, are essentially predictable once the dependency process has been initiated. Regardless of the drug used, most drug-dependent individuals and others close to them go through a similar series of emotional and behavioral changes that make them increasingly dysfunctional (Johnson, 1980; Johnson Institute, 1979; McCabe, 1978; Wegscheider, 1981).

Briefly, the early stages of dependency are characterized by a growing preoccupation with and reliance upon the drug's effects, especially during times of stress. Usual activities and relationships are neglected as the person adapts his or her lifestyle to accommodate increasing drug use. As dependence increases, the individual develops ingenious ways to obtain, use, and conceal drugs.

Blackouts, or chemically induced periods of amnesia, may begin to occur. These are associated with increasing "loss of control," where the user progressively loses the ability to stop drug use once started or to predict how he or she will act. This leads to out-of-control behavior, growing problems in different areas of life, and increasing feelings of shame, guilt, anxiety, and self-hatred. A return to the chemical for relief only initiates a vicious cycle of compulsive use, uncontrollable behavior, and adverse consequences and negative feelings. Increasing blackouts and memory distortions as well as the development of psychological defenses such as denial, rationalization, projection, and repression may bring temporary relief but put the user further out of touch with reality, and unable to see drug use as a problem.

Whatever the original problems for which drug use may have been a symptom, drug use has now become the primary problem that requires direct treatment. Unfortunately, treatment is often delayed or prevented by family members and others who, in trying to adjust to the dependent, progress through similar stages in which they learn unhealthy, defensive roles and patterns of behavior that support or contribute to the dependency. The odds of relapse are high for dependents whose families do not receive treatment but retain their own dysfunctional behavior patterns.

In the advanced stages, chemical use is continual and leads to further deterioration in all areas of life. Abrupt reduction or cessation of drug use may result in unpleasant or life-threatening withdrawal symptoms, evidence that physical dependence is complete. Without intervention to arrest the process, the dependent loses everything—friends, family, job, health, even his or her defense system—and is left with nothing but chronic pain and despair. In the end, dependency can lead to premature death or, positively, to surrender and recovery.

The costs to society of drug abuse and dependence are high. Drug abuse plays a significant role in serious crime, family violence, traffic accidents and fatalities, lowered employee productivity, poor academic achievement, and delinquency, and places a great strain upon medical, educational, and other human services. Perhaps most tragic is the amount of human suffering and untold loss to society of human potential.

2. Treatment and Recovery. *a. Intervention.* It is no longer accepted as true that the dependent must "hit bottom" before he or she can be treated and recover. Several effective techniques have been developed to intervene to bring the dependent to treatment sooner (McCabe, 1978; Johnson, 1980; Keller, 1966).

Generally, the persons who first seek help are family members or "significant others" close to the dependent. Because of their own defenses and negative feelings, however, they may be unable to see or to admit that a drug problem exists and instead present the counselor with a variety of other difficulties such as marital conflicts, financial concerns, delinquency, or illness. The perceptive pastor recognizes the symptoms of drug dependency, provides information about the disease and its effects on the entire family, encourages family members to seek help for themselves, and offers additional supportive counseling as needed. As family members learn to change their own unhealthy behavior patterns and allow the dependent to experience the negative consequences of drug use, the dependent's recognition of a drug problem and the need for outside help may be hastened.

On occasions where the pastor has an opportunity to meet with the dependent, it is essential to try to establish a therapeutic relationship that can help motivate the dependent for treatment. Knowledge of and skill in applying general counseling principles and methods as well as specific techniques for working with drug dependents are important and include building trust and rapport, accepting and accurately reflecting feelings, exploring and dealing directly with the immediate problem of drug use and its consequences rather than underlying causes, sharing information about the progressive symptoms of dependency in such a way that the dependent begins to question his or her own pattern of drug use, avoiding overprotective or other "enabling" behaviors, and, when necessary, using constructive, nonjudgmental confrontation to help the dependent see the reality of his or her condition (Clinebell, 1968; Johnson, 1980; Keller, 1966).

b. Treatment alternatives. Since drug dependency is a complex, multidimensional problem that affects persons and whole families, effective treatment must also be holistic and multidisciplinary. The wise pastor will not try to assess or to treat drug dependency alone, but will develop firsthand knowledge of community resources specializing in drug problems, know his or her own skills as well as limitations and when indicated refer to appropriate additional resources, and be willing to share responsibility for providing help and support throughout the treatment and recovery process.

Most treatment efforts today fall into one of the following categories, plus variants or combinations: detoxification; residential, drug-free; outpatient, drug-free; or chemical approaches (Glasscote et al., 1972; Mothner and Weitz, 1984; Platt and Labate, 1976). Detoxification involves the gradual reduction of drug dosages, and sometimes the administration of other drugs, in order to minimize the discomfort, pain, or potential danger associated with termination of drug use. Withdrawal from drugs is necessary before meaningful treatment can begin but does not constitute rehabilitation.

Treatment can be residential or outpatient, long- or short-term, voluntary or compulsory, chemically assisted or drug-free. Some programs treat only the dependent, but an increasing number include concerned others as well. The goal of most treatment is to break the cycle of dependency and to initiate a process of individual and family recovery in which each person learns to live a more satisfying, productive life without drugs. This generally involves helping dependents and family members recognize and relinquish their denial and other delusional defenses, accept the illness and one's own part in it, recognize and share feelings, change unhealthy behaviors and rebuild the family system, and make a commitment to an ongoing recovery program (Wegscheider, 1981).

Many dependents and families will benefit from an intensive, concentrated period of residential treatment followed by treatment in an outpatient setting. Continued involvement in a Twelve Step recovery program such as Alcoholics Anonymous, Narcotics Anonymous, or an Al-Anon Family Group is also highly recommended. Specific treatment methods vary; however, many programs utilize self-help concepts developed by groups like Alcoholics Anonymous (AA) and residential therapeutic communities that emphasize individual motivation and participation, group therapy, peer support and confrontation, and the positive role of former abusers as counselors.

Two major chemical approaches that exist in the difficult treatment of heroin addiction are methadone maintenance, a narcotic substitution method, and narcotic antagonist therapy, which uses chemical compounds to block the euphoriant effects of opiates. Numerous concerns and problems are associated with these methods; however, they may be helpful to some heroin addicts, particularly when used with other supportive services (Platt and Labate, 1976).

Accurate evaluation and comparison of various treatment approaches and their effectiveness is complicated by numerous research and methodological problems. It is apparent, however, that no single approach provides all the solutions, and that the most effective treatment is one that utilizes a variety of methods according to individual and family needs.

c. *Recovery.* Treatment of the acute phase of drug dependency is only the beginning of a lifelong recovery and growth process. During the early stages of individual and family recovery and involvement in treatment or a program like AA's Twelve Steps, the pastor's role is primarily a supportive one. In later stages, skilled pastoral counseling can play a vital part in helping dependents and families reorganize their lives without drugs and develop their full potentials as human beings. This includes individual, marital, and family counseling to help dependents and families resolve personal and interpersonal difficulties; assistance to those who request it in working on the "moral inventory" steps of Twelve Step recovery programs; and guidance and support that foster spiritual awareness and growth. Pastors are cautioned to be sensitive and to take care not to offer religious solutions too quickly to dependents lest this lead to a superficial emotional response and avoidance of personal responsibility rather than a genuine acknowledgment of the need for and acceptance of God's grace and redemptive love.

The pastor, through example and teaching, can also prepare, challenge, and encourage the church to become a place where dependents and their families can experience the acceptance, fellowship, and support that will facilitate their recovery and restore them to full relationship with themselves, with others, and with God.

3. Conclusion. The question and the challenge facing the pastor and the church today are not whether but rather how it will confront the tragic problems of drug abuse and dependence. Effective treatment requires the cooperation and help of everyone, including the pastor and the church. If drug abuse and dependence represent an attempt to satisfy spiritual and other human needs, it would appear that within the corporate body and fellowship of the church lies our best hope for both its prevention and its treatment.

Bibliography. R. Ackerman, *Children of Alcoholics* (1978). H. Barnette, *The Drug Crisis and the Church* (1971). K. Blum, *Handbook of Abusable Drugs* (1984). J. Cassens, *Drugs and Drug Abuse* (1970). H. Clinebell Jr., *Understanding and Counseling the Alcoholic*, rev. ed. (1968). R. Glasscote et al., *The Treatment of Drug Abuse* (1972). E. Gottheil et al., eds., *Etiologic Aspects of Alcohol and Drug Abuse* (1983). V. Johnson, *I'll Quit Tomorrow*, rev. ed. (1980). Johnson Institute, *Chemical Dependency and Recovery Are a Family Affair* (1979). E. Kaufman and P. Kaufmann, eds., *Family Therapy of Drug and Alcohol Abuse* (1979). J. Keller, *Ministering to Alcoholics* (1966). D. Lettieri et al., eds., *Theories on Drug Abuse* (1980). G. G. May, *Addiction and Grace* (1988); *The Awakened Heart: Living beyond Addiction* (1991). T. McCabe, *Victims No More* (1978). I. Mothner and A. Weitz, *How to Get Off Drugs* (1984). J. Platt and C. Labate, *Heroin Addiction* (1976). S. Wegscheider, *Another Chance* (1981).

J. A. BABB

FAMILY THEORY AND THERAPY. Family theory is a way to conceptualize the life of the family unit. It involves understanding the individual within the context of a dynamic family system with its own unique developmental stages, history, and cultural relatedness. Family therapy is a way of joining and restructuring a dysfunctional family system.

1. Principles of Family Theory. *a. The individual in family context.* Family system theory is based on the concept that the context in which a person lives affects the inner processes of that person. Each individual lives within the context of a family. Family system theory hypothesizes that changes in the context will produce changes in the individual.

Studies in many fields (sociology, psychology, animal behavior, and medicine) help support the connection between context and individual. Within the field of family theory, W. Toman explores the effect of birth position (firstborn, youngest, etc.) on identity and personality characteristics. J. L. Framo's studies of married couples explore the connection between husband and wife roles and expectations in each spouse's family of origin. Parental and spousal behavior is often copied from the context in which the individual is reared. Medical studies supervised by S. Minuchin indicate the relatedness of such diseases as anorexia nervosa and brittle diabetes to an individual's position within the family as well as to the dysfunction of the family system.

b. A dynamic system. In family system theory, the family is seen as a dynamic, open system, affected by the greater sociocultural system in which it exists. The family has a structure, yet that structure is always in transformation, varying between the tension of change and the calm of stability. As time passes and members join and leave the family, the system restructures itself. The family system is seen as having to adapt to changing circumstances, yet having to maintain a sense of continuity to enhance the psychosocial growth of each of its members. Both flexibility and consistency are required attributes of a dynamic family system.

c. Developmental stages. During the normal restructuring of a family system over time, the family will pass through the following developmental stages:

i. Intimacy versus idealization and disillusionment. The work of this stage is to achieve intimacy as a couple with realistic perceptions of each partner as a whole person. Partners must assume responsibility for themselves and negotiate differences to achieve mutual support and nurture in an unidealized, realistic way.

ii. Replenishment versus turning inward. At this time children are born and parenting begins. A major problem of this stage is that some mothers and fathers forget that good parenting begins with and must be maintained by a good marriage relationship.

iii. Individualization versus pseudo-mutual organization. During this stage, elementary-aged children begin to differentiate and become increasingly self-sufficient. If the movement from family interests to individual interests is inhibited, a fusion of family members occurs, producing an enmeshed, pseudo-mutual organization.

iv. Companionship versus isolation. As teenage children move into their own social peer networks, parents must reevaluate their own roles as spouses. Adolescents need parents who are fulfilled in their own adult spousal relationships.

v. Regrouping versus binding or expulsion. The young adult child moves out of the family during this stage. If the family can regroup and restructure itself, this movement away can be accomplished. If not, the young adult either is bound to the family and cannot leave or is expelled from the family and cannot return.

vi. Rediscovery versus despair. In this postparental stage, the couple must rediscover themselves and their spousal commitment. All children have now grown and left home, and the preretirement parents must form new experiences and new community connectedness.

vii. Mutual aid versus uselessness. In this final stage of family development, the retired couple mutually aid and support each other. A new sense of connectedness must be established with the family's children and grandchildren.

d. Generational histories. As one family passes through its developmental stages, another family begins. Children grow and marry, transforming parents into grandparents and initiating new sequences of family development. Parenting styles, spousing styles, coping styles, personality characteristics, and relational styles are often rooted in a three-generational history of an individual's family system. It is often helpful, therefore, to explore with an individual the history of the preceding generations to get a more complete understanding of the total family context (Bowen, 1978).

e. Sociocultural interconnectedness. Not only is the family context influenced by the individuals forming its history, it is also affected by the greater context in which it exists. Family theory is beginning to look at this greater context, that is, cultural conditions, socioeconomic status, ethnic values, religious belief systems, and governmental structures to see its effects on the development of the family and its members.

2. Principles of Family Therapy. *a. Health and wholeness within the individual and the family.* Family therapy begins with a positive premise. Within each individual there resides an energy that moves that individual forward in progressive stages of growth. If this energy is not restricted, the individual will have the ability to perceive, comprehend, and choose actions to continue the life process toward wholeness and health. Families also will move forward in progressive stages if their members are free to interact with one another in ways that do not block the flow of creative energy. The family, therefore, is a living organism with a tendency toward both maintenance and evolution.

   b. Individual problems as the result of dysfunctional family transactional patterns. Family therapy looks at the individual as part of the family. Individual problems, therefore, are conceptualized as being a result of dysfunctional interactions within the family, which alter the context and thus the inner processes of the individual living within that context. If individual problems are seen as the result of maladaptive behavior within that social unit of the family, new ways of solving individual problems can be conceived.

   c. Altering dysfunctional family patterns by changing sequences and structures. The structural school of family therapy conceptualizes the family as an organism and sees the symptoms as a reaction of the organism under stress. The goal of this school is alteration of the structure of the organism to reduce the stress. This is done by challenging the structure, the symptom, and the family view of reality.

   The strategic school of family therapy conceptualizes the problem more in terms of specific repeated interactional sequences between members of the family. The symptom is seen as a protective, sacrificial act by one family member to preserve the family homeostasis. The goal of the strategic therapist is to identify the dysfunctional aspect of the interactional sequences and to alter the sequences surrounding the symptom, thus rearranging the organization and producing change.

   d. The role of the family therapist as enabler. The family therapist is the person called upon by the family to help alter its own internal structure and functioning. The therapist must join the family system as a new member and from within assist the family in its own restructuring. Thus, the family therapist is seen as an enabler, helping the family change itself.

3. Methods in Family Therapy. *a. Working with the whole family unit.* Since individual problems are conceptualized as a result of dysfunctions within the living human organism of the family, therapy must begin with the presence of the whole family unit, including residential grandparents or other extended-family members. In separated, divorced, or second-family systems, absent family members such as a former spouse can be represented by empty chairs.

Initial sessions are especially critical since family members will attempt to align with the therapist and convince him or her of their family worldview. If important family members are not present at the initial sessions, alliances could be made between members and therapist that could prove nontherapeutic when the absent family member is introduced into the therapy.

b. Seeing the identified patient as a family symptom-bearer. It is often an individual's behavior that prompts the movement toward therapy. The identified patient is seen by the family as the problem. The family therapist must see the patient not simply as the possessor of some form of individual pathology but as a family symptom-bearer. According to the structural school, the patient is reacting to the family organism stress in a way that makes it more contained and obvious. For example, a child's bed-wetting might be seen as a reaction to a more subtle, yet more powerful family stress arising from an unresolved intimacy problem between the parents. The strategic school would more readily interpret the child's behavior as a way of drawing the family's concern to him or herself rather than to the parental dyad, thus preserving the status quo between the parents.

c. Seeing the symptom as a family metaphor. The symptom itself can be conceptualized as a metaphor for other actions causing greater stress within the family. For example, a daughter's runaway behavior could be related to her father's withdrawal from his spousal relationship. A symptom may also be a dysfunctional expression of a healthy need. A boy's fear of animals may be a mechanism for creating contact with his father since the fear prevents his leaving the house without his father. The description of the behavior of the identified patient may also be a metaphor for the behavior of another family member. A mother who describes her son, the identified patient, as disrespectful, cold, and unloving may more accurately be describing her perception of her husband's behavior.

d. Joining the family system. Since a family system is a living organism, it will attempt to incorporate the therapist as a new member of the system in a way that will continue the family homeostasis. The therapist will need to join the family system in order to earn his or her right to lead and enable the family restructuring. The therapist must join, but he or she must not be dissolved by the ego mass of the family system.

Joining can be accomplished in a number of ways. (1) Structural theorists suggest that the therapist begin by maintaining the structure already present in the family system. In this way the therapist is accepted within the current expectations and behavioral rules of the family and, once accepted, can begin to alter the structure from a position within it. Maintenance is accomplished by upholding the structure and hierarchy of the family system. Deferring to the father as the head of the household, asking permission from a husband to speak to his wife or from a mother to speak to her child continues interactional patterns already established in the family. Once joining has reached an acceptable level, restructuring can begin. When restructuring raises stress and anxiety to nontherapeutic levels, the therapist can return to joining functions, thus reducing stress and gaining new acceptance.

(2) In addition to maintaining, the therapist can join the family system by tracking. Tracking is a method of adopting the content of the family communication and following it and then using it to produce the desired restructuring. By tracking the content of the communication presented by the family, by asking clarifying questions, and by exploring and expanding the meaning of the content, the therapist gains entry into the mind-set of the individual members of the family. Using the content symbolically, the therapist can make restructuring suggestions that will be accepted by the family without their feeling challenged or confronted. (3) Therapists can also join by twinning, in which the therapist couples with the family's style, affect, and behavior. The therapist can duplicate the family's style of communication, or by duplicating body posture and movements, can affiliate with a certain family member.

S. Minuchin has suggested that joining can be done from different positions of proximity. In the close position the therapist joins by specific affiliation with individual members of the family system. In the medium position, the therapist becomes the active neutral listener, gently following and tracking the content and exploring actions that can be taken to change the behavior talked about in the content. The third or disengaged position sounds like a contradiction, yet it allows the therapist to join the family from the distanced position of an expert who makes observations or gives assurance.

e. Restructuring the family system. Having successfully joined the family system, the therapist experiences and observes the dysfunctional aspects of the family and begins the process of restructuring. The aim of restructuring is to free the family symptom-bearer, to reduce conflict and stress in the family, and to help the family learn and experience new ways of coping. There are three major ways to accomplish restructuring:

i. Challenging the symptom. Since the symptom is a result of dysfunctional family patterns of interaction, one way to challenge the symptom is to challenge the interactions of the family. Rather than settling for verbal remembrances of actions and feelings, it is far better to have interactions happen within the therapy room so that the therapist can observe the patterns, see where the sequences of behavior break down, and suggest alternatives.

Another way of challenging the symptom is to help the family focus on some dysfunctional interactional pattern other than the presenting symptom. By shifting the focus, the symptom loses some of its intensity, and the family begins to think in terms larger than the presenting symptom.

ii. Challenging the family structure. The therapist can restructure a family system by observing current family boundaries and then altering them. By observing the way the family and its subsystems interact with one another—including where family members sit, who talks, who is silent—the therapist can challenge boundaries by having family members move or by asking quiet members to talk and more verbal members to listen and observe. Homework, tasks, and directives for action outside the therapy hour continue and strengthen the new boundaries.

Another way to challenge family structure is to change the hierarchical relationships already established within the family system and its subsystems. By joining with and supporting family members who do not currently enjoy much power, the therapist can unbalance the accepted hierarchy and create new stress within the family structure.

A third method is to emphasize the complementarity of all its members. The presenting problem of the identified patient can then be relabeled as a problem of the whole family.

iii. Challenging the family reality. In restructuring a family system the subtle, yet powerful family worldview will have to be challenged and altered. The therapist must understand this worldview and be able to see how and where it encourages and supports the dysfunctional behavior of the system. One way to challenge the worldview is by using universal symbols. This allows the therapist to call on a transcendent power and allows the family to accept alternative ways of seeing things that they are not directly confronting. Another way is to challenge family myths and perceptions of history where appropriate. A third way uses the power of the therapist as expert, allowing a different explanation of reality and experience to be entered into the family thinking.

4. Implications for Pastoral Care. *a. The family as the vehicle of faith.* The Judeo-Christian faith is a faith communicated through people and through families. The OT centers around the stories of families, beginning with Adam and Eve. The faith was developed and transmitted by and through patriarchal families. The NT continues to enhance the family as the vehicle of faith through the stories of Mary, Joseph, and Jesus. Faith is proclaimed by individuals rooted in their own family structures.

In our contemporary religious community the family is still a vital part of the telling and retelling of the story of faith. Of all current institutions, the church is one of the few that serves and gathers whole families into its life. The rites of church burials, baptisms, and marriages are family events. Ministry is accomplished within the framework of the family. It is, therefore, important that the deliverer of pastoral care sees beyond the individual and perceives the context and structure of the individual's family system.

b. The pastor as family consultant and educator. The pastor, because of love and concern for the persons and families touched by his or her ministry, has the opportunity and the challenge of becoming a family consultant and educator. The pastor can develop programs, sermons, and lessons to discuss family roles. Workshops can give expertise in handling family stress through negotiation and compromise. Experts in the field of family life can be invited to discuss family issues. Church policies can be altered to allow more family interaction in services and activities. Theology can be taught through family gatherings.

c. The pastor as family counselor. Persons who are hurting often go to a pastor first to discuss their problems. A well-trained pastor will know how to assess the presented problem and either take on the counseling or make an appropriate referral. A knowledge of family system theory allows the pastor to see the person in context and, therefore, to conceptualize the problem in a way that gives greater alternatives for support and help.

d. The congregation as a family. Knowledge of family system theory and family therapy can also encourage the pastor to see the congregation as a family and to interact with it accordingly. The pastor can be aware of the developmental life stages of the congregation related to such factors as the ages of its members. Congregational events and services can be seen as extensions of family life and can be designed to involve all levels of membership. A system of congregational pastoral care can be developed in which laity are organized to support one another during developmental and situational crises. Conflicts and stress within the congregation can be explored from a systems point of view so that negotiation and compromise can be achieved between congregational subsystems. The entire life of the congregation can be experienced through the theories of family systems and can be altered beneficially through the theories of family therapy.

Bibliography. H. Anderson, *The Family and Pastoral Care* (1984). M. Bowen, *Family Therapy in Clinical Practice* (1978). H. Fishman and S. Minuchin, *Family Therapy Techniques* (1981). J. L. Framo and I. Boszormenyi-Nagy, eds., *Intensive Family Therapy: Theoretical and Practical Aspects* (1965). E. H. Friedman, *Generation to Generation: Family Process in Church and Synagogue* (1985). A. S. Gurman and D. P. Kniskern, *Handbook of Family Therapy* (1981). J. Haley, *Problem-Solving Therapy* (1976). K. J. Kaplan, M. W. Schwartz, and M. Markus-Kaplan, "The Family: Biblical and Psychological Foundations," *J. of Psychology and Judaism* 8 (1984):77–196. S. Minuchin, *Families and Family Theory* (1974). S. Rhodes, "A Developmental Approach to the Life Cycle of the Family," *J. of Social Casework* 58 (1977): 301–11. C. Stewart, *The Minister as Family Counselor* (1979). W. Toman, *Family Constellation: Its Effects on Personality and Social Behavior*, 2nd ed. (1969).

B. J. HAGEDORN

FAMILY VIOLENCE. Behavior between family members that is, in fact, criminal assault: punching, choking, knifing, shooting, and sexual assault. This violence may take various forms, such as spouse beating, child abuse, and incest. Emotional abuse and child neglect are frequently involved as well. Abuse of parents, particularly the elderly, by their grown children is also reported increasingly to hotlines and other social agencies.

There are no types of families that are exempt from domestic violence. A survey of Methodist churchwomen in 1981 revealed that 68 percent had some personal experience with family violence (Fortune, 1982).

1. Causes. The causes of domestic violence are poorly understood. However, research identifies certain risk factors. While family violence is found in every socioeconomic and ethnic group, it is more frequent in young, poor, minority, and urban families, particularly where the husband is unemployed (Schulman, 1980; Straus et al., 1980). Physically handicapped persons and pregnant women are at greater risk of being abused by family members, perhaps because their special needs also place more stress on the family's resources (Straus et al., 1980).

Many studies indicate that family violence is a learned behavior; it is the way batterers have been taught to cope. A high percentage (50 percent or more) of abusive adults were abused as children themselves or witnessed violence between their parents (Rosenbaum and O'Leary, 1981; Straus et al., 1980; Sweeney and Key, 1982).

Violent behavior in the family is not only modeled, it is also reinforced. When violent acts occur, they are often followed by positive consequences. First, there is the immediate internal release of tension that accompanies any vigorous physical activity. Batterers feel better when they have "gotten things off their chests." For batterers violence may well be their only form of emotional release, the only way they know how to relieve tension. Second, violence often produces compliance by others. Third, the negative consequences that one might expect to follow violence often do not occur for a long time or are prevented by the "forgiving" family.

Violence is often associated with alcoholism or drug abuse. However, even after successful treatment of the alcohol or drug problems, domestic violence frequently persists.

Only a small percentage of batterers appear to be psychotic. The others are frequently described as dependent, possessive people with impulse control problems. They tend to deny and minimize their violence, and try to blame their problems on others, often their families. Male batterers often have a "macho" facade, but underneath they are frequently passive people with low self-esteem, who have difficulty asserting themselves without resorting to aggression (Sweeney and Key, 1982; Walker, 1979, 1981).

2. Victims' Persistence in Abusive Relationships. Abused children or frail elderly people who are battered frequently are completely dependent on their abusers, have no financial resources that enable them to leave, and no place to go. Battered women often have similar external or social reasons. First, the woman may receive intense pressure from family and church to stay in the relationship at all costs. Second, she may be economically dependent on her spouse. Even when a woman has a job, women typically earn significantly less than men. The woman may not have a place to go where she feels safe or feels that her children are safe. Although there are shelters for homeless males, there are far fewer for women and families. Finally, the woman may be ignorant of her legal rights and the availability of shelters or services in her area.

There may be psychological factors that make it difficult for battered women to leave abusive relationships. Many appear to stay because they are virtually paralyzed by fear. This syndrome, described as "learned helplessness" by Lenore Walker, is also seen in other victims of uncontrollable violence, such as prisoners of war, rape victims, and terrorist hostages. In order to survive, they become passive and numb and try to disturb their assailants as little as possible. They may view their assailants as omnipotent and may even try to defend them to others (Walker, 1979).

Another pattern has been called the "missionary syndrome." These women stay out of a desire to reform and help their mates. Warm, maternal, and frequently devout Christians, "missionaries" endure battering with martyr-like stoicism, hoping their patient forgiveness will lead the batterer to reform. Far from eliminating domestic violence, this strategy simply provides further reinforcement for it.

Attempts to find a distinctive profile of battered women has been fruitless. However, many describe battered women as commonly suffering from low self-esteem, tending to minimize the violence, and often being unaware of their own needs and physical reactions (Walker, 1979, 1981).

3. The Church's Response. *a. Serving the victim.* As part of its traditional ministry to people in crisis, the church can provide emergency help. It can provide information about existing services and help victims obtain the legal, medical, and other aid they need through persistent advocacy.

b. *Healing the family.* The church can also help victims and their families recover from the long-term effects of violence by offering counseling services and sponsoring support groups such as Parents Anonymous, although it is important for pastors or other counseling professionals to refer violent families to experienced therapists with special training in domestic violence. Further, churches can offer violent families a chance to build positive bridges to others and break out of their isolated way of life.

c. *Challenging society.* There is a critical need for the church to offer society a nonviolent image of family life. First, family-life education programs can provide instruction in nonabusive ways of parenting and resolving conflict. Pastoral, premarital, marital, and postmarital counseling can address issues of violence prevention. The church and its leaders can model nonviolent modes of treating their own families as well as the family of God. Second, the church can be a powerful force in reducing the social stresses that enhance the risk of domestic violence. Sexism, racism, and poverty are the soil in which family violence often grows. Finally, the church has a moral responsibility to speak out against domestic violence, labeling it clearly as evil.

Bibliography. S. Bentley, "The Pastoral Challenge of an Abusive Situation," *J. of Religion and Health* 3 (1984), 283–89. D. Capps, *The Child's Song: The Religious Abuse of Children* (1995). R. Clarke, *Pastoral Care of Battered Women* (1986). M. Fortune, "The Church and Domestic Violence," *Theology News and Notes* (June 1982), 17–21. L. Hedges-Goettl, *Sexual Abuse: Pastoral Responses* (2003). C. H. Kemp and R. E. Herlfer, *The Battered Child*, 3rd ed. (1980). J. E. Korbin, ed., *Child Abuse and Neglect: Cross-Cultural Perspectives* (1981). A. Miles, *Domestic Violence: What Every Pastor Needs to Know* (2000). J. N. Poling, *The Abuse of Power: A Theological Problem* (1991). A. Rosenbaum and K. D. O'Leary, "Marital Violence: Characteristics of Abusive Couples," *J. of Consulting and Clinical Psychology,* 49:1 (1981), 63-71. M. Roy, ed., *The Abusive Partner: An Analysis of Domestic Battering* (1982). M. A. Schulman, *A Survey of Spousal Abuse Against Women in Kentucky* (1980). M. A. Straus, R. J. Gelles, and S. K. Steinmetz, *Behind Closed Doors: Violence in the American Family* (1980). S. Sweeney and L. J. Key, "Psychological Issues in Counseling Batterers," *Theology News and Notes* (June 1982), 12–16. L. E. Walker, *The Battered Woman* (1979); "Battered Women: Sex Roles and Clinical Issues," *Professional Psychology* 12:1 (1981), 81–91.

C. DORAN

GRIEF AND LOSS. The complex interaction of affective, cognitive, physiological, and behavioral responses to the loss by any means of a person, place, thing, activity, status, bodily organ, and so on, with whom (or which) a person has identified, who (or which) has become a significant part of an individual's own self.

The power of grief to disrupt the total life of a person derives from the interaction between the physiological inheritance of an infant and growing child with the significant other people and events of her or his life. As a part of this process, attachments are formed and the individual self is developed from the perceived attitudes of significant others toward oneself. The breaking of these attachments in grief, the loss of the other, is experienced as one's own breaking, the death of significant aspects of one's own self.

Grief is a process with identifiable stages during which one gives up that which is lost, withdraws emotional investment in the physical reality of the other, effects gradual reinvestment of one's self in the images of the other that are a part of the self, and renews meaningful activities and relationships without the lost one. All of the stages must be gone through at the person's own pace in order for positive reorganization to take place.

Pathological grief refers to the blocking of the usual movement through the process, with the person fixating on one or a few feelings or behaviors of some stage prior to resolution. Intense ambivalent feelings toward the deceased have been repressed, and this repression stands in the way of the mourning that needs to take place.

Pastoral care of the bereaved attempts through frequent conversations to facilitate grieving: expressing feelings, remembering, accepting the reality of physical death, experiencing one's own value as an individual, and discovering meaning in one's life in the midst of the events. The funeral is also considered to be a part of the pastoral care of the bereaved.

1. The Dynamics of Grief. *a. Psychoanalytic theory.* Freud spoke of mourning as the process of withdrawing libido that had been directed toward the lost loved object and redirecting it toward another object. An internal reaction is triggered, since the lost object had in some sense become a part of the person's own ego. The process of freeing the libido and redirecting it takes place bit by bit over a period of time (Freud, 1914).

The pastoral psychologist Edgar Jackson (1957) built his approach on that of Freud, but made additional contributions in his discussion of the relationship between the child's early experiences of deprivation and the later loss of the person by death, of the death of an emotionally related person as a reminder of one's own finitude, and of the significant role in one's life of a system of values for providing meaning and coherence for all of life's experiences.

J. Spiro, a rabbi, also elaborates a psychoanalytic approach particularly relevant to the pastor. Spiro relates Jewish mourning customs to the social and the unconscious personal needs of the bereaved (Spiro, 1967). A more recent, detailed psychoanalytic exposition of the dynamics of grief that also pays attention to sociological factors, theological issues, and the minister's role, is that of Spiegel (1978).

b. Interpersonal theory. D. K. Switzer (1970) has made a synthesis of the ideas of several theorists with particular relevance to understanding grief. Switzer sees the development of the self as arising from the interactions of a particular human being with the particular physical and social environment. The learning of attitudes toward one's self and the external world, including other human beings, derives from the perceived behavior of the primary caregiving person(s) toward the infant and small child. Among the very important early behaviors of these caregiving people are the "going away" and "being absent" behaviors. From the very beginning of extrauterine life the infant learns that the absence of the caregivers inevitably produces physical discomfort and even pain, which quickly is learned as psychological discomfort, the threat to one's well-being when the caregivers leave or prepare to go. From this base Switzer develops a theory of grief as the reactivation of the early experiences of separation anxiety by a contemporary loss. Guilt as moral and existential anxiety, as fear for our own being rising out of our awareness of our finitude, our helplessness in certain situations, and our mortality, contributes to the overwhelming disruptive power of the experience, since the loss of the other is experienced as the loss of one's own self.

R. S. Sullender (1979) criticizes Switzer's failure to note unique differences between infantile mourning and adult grief. While Switzer's work does note some striking differences between them (the various aspects of existential anxiety, for example), other differences between infantile and adult separation experiences need to receive more attention. In addition, a predominant reaction in grief, the affect of sorrow, is not accounted for, and probably is not directly related to separation anxiety as such.

c. Biological-psychological conceptions. J. Bowlby and C. Parkes are major contributors to an understanding of grief based upon a combination of ethologists' studies of the behavior of animals, using these findings to make suggestions concerning the source and meaning of human experiences of attachment and separation, and upon some of the interpersonal and psychoanalytic approaches already mentioned. The bonding of infants to adults is a need passed on to human beings from higher primates by patterns of imprinting, and there is an inherent striving toward the accomplishment of this process (Bowlby, 1969). The breaking of attachments calls forth typical searching and mourning behaviors that have resulted from imprinting, and requires the processes of detachment and reattachment.

Parkes states that "the pining or yearning which constitutes separation anxiety is the characteristic feature of the pang of grief" (1972, 6).

d. Summary. Any comprehensive theory that assists in understanding the reaction of grief will need to take into account both the common and the unique physiological givens of the human being as a particular personality is developed in the interaction of that human being with the primary caregivers and with other persons and events. Psychoanalytic emphases on internal psychic processes must also be integrated into such a theory.

2. Grief as a Process: Stages and Behaviors. Parkes stated it most clearly: "Grief is a process and not a state. Grief is not a set of symptoms that start after a loss and then gradually fade away. It involves a succession of clinical pictures which blend into and replace one another" (1972, 6–7).

In the highly selective review that follows, it will be noted that there is no reference to the popular work by Elisabeth Kübler-Ross (1969). Some writers have referred to the stages of dying she describes as stages of grief. While there are some similarities in behaviors, there are some very significant differences as processes. To attempt to force her stages of dying on post-loss grieving is distorting and misleading.

a. Stages. As early as 1955, pastoral theologian Wayne Oates proposed a very helpful theory of grief outlining a progression of stages: (1) The shocking blow of the loss in itself; (2) the numbing effect of the shock; (3) the struggle between fantasy and reality; (4) the breakthrough of a flood of grief; (5) selected memory and stabbing pain; and (6) the acceptance of the loss and the affirmation of life itself (1955, 52–55).

A more thoroughly developed picture is provided by Y. Spiegel. (1) Spiegel notes *shock* as the first stage, including disbelief, emotional numbness, occasional outbreaks of pain and tears, a frequent lack of awareness of external events and conversations, and difficulty in thinking clearly. (2) The *control* stage follows, characterized by both the self-control of the grief-stricken and that which is demanded by other persons with whom one must deal. Spiegel describes the person as often passive, having difficulty in carrying out decisions, experiencing distance between one's self and the external world, a sense of the unreality of it all, a depersonalization, feeling empty or dead inside, and trying to act as if the loss had not occurred.

(3) The third stage he refers to as *regression*. The organization of the self that had been based upon interaction with the other can no longer

be sustained under the impact of the reality of the loss. Earlier forms of feeling and reacting begin to dominate and are often independent of the realities of the present environment. There are experiences of pain, uncertainty, fragmentation, heightened emotionality of all kinds, weeping, anger, complaining, becoming exhausted and withdrawing, seeming apathy, self-centeredness, preoccupation with and often idealization of the deceased, grasping at simple explanations including religious ones, a pervasive sense of helplessness, and a variety of control and defense mechanisms directed against the pain and the fear of loss of control.

(4) The final phase is *adaptation,* the step-by-step giving up of regressive behaviors. In their place more adaptive responses arise as the loss is recognized to its full and final extent. This makes necessary the very painful giving up of expectations of interaction with the deceased, accompanied by a restoration of the person within one's own individual personality. In so doing, recontact with the present external world takes place (Spiegel, 1978, 62–83).

Many of the behaviors mentioned by Spiegel and others are also described by Parkes, but Parkes's stages contribute additional understanding because they grow out of empirical research. His first stage is *numbness and denial,* although elements of denial operate in the other stages as well. Parkes's research indicates that the usual period of time for this stage is five to seven days.

The second stage is *yearning,* intense painful longing for the deceased, preoccupation with thoughts of that person, searching behavior, illusions of thinking that one has seen the person, dreams and fantasies, auditory and occasionally visual hallucinations, self-reproach, identification with behaviors, activities, or illness of the deceased (especially a terminal illness), and thoughts and feelings of suicide. This stage usually lasts for several weeks.

The third stage is *disorganization and despair,* beginning with some reduction of the intensity of yearning, the diminishing of the magnitude of the other emotional reactions. There are various degrees of apathy and aimlessness, and the inability to see a positive future. The majority of respondents in the research were still in this stage a year following the loss.

Finally, there is *reorganization.* The internal task of removing one's energy from the person who has died, while not necessarily finally accomplished, and perhaps never is, is substantially accomplished, and the bereaved person begins to see a hopeful future without the physical presence of the deceased and to experience the present as meaningful. Parkes's study of widows indicates that even after thirteen months the majority of his research subjects could not be said to have completed their grieving process.

b. Comments on process, stages, and behaviors. Since grief is a process with stages, it is essential for a person to go through each one of the stages completely in order to reach a positive resolution of the whole grief reaction. This reorganization is accomplished when the person is capable of living approximately as meaningfully, happily, and effectively as prior to the loss. To continue to repress and suppress the feelings involved in grief, to go about one's usual business as if there had been no loss, to attempt to skip stages or not do what needs to be done to work out the internal psychological tasks and the external social tasks is to thwart the process of resolution and reorganization.

Grief understood as a process also communicates to us that it is usually a transient, although not smoothly and rapidly moving, period of time. This means that the feelings and thoughts and most of the behaviors of grief as they appear *during the process* are normal. Many powerful ones may be experienced at the same time, some may be in conflict with one another, and together they may be absolutely overwhelming to the individual. These reactions are in themselves not to be feared; even reactions such as hallucinations, if they do not persist, do not seriously interfere with one's daily activities or the process of grief, and are not harmful as long as one does not base one's decisions and behavior upon them. While it is not uncommon for grieving persons to feel intense anger or to have thoughts of suicide, the actual behaviors of violence and suicide have to be resisted.

It is crucial that the minister be aware of these data in order to evaluate where a person is in the process, to facilitate the movement of the process without seeking to force it too rapidly, to be alert to a person's attempts to leap over a stage, not to be frightened in the presence of behaviors unfamiliar to the minister herself or himself, to be able to assure persons that they are not losing their minds, yet to be able to take with utmost seriousness their suicidal thoughts and feelings and potential violence toward others.

3. Pathological Grief. Pathological (morbid, atypical, unresolved) grief is that condition of the bereaved in which he or she does not reach the final stage of the process or is not continuing to make progress toward positive resolution within six to eight months after the loss. Given this approximate period of time, a fixation on a particular symptom or a particular segment of a specific stage of the normal grief process may be noted (usually either stage two or stage three of Parkes's scheme), with the adoption in a rigid and inflexible manner of one or a small select number of the mechanisms or behaviors of that stage. This fixation is in contrast with the usual grief process when there is the experimental testing of the various behaviors over a period of time, discarding those that are not functional in the maintenance and the restructuring of the self, and then going on to utilize in a constructive and adaptive way several of those that facilitate self-maintenance and growth.

Researchers have pointed out certain distinguishing dynamics of pathological grief. Parkes indicated that as a result of his comparison of the grief of psychiatric patients and that of widows from the general population, the only discernible differences were that the psychiatric patients had a greater intensity of guilt and that the behavior of self-reproach persisted for a longer period of time. There was also the tendency for the early grieving of this group to be delayed, that is, displaying a lapse of two weeks or more between the loss and the beginning of the pangs of grief (1972, 107–8).

V. Volkan (1970) specifies the universality of a love-hate ambivalence in the persons with pathological grief whom he has treated, though such ambivalence is involved at least to some degree in all grief. Obviously it is quite minimal in some; thus it is the presence of *intense, exaggerated,* or *repressed* ambivalence that seems to be involved in pathological grief.

This condition may look like any one of a number of disorders or forms of human unhappiness: depression, bitterness, anxiety attacks, general irritability, outbursts of anger, or even more severe symptoms of emotional disorder.

Ministers can play a very important role in identifying such persons and being effective pastors to them. Understanding the source of their unhappy and often difficult behavior can give a different perspective on the way in which they relate to others and therefore can lead to the pastor's establishing a more constructive relationship with them. More frequent visits and conversations with those persons may eventually begin to focus on the relationship of their present unsatisfactory lives to their incomplete grief. Even though there is a possibility that the person will resist the minister's efforts, the minister may discover that the person's intensity of dissatisfaction with her or his present life is sufficient to overcome the threat of feeling the pain and the person may be open to referral to the appropriate helping professional.

4. Needs of the Bereaved. Since many of the needs of the grief-stricken have been referred to in the foregoing discussion, it remains only to gather them together in summary form. The list is somewhat, but not precisely, chronological. The needs are: (1) to accept in one's own mind the reality and finality of the physical death; (2) to become aware of and express all of the feelings one has toward the deceased person, the loss of the person, and sometimes concerning the mode of death (lingering and painful illness, sudden accident that seems to be the clear fault of the deceased or some other person, suicide, etc.); (3) to break the emotional ties with the deceased in the sense of not attempting to invest emotionally in that person and behave toward the person as if he or she were still physically present; and by not seeking to get one's continuing needs met directly through that person; (4) to break habitual patterns of speech and other behaviors that assume the other's continued physical existence; (5) to affirm one's own self as worthwhile in and of one's self apart from interaction and connection with the deceased; (6) to reaffirm and therefore to allow to come back to life those characteristics and behaviors of the deceased with which the person had previously identified, and that can now be experienced as continuing to contribute to the ongoing and growing life of the grieving person; (7) to cultivate both old and new family relationships and friendships; and (8) to rediscover meaning in and for one's own life.

In meeting the first seven needs, the emotional and relational meaning foundation of the person's life is already being reestablished. In addition, the human being strives naturally and constantly toward ways of thinking about human experience that bring some sense of coherence, that help the person understand her or his own experience and lead to the effective sharing of that experience and that meaning with others, and that are also stimulating and reinforcing to the entire grieving process.

5. Pastoral Care of the Bereaved. Effective pastoral care for bereaved persons is based upon the capacity of the pastor to relate closely to persons undergoing intense emotion; a knowledge of the dynamics, stages, and behaviors of grief and the needs of the bereaved; and an awareness of findings like those of Parkes that make clear that early full grieving, allowing oneself to feel and to express those feelings both verbally and nonverbally, tends to lead to the most constructive resolution of the process, while the repression or suppression of the early reactions to the loss tend to lead to a greater severity of the grief symptoms later (Parkes, 1970, 450).

The process by which pastoral care is accomplished is by frequent visits with the grieving, assisting persons to express themselves by asking about what has taken place, and by responding with accurate empathy. The pre-funeral visit can be a time of assisting people to talk about the deceased so that their own memories are activated, the feelings and expression of emotions are facilitated, and in the process, the minister is gaining information about both the deceased and the bereaved that will lead to the development and execution of a more pastorally effective funeral.

The funeral should be viewed as a worship service of the community, yet also as a part of the pastoral care process. Its goals are to affirm the reality and finality of the physical death of the person, to encourage remembering and the sharing of memories, to facilitate the identification and expression of feeling, to bind persons to one another in community, to provide conditions and resources that may assist growth in faith and hope, and to celebrate the life of the deceased before God in context of appropriate religious meanings and ritual expressions.

In continued pastoral visits, it is helpful to ask the bereaved about what their feelings are right at the moment, review the death and the events surrounding the death, and discuss their most vivid memories of the person and the feelings connected with those memories.

One difficult task of many grieving persons, which is especially difficult in terms of pastoral guidance, is allowing sufficient time for mourning, not covering it up by premature decisions to move and to get rid of all reminders or working and filling time with a flurry of activities, yet at the same time beginning to return, as quickly as one is actually ready, to daily activities, responsibilities, and the reestablishing of old or developing new relationships.

In many situations an awareness of family systems dynamics is critical. Each individual family member must be ministered to, but the family as a whole needs also to be considered. Children of whatever age must not be overlooked by the pastor. Though their grief is not identical to that of adults, nor the way they express it, the impact of the loss upon them may be at least as great. Adults often need encouragement to give extra loving attention to children in the family at a time when the adults themselves feel as if they have less to give. Unfortunately, some families expect sameness in thinking and feeling among their members and become angry with or ostracize one another for differentness. The pastor may be able to help by pointing out differences in grief reactions of people of different ages and with different relationships to the deceased. The pastor can help family members understand and tolerate differences, and communicate more fully and clearly with one another.

Finally, families face difficulties in reassigning both instrumental and affectional roles. A perceptive pastor can call to their attention the need for whole-family negotiation and help family members resist the undiscussed assignment of particular new rules to various members who do not want them or who are not developmentally mature enough for them, or the undiscussed taking over of certain roles of the deceased by one family member (see Switzer, 1974, ch. 5).

Bibliography. J. Bowlby, *Attachment* (1969). S. Freud, "Mourning and Melancholia," *SE* 14 (1914), 125–53. E. Jackson, *Understanding Grief* (1957). E. Kübler-Ross, *On Death and Dying* (1969). K. Mitchell and H. Anderson, *All Our Losses, All Our Griefs* (1983). W. Oates, *Anxiety in Christian Experience* (1955). C. Parkes, *Bereavement* (1972); "The First Year of Bereavement," *Psychiatry* 33 (1970), 444–67; "'Seeking' and 'Finding' a Lost Object," *Social Science and Medicine* 4 (1970), 187–201. Y. Spiegel, *The Grief Process: Analysis and Counseling* (1978). J. Spiro, *A Time to Mourn* (1967). R. S. Sullender, "Three Theoretical Approaches to Grief," *J. of Pastoral Care* 33 (1979), 243–51. R. Sunderland, *Getting through Grief: Caregiving by Congregations* (1993). D. K. Switzer, "Awareness of Unresolved Grief: An Opportunity for Ministry," *The Christian Ministry* (July 1980), 19–23; *The Dynamics of Grief* (1970); *The Minister as Crisis Counselor* (1974), rev. and enlg. (1986). V. Volkan, "Typical Findings in Pathological Grief," *The Psychiatric Quarterly* 44 (1970): 1–20.

D. K. SWITZER

INTERSUBJECTIVITY, COUNTERTRANSFERENCE, AND USE OF THE SELF IN PASTORAL CARE AND COUNSELING. Based on the work of Sigmund Freud, *countertransference* is classically defined as the unconscious distortions in a therapist's or other caregiver's perceptions about the client or person being helped, due to unresolved internal issues usually rooted in the helper's early childhood. In this view, countertransference is a hindrance, because it removes the caregiver's objectivity, and therefore needs to be neutralized or eliminated. The concept originated as the counterpart to the *transference*, Freud's term for the patient's projecting (unconsciously transferring) early childhood experiences of parents and other authority figures from the past onto the person of the therapist (or caregiver, helping professional, or other authority figure). A caregiver working from this classical theoretical perspective would work to manage his or her countertransference so that it would do no harm. This work normally takes place initially in personal psychotherapy with a psychoanalytically trained therapist, in order to recognize and resolve neurotic tendencies and blind spots. A professional habit of self-examination then continues throughout the caregiver's professional life in the form of ongoing attentiveness to one's personal vulnerabilities and trigger points, supplemented by professional supervision or peer consultation as needed.

This focus on the importance of self-awareness and self-analysis has been a cornerstone of clinical pastoral training in the mainline Protestant denominations since the early twentieth century. To this day, pastoral caregivers and counselors from a variety of theological and ecclesial traditions, and theoretical orientations ranging from psychodynamic, Jungian, and family systems, to Rogerian, existential, and more eclectic approaches to care, hold self-knowledge to be one of the central foundations of effective and ethical care.

Recently, an expanded view of countertransference has begun to be appropriated into pastoral care and counseling. This view, sometimes termed "Totalist," incorporates this original classical understanding but also widens it beyond simply the negative or neurotic elements in the caregiver's personality. In this expanded definition, *countertransference* is the sum total of *all* the helper's thoughts, feelings, fantasies, impulses, and bodily sensations, conscious and unconscious, related to the client. It still includes preconditioned patterns of relating developed in the helping professional's own childhood but also recognizes that the caregiver's responses may also be strongly influenced or even evoked by the *transference* of the helpee. *Transference*, in this model, is similarly defined as the sum total of the *helpee's* thoughts, feelings, fantasies, impulses, and bodily sensations, conscious and unconscious, toward the helping professional, and may include, but again is not limited to, preconditioned patterns of relating developed in childhood.

This "new" understanding goes at least as far back as the 1950s, with psychoanalysts in the first and second generation after Freud (including Sandor Ferenczi, D. W. Winnicott, and especially Paula Heimann). It was little appreciated in the psychoanalytic world until the last two decades, with the advent of "intersubjectivity theory" within self psychology, and "relational psychoanalysis," which emerged from object relations and interpersonal psychoanalysis in the United States. With the diffusion of theoretical approaches and the waning of influence of psychoanalysis within pastoral care and counseling beginning in the 1960s and 1970s, these developments were generally unknown or disregarded until very recently. In the early twenty-first century, however, both in pastoral practice, and in psychotherapy more generally, there has been a reemergence of attention to countertransference, and the *use of the self* in care and counseling.

In this contemporary view, transference and countertransference operate together to form a complex interrelation between helper and helpee (and indeed, in all human relationships). This complex interrelation has come to be known by the term "intersubjectivity." The psychodynamic worldview underlying this understanding of mutual influence in relationships presupposes the presence of an unconscious as well as conscious relationship in all human interconnections. Intersubjectivity is not merely experienced at the conscious level of mutual observation, perception, and communication, but also unconsciously, through fantasies, dreams, symbolic communications, and nonverbal enactments. Conceptions of "self" and "other" are intertwined in a relational matrix. Aspects of both "self-ness" and "otherness" may be discovered in one's subjective experience of both oneself and the other; as well as in the "between" of the relationship itself—the interstices of the relationship as it is continually being *co-constructed*. This complex interrelation informs and generates patterns of both meaning-making and enactment, and also directly shapes the quality (positive or negative) of growth and healing that evolves in the helping relationship over time.

Countertransference in this construction is regarded not only as a hindrance but also as a valuable tool. Classical countertransference remains a central component within the Totalist definition, and remains as a safeguard for appropriate professional boundaries and ethical treatment of patients, clients, and parishioners. Self-examination is still centrally important for understanding one's own neurotic vulnerabilities and tendencies toward emotional and behavioral reactivity (from which no one is immune). At the same time, in contemporary practice theory, countertransference is understood as a valuable instrument for listening for the other through the unconscious relationship that grows between helper and helpee. The helper's own thoughts, feelings, and fantasies are understood to absorb the thought life of the other, through careful and care-full immersion in the intersubjective pool of unconscious communication and experience between helper and helpee. The caregiver or counselor thus uses himself or herself as an instrument, resonating with the other and absorbing the other's thought-world, feelings, and experiences. Shared wisdom is exchanged at both conscious and unconscious levels across the continuum of the helping relationship.

Attentiveness by the caregiver to his or her own shifting affect states thus can generate insights about the possible distortions and reactivity that can disrupt or even damage care, but also can attune the helper more empathically toward an understanding of the helpee's inner world. The use of the self in pastoral care and counseling therefore requires maintaining a balance between the classical and Totalist understandings of countertransference, and calls for alertness and sensitivity to signals, both conscious and unconscious, that may arise anywhere along the spectrum of self and other within the helping relationship.

A specifically *pastoral* intersubjective model, moreover, in order to be pastoral, must recognize theological reflection as a further tool for empathic understanding of both helper and helpee. A distinctively pastoral method of working intersubjectively would include: (1) *self-care*, including seeking out sources of relational support and consultation as needed, quiet time to reflect, and centering prayer; (2) examination of countertransference in the *classical* sense, to become aware of reactions in the helper's self that might distort or impede an empathic understanding of the other's reality; (3) preliminary *pastoral assessment* focusing on the other's actual needs; (4) examination of countertransference in the contemporary *Totalist* sense, recognizing that any of one's own subjective feelings and experiences of the other may be drawn from a shared pool of meaning and experience, conscious and unconscious, and may contain insights that can increase empathic understanding of the other; (5) *theological reflection* that uses a free associative process or reverie to discern how God/Christ/or Spirit might be perceived within the intersubjective movements of the relationship; and (6) integrating insights from all these sources to glimpse previously unconsidered dimensions of the pastoral relationship, and to imagine further possibilities for *pastoral praxis*. While these steps may work best in sequence, so that self-awareness is engaged early in the helping process as a guardian to its ethical integrity, experienced practitioners frequently engage all these levels more or less simultaneously and continually as the pastoral relationship continues to deepen and unfold.

Bibliography. L. Aron, *A Meeting of Minds: Mutuality in Psychoanalysis* (2001). L. Aron and S. A. Mitchell, *Relational Psychoanalysis: The Emergence of a Tradition* (2001). P. Cooper-White, *Many Voices: Pastoral Psychotherapy in Relational and Theological Perspective* (2007); *Shared Wisdom: Use of the Self in Pastoral Care and Counseling* (2004). L. Epstein and A. Feiner, *Countertransference: The Therapist's Contribution to the Therapeutic Situation* (1979). S. Ferenczi, "The Confusion of Tongues between Adults and the Child: The Language of Tenderness and Passion" (1933) in *Final Contributions to the Problems and Methods of Psycho-Analysis,* (1955); *Further Contributions to the Theory and Technique of Psycho-Analysis* (1926). S. Freud, "The Future Prospects of Psycho-Analytic Therapy," in J. Strachey, ed. and trans., *SE* 11 (1910), 141–51; "Observations of Transference-Love," *SE* 12 (1915), 157–71. P. Heimann, "Counter-transference," *British J. of Medical Psychology* 33 (1960), 9–15; "On Counter-transference," *International J. of Psycho-Analysis* 31 (1950), 81–84. O. Kernberg, "Notes on Countertransference," *J. of the American Psychoanalytic Association* 13 (1965), 38–56. K. Maroda, *The Power of Countertransference: Innovations in Analytic Technique,* 2nd ed. (2004). D. M. Orange, G. E. Atwood, and R. D. Stolorow, *Working Intersubjectively: Contextualism in Psychoanalytic Practice* (2001). R. D. Stolorow and G. E. Atwood, eds., *Faces in a Cloud: Intersubjectivity in Personality Theory,* rev. ed. (1994). R. D. Stolorow, G. E. Atwood, and B. Brandchaft, eds., *The Intersubjective Perspective* (1995). M. J. Tansey and Walter F. Burke, *Understanding Countertransference: From Projective Identification to Empathy* (1989); D. W. Winnicott, "Hate in the Countertransference," *International J. of Psycho-Analysis* 30 (1949), 69–75. B. Wolstein, ed., *Essential Papers on Countertransference* (1988).

P. COOPER-WHITE

PREMARITAL COUNSELING. Premarital counseling most often refers to the ministry offered by a pastor to a couple prior to officiating at their marriage. It is more often a type of pastoral care, guidance, and interpretation rather than counseling because the majority of couples who come to the pastor have no awareness of "having a problem"—the condition presupposed by the concept of "counseling." In fact, the time immediately prior to the marriage, when most couples receive premarital pastoral care is likely to be a time of denial of problems and the negative side of their ambivalence about the marriage.

1. Purpose. The primary value in premarital pastoral care is in assisting a couple to surface assumptions about themselves, their families of origin, and the religious community that—at least through the minister—they are asking to bless their marriage. Its secondary value is to provide the couple with an opportunity to develop a significant relationship to the minister and thence to the religious community. Premarital pastoral care may become counseling, and is most likely to, when one or both persons in the couple have been previously married; when the couple has had a long relationship, perhaps having been living together; when one or both are resistant to marriage; or when at least one person fears that a past individual experience may influence the relationship in a negative way. Under such circumstances premarital work is not focused upon preparing for a marriage for which a date already has been set but upon examining some of the areas of concern that the couple has acknowledged.

It can be argued that premarital pastoral care developed more out of the church's concern to preserve the institution of marriage than from a pastoral concern for individuals. Its identification of this ministry as "counseling"—in addition to the popularity that the word, *counseling*, developed in the 1950s—may be attributed to the church's preference to locate the problem of marriage in the couple rather than in its view of marriage or its effectiveness in blessing it.

2. Approaches. K. R. Mitchell and H. Anderson have argued that the most important task of premarital care is assisting the couple in appropriate disengagement from their family of origin. "You must leave," they say, "before you can cleave" (1981). Couples intent on being married may be reluctant to examine their own relationship. Discussing their families of origin is less likely to produce resistance and more likely to yield fruitful results for the couple; therefore, it is also an effective means of surfacing assumptions about what marriage is and what their particular marriage is likely to be. Adapting the work of family system theorists, such as M. Bowen (1978) and J. L. Framo (1982) to their purposes, Mitchell and Anderson describe their family system approach to premarital pastoral care and suggest a variety of methods for implementing it. Preparing and interpreting genograms, examining triangles within the families of origin, discussing family myths and traditions as well as the role of various family members and the explicit and implicit rules for family behavior are among the suggestions made for the structure of the interview.

Consistent with such an approach, a couple might be asked to write a story about the past, for example, the myth of their parents' marriage or some other significant marriage; or a story that characterizes their present relationship and a story about the future. In the telling and interpretation of these stories there is practice in the use of the imagination needed for creating a life together. Moreover, these efforts also help put this particular couple's story into the historical context of other stories—with those who have taken similar vows—and help suggest the common story of those who are seeking a Christian blessing for the journey they are undertaking.

3. Exploring Religious Tradition. Related to this is the discovery or rediscovery of the story of the religious tradition from which they come and of the one that they are asking to bless their marriage. As is often the case even with couples from the pastor's own parish, assumptions about their religious tradition are not what one might expect. In order to bring together couple and tradition in an honest and meaningful wedding service, religious assumptions and traditions need to be explored and interpreted. It is the minister's responsibility to interpret what the religious community has said and is saying about marriage in the wedding service. Most often there needs to be an interpretation of the history of the various elements, its meaning, and how it might be related to the couple to be married. Optimally, this interpretation may elicit dialogue about the couple's view of the elements in the marriage service, sometimes restating them so that they may be participated in with honesty and conviction.

The minister's responsibility in pre- or postmarital pastoral care might be described as providing a hermeneutical bridge between the couple's present life situation, their families of origin, and the way that the church has historically offered blessing to a marriage. That bridge or relationship, which can seldom be used for counseling prior to the marriage, may be an important basis for establishing a counseling relationship later on when the circumstances of life and marriage make the couple aware of their need for such a ministry.

Bibliography. M. Bowen, *Family Therapy in Clinical Practice* (1978). W. J. Everett, *Blessed Be the Bond* (1985). C. A. Gallagher, G. A. Maloney, M. F. Rousseau, and P. E. Wilczak, *Embodied in Love: Sacramental Spirituality and Sexual Intimacy* (1983). J. L. Framo, *Explorations in Marital and Family Therapy* (1982). R. Haughton, "Marriage: An Old, New Fairy Tale," in J. J. Burtchaell, ed., *Marriage among Christians* (1977). W. J.

Lederer and D. D. Jackson, *The Mirages of Marriage* (1968). D. R. Mace, *Getting Ready for Marriage* (1985). K. R. Mitchell and H. Anderson, "You Must Leave before You Can Cleave: A Family Systems Approach to Premarital Pastoral Work," *Pastoral Psychology* 30:2 (1981), 71–88. T. S. Nease, *Premarital Pastoral Counseling Literature in Protestantism, 1920–71*, PhD dissertation, Princeton Theological Seminary, University Microfilms (1973). T. K. Pitt, *Premarital Counseling Handbook for Ministers* (1985). D. J. Rolfe, "Developing Skills and Credibility in Marriage Preparation Ministry," *Pastoral Psychology* 33:3 (1985), 161–72. C. J. Sager, *Marriage Contracts and Couple Therapy* (1976).

T. S. NEASE
J. PATTON

SUICIDE (Pastoral Care). Suicide is the deliberate human act of self-inflicted, self-intentioned death. It is to be distinguished from the instinctive activity of some animals that leads to their death, and from the self-destructive activities of humans who are not consciously intending to die. Therefore, this discussion does not consider concepts of unconscious motivation, death instinct, self-destructive carelessness, and accident-proneness. The term refers only to a fully conscious human act carried out with the intention of terminating one's own life in the immediate future.

The question of why some people are suicidal is as complex as is the etiology of any human behavior, and any explanation depends on the viewpoint of the person offering the explanation. Suicide has been described as a weakness, a noble act, a sin, a crime, a disease, and a natural choice. It has been discussed by philosophers, theologians, anthropologists, sociologists, psychologists, novelists, and poets. The 25,000 annual suicides in the United States leave in their wake confusion, fascination, aggravated grief reactions, and often additional suicides. Usually an intensive, lonely activity, it is sometimes performed in consort with a beloved in a love pact, and sometimes in mass numbers. It is often the result of mental disease such as psychotic depression or schizophrenia.

1. Historical Attitudes. *a. Greek.* The early Greeks (Homer and others before 700 B.C.) regarded the act of suicide as being good and admirable, whereas the later Greeks began to think of it as a political offense because it deprived the state of a citizen. Pythagoras (582–507 B.C.) thought all men were soldiers of God and had no right to take their own lives. Socrates, Plato, and Aristotle (469–322 B.C.) wrote against suicide except in cases of extreme poverty, sorrow, or disgrace, or unless it was ordered by the state. Still later in Greek tradition thinking was again changed and the Stoics and Epicureans encouraged suicide as a quite natural solution to many problems.

b. Religious. The OT records six suicides (Judg. 9:54; 16:28–31; 1 Sam. 31:1-6; 2 Sam. 17:23; 1 Kings 16:18, 19) and the NT one (Mt. 27:3-5), none making any value judgment. Suicide was a fairly common occurrence in the early church, which tended to approve of self-sacrifice and martyrdom, and it was not until St. Augustine (354–430) wrote strongly against it that the church began taking a different view. Several church councils from 533 then condemned suicide, and St. Thomas Aquinas (1225–74) reaffirmed the Augustinian view that suicide is a sin.

c. Contemporary. Another shift in attitude began with Sir Thomas More (1478–1535) and continued through the writings of Donne, Hume, and Kant, all of whom opposed the church's condemnation of suicide as a sin and began to think of it as an aberration of mind that should be treated tolerantly. From this tolerance grew the modern view that suicide represents disease and should be treated as such. There is today, however, a strong minority view that holds that suicide represents neither a sin nor a disease but is rather a rational choice.

2. Pastoral Understanding. a. Depression and isolation. Most suicidal persons are lonely, depressed individuals experiencing strong feelings of hopelessness and helplessness, usually with strong underlying anger. Characteristically they have been experiencing suicidal thoughts for months or years as they have tried a variety of solutions for their emotional pain. Work, prayer, medication, and alcohol have failed as solutions, and they experience their lives withering away along with a diminishing capacity to cope with their pain and stress. Usually the depression is in response to some loss or series of losses that are emotionally significant to them, such as loss of a relationship, job, health, or reputation.

b. Ambivalence. Even at advanced stages of the development of suicidal ideation, most suicidal persons are highly ambivalent about dying. That is, simultaneous desires for life and death are in conflict. This ambivalence is seen in conflicting behavior (making suicide attempts in places where rescue is likely), in suicide notes ("if you love me, wake me up"), and in interviews with those who have survived serious attempts ("I finally decided to take the pills and leave it up to fate"). Most suicidal persons are not so much wanting to die as they are willing to die as a necessary price to escape the seemingly endless pain.

c. Crisis. Most suicidal persons will make a serious attempt only during a relatively brief period of time when the emotional pain peaks and when coping skills are low. The duration of this emotional crisis may be only a few hours, or at the most a few weeks. Clinical experience has consistently shown that if the crisis is survived because of someone's intervention or because of some other factor, the suicidal person does not soon return to the high-risk stage.

d. Communication. As desperate and depressive feelings develop, suicidal persons make many covert and overt attempts at communicating their pain and their suicidal thoughts. This attempt at communication has been called "the cry for help." Verbal expressions of depression and uselessness, visits to physicians with complaints of vague symptoms, making a new will, giving away valued possessions, being careless in the use of medications and other drugs, and nonlethal suicide attempts and gestures can all be attempts on the suicidal persons' part to communicate their distress and their developing resolution to take their own life. They are all examples of the cry for help aimed toward loved ones, the general community, or to God. Contrary to the popular myth that the person who talks about suicide seldom commits it, the fact is that most persons who commit suicide have expressed their intention to do so.

3. Pastoral Intervention. *a. Listening.* Because most suicidal talk and behavior is at heart an attempt to communicate distress, most suicidal people respond well when that communication is received by a sensitive, concerned listener. If the listener can put aside all other concerns and gently inquire into the suicidal thoughts of the distressed person, the first important step in the intervention process will be achieved.

b. Evaluating suicidal risk. Because not every person who is depressed or who thinks about suicide represents a high suicidal risk, it is important to determine who among that population is about to take action so that appropriate response can be made. The key element in this determination is the suicidal plan the person has developed. Most persons who are seriously suicidal have thought carefully about the way they plan to die and have carefully prepared the means and the time, perhaps even having rehearsed the act. Because they are ambivalent about dying, most suicidal persons will be honest about the extent of their planning when a listener with genuine concern inquires. The more specific, deadly, and available the means are, the higher the risk will be. The use of pills is the most common means of suicide in the United States, with guns the second most common. Both represent high-risk means. Other factors to be considered in evaluating suicidal risk include high-stress factors, low personal resources, a history of previous suicide attempts, and the use of alcohol.

c. Intervention plan. Because most people in a suicidal crisis represent a high risk for a relatively short period of time, the intervention plan should focus on immediate issues and be implemented quickly. The plan should take into consideration areas of perceived stress, present crisis factors, and should seek to develop immediate, if temporary, solutions. A list of all existing resources should be developed, including personal relationships, professional relationships, and community resources. The suicidal person should participate fully in every phase of plan development and implementation. Good follow-through is essential so there is no opportunity for feelings of abandonment.

d. Referral. In all high-risk situations, and in all situations in which there is doubt about the severity of risk, professional consultation should be sought. In many communities suicide prevention centers have been established and these are normally excellent resources for consultation or referral. Some are twenty-four-hour telephone services and others provide walk-in capacity. Community mental health centers and private psychiatric and psychological services are also available in most communities.

Bibliography. L. D. Hankoff and B. E. Einsidler, *Suicide: Theory and Clinical Aspects* (1979). C. L. Hatton, S. M. Valente, and A. Rink, *Suicide: Assessment and Intervention* (1977). J. Hewett, *After Suicide* (1980). E. S. Shneidman and N. L. Farberow, *Clues to Suicide* (1957); *The Cry for Help* (1961). E. S. Shneidman, N. L. Farberow, and R. L. Litman, *The Psychology of Suicide* (1976).

P. W. PRETZEL

6

PASTORAL THEOLOGICAL METHOD

Beginning with Anton T. Boisen, the method of pastoral theology that informs the practice of pastoral care and counseling has been a central discussion in the field. Boisen's method was to bring individual human experience and social movements, studied with the tools of behavioral science, into dialogue with biblical study and theology. Seward Hiltner furthered the use of the "action-reflection-action" method of clinical learning in constructing an operational theology that informs praxis. Even in the postmodern updates to these early methods (as noted in chapter 2), the answer to the question of whether pastoral theology is "content" or "method" is "yes," in that both are equally involved in informing the work of care. Below are reflections of theology (content) and method that provide valuable assistance for practice.

CASE STUDY METHOD. An organized and systematic way of studying and reporting various aspects of a person, family, group, or situation using a predetermined outline of questions or subjects. In clinical supervision the case study method is frequently used as a method of reporting, analyzing, and evaluating a pastoral encounter or counseling session. It is also used as a teaching method in many disciplines, including theological education, where a particular pastoral situation is reported and discussed in a classroom setting.

1. Development and Use. The use of stories or parables for purposes of instruction is an ancient precursor of the modern case study method. The prophet Nathan, for instance, used a story of a rich man and a poor man to confront King David with the meaning of his behavior (2 Sam. 12:1-6), and Jesus used stories like those of the good Samaritan (Lk. 10:29-37), the householder (Mt. 21:33-41), and the man with two sons (Lk. 15:11-32) to teach about the kingdom of God.

a. Psychology. The case study has been especially important in the field of psychology as a means of describing, analyzing, and interpreting clinical issues in the lives of individuals. Freud wrote extensive case histories to illustrate and describe his clinical findings. These were typically a chronological account of Freud's sessions with a patient, giving data concerning presenting problems, behavior, symptoms, and therapeutic interventions, and concluding with a clinical discussion and analysis of the case. Other case studies in psychology have utilized categories such as present illness, personal history, family history, psychiatric findings, hospitalizations, psychometric findings, and clinical summary. In psychology, a distinction is made between the case study, which usually deals with a problem of adjustment during a relatively short period of time, and the life history, a more comprehensive, long-term analysis of a person's life issues (see Bromley, 1977). Erikson (1975) published psychohistorical case studies exploring the psychosocial development of Martin Luther, Gandhi, and Thomas Jefferson.

b. Pastoral theology. The case study method has been important in the conceptualization and teaching of pastoral theology. S. Hiltner (1958) used the detailed pastoral notes of Ichabod Spencer, a Presbyterian minister in the mid-nineteenth century, to define and illustrate the functions of shepherding. Hiltner believed that one-to-one relationships could provide the starting point for the study of basic principles in pastoral theology. E. E. Thornton (1964) used an extensive case study of "Mr. Mills" to approach subjects such as repentance, salvation, and faith. W. E. Oates (1970) provided vivid case examples to describe the relationship between religion and mental illness.

c. Clinical Pastoral Education (CPE). *i. Anton T. Boisen.* The use of the case study method in CPE originated with Anton T. Boisen, the founder of CPE. His belief that the study of theology in the classroom must be supplemented with a reading of the "living human documents" led him to recruit four theological students for the first unit of CPE at Worcester (Massachusetts) State Hospital in 1925. His case studies of mentally ill people were motivated partly by his desire to understand and validate his own experience of mental illness. (See Boisen 1936, 1946,

1955, and 1960 for examples and applications of his case study method with individuals and social groups.)

Boisen first became acquainted with the case study method while studying with George Albert Coe at Union Theological Seminary in New York (1909–10). In Coe's seminar on mysticism, Boisen read Delacroix's careful case analyses of Saint Teresa, Madame Guyon, and Heinrich Suso. Another major influence on Boisen's method was Richard C. Cabot, with whom Boisen studied at Harvard Divinity School. Cabot's book *Differential Diagnosis* was based on his clinical pathological conferences at Harvard Medical School. This educational procedure pointed to diagnosis on the basis of known facts as the most important part of learning from the "human documents." Boisen attended Cabot's social ethics seminar on preparation of case records for teaching purposes (1922–23). Boisen also learned the case study method in social work from Susie Lyons of the Social Service Department at Boston Psychopathic Hospital (1923–24). By applying case study principles as a social worker, Boisen found that he could study the whole person in his or her social setting and deal with significant factors such as motives, values, and religious experience.

In CPE, Boisen's basic goal was to help theological students form their own theology from an empirical base. In the introduction to an unpublished collection of his case studies, which he distributed to CPE centers, Boisen noted that their use was not primarily for students to learn skills but rather to enable students to build a theology through a careful study of religious experiences and beliefs. He believed that a detailed survey of a patient's family, religious, and developmental history, as well as the present illness, was the most important activity for CPE students because it would enable them to understand the patient and provide a basis for discussing the meaning of the patient's illness and treatment. In this way, students were able to read the "living human documents." (For a more detailed description of Boisen's case method, see Asquith, 1976 and 1980.)

ii. Russell L. Dicks. Beginning his work as chaplain at Massachusetts General Hospital, Dicks developed another approach to the case study method: the "verbatim." Adapted from social work, though with precursors in earlier centuries of pastoral care, the verbatim was more suited to short-term pastoral care in a general hospital, where Boisen's life history method would have been difficult and, in many cases, less relevant to crisis intervention during physical illness.

In the verbatim, Dicks sought to reproduce, as closely as possible, the actual conversation between chaplain and patient (see Cabot and Dicks, 1936). Such a focus became the cornerstone for supervision and evaluation of pastoral work in CPE. It enabled reflection upon the effectiveness, appropriateness, and congruence of the pastor's response to a person in crisis. While Dicks was indeed concerned about the ways in which a person's religious beliefs functioned during illness, his verbatim dealt more with method and practice than with the theological reflection inherent in Boisen's life histories. Boisen, while affirming the importance of good pastoral care, became increasingly concerned, as the CPE movement progressed, that it was focusing more on psychological method than on theological understanding of human experience. Nevertheless, the testing and formation of a student's theology continues to be a basic purpose of CPE, and the case study method remains as one of the primary tools by which this objective is achieved.

2. Methodology. *a. Format.* The most frequently used type of case study in pastoral care and counseling is that of the student's own experience. This may be recorded according to the following outline.

I. Background Information
  A. Basic facts about the person or situation
  B. Conditions leading to the pastor's involvement
  C. Summary of pastor's relationship to person or situation up to the point of the report, including other persons or professionals involved
  D. Nature of pastor's preparation for the visit, session, or situation, including intended goals
  E. Physical description of the person(s), environment, and first impressions at beginning of event
II. Description of Event
This may take one of several forms:
  A. Verbatim account of entire session, including pauses, nonverbal communications, exterior events, and so forth, with each statement labeled and numbered according to persons involved
  B. Process report of event, written in prose form summarizing the content of all verbal and nonverbal interchanges
  C. Combination of verbatim and process reporting, which gives verbatim account only of short, critical segments of event
  D. Audio or video recording of event, or segment of it

III. Evaluation
  A. Identification of theological and psychological issues inherent in the session
  B. Evaluation of pastor's role in the event in light of stated goals and in terms of strengths and weaknesses of method, including a statement of what was learned or resolved in the event
  C. Citing of relevant literature that may assist the pastor in dealing with this and future events
  D. Questions for discussion of the case

b. Guidelines for use. A study of historic and contemporary uses of the case study method suggests several guidelines for its use in pastoral care.

(1) Discussion and analysis of case studies should make use of, but also *transcend*, behavioral science perspectives. In the pastoral care movement it has been the temptation to rely heavily upon the behavioral sciences for understanding a person's life issues and to give only secondary attention to theological themes that might be inherent in the case. This can be addressed by examining the goals for use of a case study; is it being studied to make one a better therapist or a better theologian? The former is not pastoral care without equal attention to the latter.

(2) A case used in pastoral care should be *theologically provocative*, having inherent issues that stimulate theological thinking among those using the case. Initially, it often requires skill and effort on the part of the teacher or supervisor to make such theological issues apparent to students in pastoral care; ultimately, a case study should enable students to make this identification on their own and thus gain skill as pastoral theologians. If this cannot be done without a great deal of effort and speculation, then the case may not be suitable for use.

(3) Some principles should emerge out of a case study with *universal* application to the pastor's work. The case should not be too narrow in focus but should have wider application to an understanding of theology and basic life issues.

(4) The case should be interpreted from an *informed* perspective. While Boisen asserted the importance of studying the nature of human experience, he also disapproved of students who did not read to supplement their clinical learning. Theological and psychological dynamics can only be accurately identified from the foundation of a basic body of knowledge. To be fully effective, a case study should stimulate and make use of clinical reading on the issues raised in the case.

(5) A final concern in case studies is *confidentiality*. Deep and sensitive material about a person's life is usually presented. The presenter often feels a sense of betrayal of confidence, which can cause resistance in reporting the full story. In situations where the identity of the counselee, parishioner, or patient must be disclosed, recordings or materials should be erased or destroyed after use. When the identity of the person is not necessary, it should be disguised. In supervision, the person is frequently not the central focus; the main emphasis is rather upon the presenter of the case. The case study is a tool for facilitating growth and skill in identifying and dealing with the various dynamics present in the case.

The regular use of the case study method can also add depth to the practice of pastoral care and counseling. In the face of many responsibilities, the pastor is often tempted to make superficial judgments based on inadequate information. The investment of time spent in learning the history and details of a person's situation will enable the pastor to be more prescriptive, and therefore more effective, in his or her pastoral care and counseling.

Bibliography. G. H. Asquith Jr., "The Case Study Method of Anton T. Boisen," *J. of Pastoral Care* 34 (1980), 84–94; "The Clinical Method of Theological Inquiry of A. T. Boisen," unpublished dissertation, Southern Baptist Theological Seminary (1976). A. T. Boisen, *The Exploration of the Inner World* (1936); *Out of the Depths* (1960); *Problems in Religion and Life* (1946); *Religion in Crisis and Custom* (1955). J. Breuer and S. Freud, "Studies on Hysteria," SE 2 (1955). K. Bridston et al., *Casebook on Church and Society* (1974). D. Bromley, *Personality Description in Ordinary Language* (1977), ch. 8. R. C. Cabot and R. L. Dicks, *The Art of Ministering to the Sick* (1936), ch. 18; *Cases in Theological Education* (1981). C. S. Calian, "Case Study Materials and Seminary Teaching," *Theological Education* 10 (1974), 136–217. N. Cryer and J. Vayhinger, *Casebook in Pastoral Counseling* (1962). E. Draper et al., "On the Diagnostic Value of Religious Ideation," *Archives of General Psychiatry* 13 (1965), 202–7. E. Erikson, *Life History and the Historical Moment* (1975). W. Fallaw, *The Case Method in Pastoral and Lay Education* (1963). S. Freud, *Three Case Histories*, ed. P. Rieff (1963). J. Glasse, *Putting It Together in the Parish* (1972), chs. 7–8. S. Hiltner, *Preface to Pastoral Theology* (1958). M. McNair, *The Case Method at the Harvard Business School* (1954). W. E. Oates, *When Religion Gets Sick* (1970). R. Perske, "The Use of a Critical Incident Report," *J. of Pastoral Care* 20 (1966), 156–61. P. Pigors and F. Pigors, *Case Method in Human Relations* (1961).

G. Rosell, "Clio in the Classroom: The Use of Case Studies in the Teaching of History," *Theological Education* 13 (1977), 168–74. W. Runyan, *Life Histories and Psychobiography* (1982). V. Satir, *Conjoint Family Therapy*, rev. ed. (1967), 112–35. E. E. Thornton, *Theology and Pastoral Counseling* (1964). R. Veatch, *Case Studies in Medical Ethics* (1977).

G. H. ASQUITH JR.

ESCHATOLOGY AND PASTORAL CARE. The doctrine of "the last things," that is, of the end of this world-epoch and of the beginning of God's new world order, the doctrine of the end and goal of humankind and of the cosmos. It is a theological doctrine of the future because it looks for the end and consummation of the world from God who is the Creator and also the creation's Redeemer. It is the Christian doctrine of the future insofar as it derives from God's faithfulness revealed in the history of Christ, in his death, and in his resurrection from the dead, and insofar as it hopes for the future as Christ's Parousia. Since this hope for the coming of Christ is grounded in the remembrance of Christ's history and in its representation in the gospel and in the Eucharist, it is neither a speculation nor a dream but a grounded promise. Personal and social hopes for the future, as well as personal and social fears of catastrophes, must be oriented to the grounded promise of Christ, if they are properly to be called Christian.

Christian eschatology, which at its core speaks of "Christ and his parousia," stands in a historical and logical relationship to Jewish eschatology, which derives from the Torah and the kingdom of God, and to Islamic eschatology, which hopes for a universal reign of God. If Abraham is the father of the Jewish, Christian, and Islamic faiths, then these three religions are aligned eschatologically through Abraham's promise.

By virtue of the representation of Israel's history and the history of Christ, Christian eschatology opens up three horizons of expectation for the future: (1) individual eschatology—life until death and eternal life; (2) collective eschatology—history and the kingdom of Christ, judgment, and the kingdom of God; and (3) cosmic eschatology—creation and nature, the destruction of this world order and the creation of the new heaven and the new earth.

1. History. In the development of the church and of theology in the West, cosmic eschatology was reduced to the eschatology of history, and collective eschatology was reduced to individual eschatology. Consequently, pastoral care was reduced to the "care of souls" (*cura animarum*) and became centered on the preparation of individuals for a "good death" and on the eternal life "after death." For a long time, the salvation of the soul in "the beyond" functioned as the eschatology of the pastoral care of the souls. Only in certain messianic groups was a collective eschatology preserved. They expected the bodily resurrection of the dead on the Last Day and therefore assumed that the soul either dies along with the body or falls into a state of "soul-sleep."

Only in the twentieth century, with the rediscovery of biblical eschatology, did hope as preparation for the coming kingdom of God come to the fore: pastoral care was understood as the "call to the kingdom of God" (Christoph Blumhardt, Eduard Thurneysen) encompassing body and soul, individual and community, community and society, society and nature. The "salvation of the soul" was tied to the *diakonia* of the body; the awakening of faith was bound up with working together in God's kingdom in the world. Thus pastoral care can no longer be only the individual care of souls but must be extended to a corporate care of souls, that is, the establishment of a brotherly and sisterly community. The care of souls by the pastor must be embedded in group care of souls and in the therapeutic ethos of the community. Then, pastoral care occurs as Luther explains it in the "Schmalkald Articles" III/4 (1537): "*per mutuum colloquium et consolationem fratrum,*" the care of souls is a task of the entire community and happens in "mutual conversation and consolation among brethren." It addresses the personal problems of individuals, the common problems of families, the social problems of society, the problems of the natural environment and of one's own embodiment. The more theology rediscovers today the necessity and the meaning of collective, historical, and cosmic eschatology, the more pastoral care will liberate itself from its traditional, individualistic narrowness and become a comprehensive care for the kingdom of God. For we always care only as far as we are capable of hoping.

2. The Spirit of God in Life and in Death. From very early times Christian individual eschatology adopted the Platonic doctrine of the immortality of the soul. Thereby, however, it let its Christian character slip away. According to Plato, death is "the separation of the soul from the body." Whether this separation is mourned as a loss or is celebrated as a liberating, festive occasion, this concept presupposes an ontological dualism: the soul is immortal, everlasting, incapable of suffering; the body is mortal, transitory, and subject to suffering. In death, only the mortal part of the human being passes away, while the immortal soul returns to the realm of ideas. Through an imaginative (*geistige*) anticipation of death (*meditation mortis*), the individual becomes conscious of his or her immortal soul. "Know thyself," that is, "remember that you will die." One's entire life, therefore, serves to prepare one for death. The Christian *ars moriendi* literature has its origin in this Platonic teaching about the soul and about death.

When the early Christian expectation of the immediate Parousia of Christ disappeared, the hope for the bodily resurrection of the dead was replaced by this individual hope for the deliverance of the soul through death in a "life after death." Even in the NT there is the individual hope for being wholly with Christ immediately after death (2 Cor. 5:6; Phil. 1:23). Yet this individual hope does not exclude universal hope; it rather includes it. Hope for the redemption of the soul and hope for the redemption of the body supplement each other (Rom. 8:23).

But where, then, does the soul remain after the individual death and before the general resurrection of the dead? Medieval theology resolved this problem with the assumption of an "intermediate state," the *purgatorium*: after death, souls enter into a fire of purification in order to be united with the resurrected body on the Last Day. This conception does, indeed, provide persons with hope for redemption beyond individual death, but it also empties universal hope, because everything depends on the purification of the soul.

However, only that which does not live bodily can be immortal. Only bodiless (i.e., unlived, empty) life cannot die. The doctrine of the immortality of the soul is, in reality, a teaching about unlived life. In contrast to this, the NT uses the image of the grain of seed, which falls into the ground and dies—otherwise it remains solitary. And when it dies, it bears a rich harvest (Mt. 10:39; Lk. 17:33; Jn. 12:23; 1 Cor. 15:42-44). In other words, life that is not being lived and does not die remains solitary and barren. That is death before life. Lived and therefore mortal life, however, is hopeful and productive. It is life before death.

Human life is alive insofar as it is being loved and affirmed. The more passionately we live, the more we experience the joy and rich abundance of life. But along with this we also experience the pain of dying. Only life truly lived can die. Unlived life cannot die. The modern "denial of death" is the price paid for the apathy of modern life. The true *ars moriendi* is not the preparation of the soul for the hereafter but the devotion of body and soul in love, that is, the *ars amandi*. In hope for the God who resurrects the dead, humans can wholly live their lives in love and can also wholly die.

Is there, then, no *"intermediate state" for the soul?* That old conception transfers the time of the living to the dead. That is misleading. For the dead themselves, the time between their individual deaths and the day of the resurrection is only "a moment" (M. Luther). *Where, then, are the dead now?* According to Paul, they are under the ruling power of Christ, which now extends over the "living and the dead" (see Rom. 14:8-9). Christ will lead the dead to the resurrection and, eventually, destroy death (1 Cor. 15:55-57). *Does something immortal exist* already in this life prior to death? The soul is not immortal but the *spirit of God* is immortal, which, already here, in this life, fills believers with the power of the Resurrection (Rom. 8:11). Wherever the life-giving Spirit is experienced, there eternal life is experienced before death. Wherever persons get close to the creative ground of lived life, death disappears and they experience continuance without perishing. "If a man has faith in me, even though he die, he shall come to life" (Jn. 11:25 NEB). The same is also valid for love.

What, then, is death? Death, then, is neither the separation of the soul from the body nor the end of body and soul but the transformation of the spirit of life, which fills body and soul, into the new, transfigured world order of God. Death is no end and no separation, but a transformation into the life eternal. Dying persons experience "the way through the gate" (Kübler-Ross, 1974), and those who mourn for the dead participate, in their grief, in this transformation. Christian care of "souls" is in reality care for the spirit of life that, here and now, makes body and soul alive in love and that, penetrating through and beyond death, will transform the entire lived life into the life everlasting.

3. The Redemption of the Body and the New Creation. The experience of the presence of God's *spirit* grounds the hope for the kingdom of God in which soul and body, heaven and earth will be redeemed. Paul has developed this universal *cosmic eschatology*: "For the creation waits with eager longing for the revealing of the sons of God." (Rom. 8:19). The Revelation of John promises "a new heaven and a new earth" (21:1). That includes hope for "the redemption of our bodies" (Rom. 8:23). If we disregard the time-bound apocalyptic conceptions, this means there is no personal hope in God's spirit without the bodily, the social, and the cosmic hope for the kingdom of God.

In the experience of God's Spirit persons are not being separated *from* their bodies in a Platonic manner but they wait for the redemption *of* the body, that is, they wait for the new body entirely permeated by God's Spirit—the "spiritual body." This bodily hope can only be fulfilled when not only believers but also the entire Creation becomes free. Therefore, hope for the "redemption of the body" is always bound up with hope for "the new earth," in which "there shall be no more death...nor crying...[nor] pain" (Rev. 21:4 KJV). There is no realistic individual eschatology without this cosmic eschatology. The destiny of the individual person is inseparably tied to the destiny of God's entire creation. Therefore, Christians look not for the destruction but for the transformation of creation into the kingdom of God. God's judgment over all godless beings is the beginning of this eschatological transformation.

Christian hope brings persons into a deep solidarity with the whole suffering Creation, binding humanity to the earth itself. From this there follows a care for peace over against the nuclear destruction of the world; for justice over against the progressive oppression of peoples of the developing world; for the life of creation over against the proliferating destruction of the natural environment.

Pastoral care in this wide horizon is the engagement of the entire community of Christ on behalf of the life of the Creation against universal death and against the powers of death in the midst of life. Whoever surrenders and renounces the hope for the kingdom of God collaborates with the powers of death. Such is the temptation of the religious and political apocalyptic of the impending global catastrophe: "Armageddon in our generation." Christian hope is no blind optimism but a knowing resistance: whoever knows the danger hopes for deliverance, and whoever hopes for deliverance resists the paralyzing fear. "If the world perished tomorrow, I still would plant an apple tree today," Luther is said to have remarked.

The apocalyptic system of fear, then, only has a Christian meaning if it serves the establishment of a messianic system of hope. Over against apprehensions of a nuclear, economic, and ecological holocaust, which are widespread these days, the Christian community will assert its hope for the kingdom of Christ crucified for the world, in order that humanity may in time turn back from death to life. Turning back in personal and in public life is the praxis of Christian hope.

Bibliography. P. Althaus, *Die letzten Dinge: Lehrbuch der Eschatologie* (1957). O. Cullmann, *Immortality of the Soul or Resurrection of the Dead?*

The Witness of the New Testament (1958). V. Eller (ed.), *Thy Kingdom Come: A Blumhardt Reader* (1980). C. Gerkin, *Crisis Experience in Modern Life* (1979). J. Hick, *Death and Eternal Life* (1976). E. Kübler-Ross, *Interviews mit Sterbenden* (1981); *Was können wir noch tun?* (1982) [ET, *Questions and Answers on Death and Dying* (1974)]. J. Moltmann, *The Crucified God* (1974); *Theology of Hope* (1967). J. Robinson, *In the End, God* (1950). E. Thurneysen, *A Theology of Pastoral Care* (ET, 1962). F. Wright, *Pastoral Care for Lay People* (1982).

J. MOLTMANN

HEALING. The process of being restored to bodily wholeness, emotional well-being, mental functioning, and spiritual aliveness. Christian modes of healing have always distinguished themselves by achieving a spiritual advance in connection with the healing process. Healing may also refer to the process of reconciling broken human relationships and to the development of a just social and political order among races and nations. In recent times, healing and wholeness have become metaphors for religious views of salvation.

1. Old Testament View of Healing. For Christians, concern for healing has its roots in the OT. The Hebrews pictured the world as good. There was a unity of mind and body, created by God. Whereas health was viewed as a blessing from God, a reward for righteousness and faithfulness to the Mosaic covenant, illness was often regarded as divine punishment or chastisement for transgression. Health and holiness were therefore positively related and were united in the concepts of shalom and righteousness. Holiness refers to a sense of personal unity and integration of one's being in dynamic relationship to God, world, and community out of choice. It eventuates in the notion of a centered and covenanted life, set apart for a morally committed existence in the world. This existence is characterized by *shalom*, or bodily wholeness and being at peace with self, God, and neighbor. It is a righteous life inasmuch as it is characterized by deliverance from one's enemies, personal integrity, and living fitly in the world as a member of the covenant community with God. There is a social dimension to salvation and the health that attends it, extending to relationships among nations as well as an ecological dimension involving stewardship of the earth. Thus, healing and salvation are linked insofar as they both involve restoration to dynamic wholeness in body, mind, spirit, society, and the world, and derive from being in proper relation to God. The book of Job revises the view that all illness and affliction are divine punishments upon sin and adds the perspective that illness results from an evil agency deriving its power indirectly from God and operating apart from human intention and virtue. Rather than necessarily reflecting a broken relationship with God, bodily and emotional affliction may overtake the faithful and may eventuate in a spiritual and theological advance whether or not physical healing actually occurs.

2. New Testament View of Healing: The Ministry of Jesus. The NT portrays Jesus as vitally concerned with healing the physical, moral, and mental diseases of persons, and commanding his followers to do the same. About one-third of the Gospel accounts describe various healings performed by Jesus, and the early church reported dramatic healings by its leaders and members. The NT regards healing as an indication of the presence of the kingdom of God, in which restoration of bodily wholeness, emotional well-being, and mental functioning take place in the context of a spiritual advance. Jesus and his followers believed that sickness and disease resulted from demon possession rather than from divine punishment of personal or corporate sin. Illness and disease were regarded as forms of bondage to evil forces, taking place in the depths of personal being apart from personal choice or control. Jesus' method of healing evoked latent attitudes of faith and the desire for wholeness and linked these with the healing power of God, who hates evil in all its forms. Thus, Jesus provided an opportunity for human faith and divine power to coalesce in creating a new order. Restoration of bodily, emotional, and mental capacities was not the only concern of this new order, but restoration of these faculties was included in it. As in the OT, salvation and health were integrally related; both were seen as blessings from God, who opposes sin and evil, of which sickness and personal disorder are expressions. The mind, body, and spirit were understood to compose a dynamic unity. The witness of Jesus, however, also advanced the idea that though personal attitudes play a part in the healing process, they may be overwhelmed by evil agents that distort the personality and cause bodily, emotional, and spiritual disorder. Further, Jesus commanded his followers to heal the sick.

3. Contemporary Issues of Brokenness and Healing. In the twentieth century there were converging religious and secular forces that recaptured some of the Jewish and early Christian views about the unity of body, emotions, spirit, society, and the cosmos in the process of disease and healing. Individuals, societies, and nations are described in some important Christian literature, notably that of the World Council of Churches, as in need of healing from their brokenness and liberation from bondage to forces of evil that have captured them. The dualistic and deterministic worldview is in itself regarded as an expression of sin's estrangement inasmuch as it divides and fragments that which God created to be related. In individuals, this brokenness is expressed in unabated identity crises, in persistent estrangement from one's roots, in ongoing difficulties with what it means to be male and female and how to relate to families, in struggles over depression arising from frustrated aspirations, aging, illness, and a sense of meaninglessness and isolation. On a national and global scale it is characterized by oppression, lack of education and jobs, and the selfish, greedy use of the earth's resources eventuating in the pollution of air, water, and land.

According to recent World Council of Churches' statements, the religious call in the modern world is to share, to be a healing presence where it is needed, whether between cultures, races, generations, women and men, races and religions, or oneself and one's family. Healing has once again, as in its biblical rootage, become connected with salvation, shalom, and holiness, and with the transformation of the personal and the social fabric of existence.

4. Pastoral Theology and Therapy for Healing. The theoretical and practical contributions of S. Hiltner, J. N. Lapsley, and others have both reflected and spawned a major concern for health and healing in modern pastoral practice. Nearly all seminaries have major curricular offerings in pastoral care and counseling, and much of the average minister's time is taken in ministries related to the restoration of bodily wholeness, mental functioning, interpersonal reconciliation, and spiritual aliveness. A number of programs training pastoral care and counseling specialists have emerged to support the growing number of persons focusing their ministries in the area of personal and interpersonal healing. The College of Chaplains of the American Protestant Hospital Association, the Association of Clinical Pastoral Education, and the American Association of Pastoral Counselors are but a few of the professional groups that support the various healing ministries in today's religious world. Though their emphases and methods may vary, persons in these groups are united in the conviction that illness and personal distress is an opportunity for the healing power of God to work in a transforming manner. The mind, body, and environment are understood to be interconnected in the processes of disease and healing, and religious perspectives and methodologies are broadly interpreted to play a potentially important role in the healing of persons.

5. Modern Pastoral Approaches to Healing. Within current pastoral practice, there are two major approaches to the processes of healing, with variants and nuances of interpretations within them. One is the practice of spiritual-charismatic-sacramental healing. Morton Kelsey has interpreted this mode in many of his books, especially in *Healing and Christianity in Ancient Thought and Modern Times*. The other is the pastoral counseling or pastoral-psychotherapy approach, which draws upon modern psychotherapeutic modes for much of its self-understanding and methods. Seward Hiltner, James Lapsley, Wayne Oates, Howard Clinebell, Carroll Wise, and others have written about and practiced this mode of pastoral healing.

a. Spiritual-charismatic-sacramental healing. Akin to the relatively direct form of healing ascribed to Jesus and the early church, it has been carried forward by great healers throughout the history of the church. Of the numerous forms of this healing, nearly all involve a combination of bodily restoration and emotional renewal with an attendant spiritual advance. It is usually performed by a recognized healer and carried out in a communal context involving a variety of religious practices. Occasionally, exorcisms are performed by those having the gift of healing. The processes involved in spiritual healing include spiritual discernment on the part of the healer, washing and anointing, laying on of hands, prayer—sometimes in tongues—confession of sins, singing praises to God, and meditation. The Eucharist is sometimes celebrated at healing services. It is theorized that the latent faith and desire for wholeness on the part of the ill person are awakened by the healer in the healing context, and linked with the saving and healing power of God who works through persons with special gifts. It still constitutes a frontier for critical examination in order to assess more fully its distortions and excesses, as well as its achievements and potential for being incorporated into other models and practices of healing in the church.

b. Pastoral counseling and pastoral psychotherapy. With roots in the guidance of penitents in the Middle Ages, this approach has evolved in its modern form through dialogue primarily with the psychologies of Freud, Jung, Rogers, Erikson, Berne, and, more recently, with some of the family systems perspectives delineated by Satir, Ackerman, Bowen, Minuchin, and others. This dialogue has allowed the pastoral care and counseling movement to recapture its classical understanding that the body, mind, spirit, and environment are dynamically related and that for healing to occur pastoral counseling must engage the depths of the personality and its situation in the world. These perspectives make it clear, once again, that healing involves a liberation from bondage to forces that work in spite of conscious, willful, or rational intentions. The pastoral counseling movement has thus rediscovered that healing involves a new relation to oneself, to one's neighbor, and to God. In relation to self, one is enabled to overcome crippling dependencies and counterproductive strategies of living, to be released from destructive negative emotions, to find a sense of purpose and direction, to experience the harmonious working of one's personal aspirations and natural instincts, to be reconciled to one's limitations, and to be aware of one's continuity with and participation in the human race and its enterprises. In relation to one's neighbor, egocentricity is abated; compassion and empathy increased; one's behaviors become less dominated by anxiety, fear, and hostility; and a growing capacity for cooperation and collaboration result. Differences of opinion and conflict are regarded as opportunities for enrichment. One is better able to balance giving and receiving, work and pleasure, the conscious and the unconscious, the personal and the social. In relation to God, one experiences acceptance rather than punishment, rejection, or indifference. An awareness of God's continual providence may emerge, as well as a sense of being called or drawn to new patterns of living and new forms of work. An inner freedom in relation to God predominates, which eventuates in a spontaneous confidence and an impulse to worship joyfully. One begins to identify with God's compassion for all of the living and to see the world in inclusive rather than chauvinistic terms. Since the healing of one's relationship with God often involves a radical restructuring of one's concepts of God, one becomes more tolerant of other religious perspectives, and capable of being influenced by them without losing one's own rootedness.

6. The Role of the Caregiver in Healing. The pastoral caregiver, counselor, or therapist is not the healer, but is the one who takes the major responsibility for creating the conditions by which healing may occur in the special relationship between the pastoral healer and those seeking assistance. The relationship of openness, trust, mutual exploration and learning, acceptance, and establishing limits between the parties allows the depths of the predicament and the latent impulses toward healing in the parishioner, or the parishioner's milieu, to become apparent and to effect a healing process. Sometimes the caregiver helps families or groups restructure their relationships in such a way that the conditions for health are more optimal, and helps interpret the religious dimensions of the disease and healing processes. This interpretation generally affirms that the pastoral helper represents or reflects God's incarnational presence in the sufferings of the world and points to God's saving and renewing work in the structures of this world. Religious interpretation, in addition, involves the difficult assignment of helping parishioners discover how internalized theologies and religious practices contribute to attitudes and behaviors that maintain their illnesses. The healing process therefore often involves considerable theological reworking at the dynamic level of the personality.

7. Future Directions in Modes of Healing. One frontier confronting the church is the need to bring together both modes of healing, addressing each other at both the conceptual and practical levels. In current practice, they tend to reflect the sacred/secular split so endemic in the modern world, and to operate out of worldviews that do not tend fully enough to healing in all the dimensions of human experience. The charismatic-spiritual mode tends to neglect the emotional, cognitive, and relational dimensions of experience, while emphasizing the physical and the spiritual. It emphasizes continuity with historic theological interpretations and is in tension with modern viewpoints. The pastoral-psychotherapeutic mode minimizes the spiritual and bodily in favor of the emotional, cognitive, and relational dimensions of experience. It is more comfortable with contemporary worldviews, and sometimes appears to be in tension with historic Christian views.

Another frontier is the need to develop models of healing that bring the social, political, economic, and ecological dimensions of health and healing into dialogue with the spiritual, emotional, and physical. Neither the charismatic-sacramental nor the pastoral-psychotherapeutic approaches has transcended its foundations in individual psychology and Western bourgeois culture.

In addition, there is a need for pastoral theological interpretations of healing to incorporate perspectives and practices from Native American, Asian, African, and Spiritualistic sources. Rather than being seen as superstitious and primitive, these powerful orientations may enable us to further regain the holism of our early Judaic and Christian heritage and to more fully witness to the saving power of God in the world.

Bibliography. F. Capra, *The Turning Point: Science, Society, and The Rising Culture* (1982). W. A. Clebsch and C. R. Jaekle, *Pastoral Care in Historical Perspectives: An Essay with Exhibits* (1964). S. Hiltner, *Religion* *and Health* (1943); *Preface to Pastoral Theology* (1958). M. T. Kelsey, *Healing and Christianity in Ancient Thought and Modern Times* (1973). J. N. Lapsley Jr., *Salvation and Health: The Interlocking Processes of Life* (1972). A. Weil, *Health and Healing: Understanding Conventional and Alternative Medicine* (1983). World Council of Churches, "Healing and Sharing Life in Community," Issue Paper 4 (1983).

L. K. GRAHAM

INTERPRETATION AND HERMENEUTICS, PASTORAL. Pastoral interpretation is that process by which the pastor attaches meaning to the events and relationships that occur in any context in which pastoral ministry takes place. Hermeneutics is "the study of the methodological principles of interpretation and explanation; *specifically* the study of the general principles of biblical interpretation" (*Webster's Third International Dictionary* [Springfield, Mass., 2002, s.v. "hermeneutics"]).

Modern usage of *hermeneutics* began in the sixteenth and seventeenth centuries with the post-Reformation need for guidelines for interpreting Scripture. In ancient times the Greek verb *hermenuein* and noun *hermeneia* were derived from the myth of Hermes, the wing-footed messenger-god. Various forms of the word "suggest the process of bringing a thing or situation from unintelligibility to understanding" (Palmer, 1969, 13). In modern usage the discipline of hermeneutics has broadened to include issues related to all processes of human interpretation, understanding, and explanation.

1. General Features. Pastoral interpretation includes both the pastor's activity as interpreter of the faith tradition, particularly the Bible, and the interpretation of present events and relationships. The pastoral hermeneutical task therefore concerns itself with ways of seeing and responding to situations of contemporary life that comport with the vision of life that emerges from Scripture and tradition. The modern context of ministry, however, requires that this Christian vision be supplemented and critically related to the perspectives on contemporary life coming from modern secular thought, especially those coming from the social and human behavioral sciences.

Pastoral interpretation most often involves some practical purpose, for instance, the preparation of a sermon addressing a pastoral issue or concern, or the question of appropriate pastoral response to a situation in the life of a parishioner. But in addition it is concerned with the questions of appropriate descriptive language and normative judgments as to what constitutes the good.

Pastoral interpretation likewise goes on at many levels, sometimes formal and explicit, at other times quite informal and unself-conscious. As persons embedded in particular cultural ways of seeing and giving significance to phenomena, pastors are often prone to fall into popular interpretations of common events and relationships. The art of pastoral interpretation involving more critically reflective understanding makes use of theological, ethical, psychological, social-scientific, and other languages of interpretation. These more critical understandings, however, can only be acquired by the disciplined process of careful observation and reflection, as well as by the equally rigorous process of learning the appropriate language and conceptual tools provided by the various disciplines applicable to pastoral practice. As a disciplined art, pastoral interpretation therefore is inherently an interdisciplinary activity that makes appropriate use of the images, themes, concepts, and descriptive modes of a number of sometimes disparate languages, while sustaining the theological and ethical perspectives central to the Christian vision as normative warrants for pastoral understanding and action. The pluralism of languages by which any event or relational situation may be interpreted in the modern world thus presents an opportunity for enrichment of the pastoral perspective and also the problem of making judgments concerning the most appropriate and helpful languages to be utilized.

A broad interdisciplinary approach to pastoral interpretation or hermeneutics can assist the pastor in avoiding both the superficiality of popular cultural interpretations of the events of everyday life and the tendency toward reductionism—the apparent simplification of explanatory interpretation by reducing explanation to a single set of language images, which are often set in a language of causation. However, an interdisciplinary approach to pastoral interpretation also sets before the pastor the task of determining how to integrate the various available languages, each of which may illuminate a particular facet of meaning or explanation of the problem at hand. The problem of deciding which items among a welter of perceptual data, factual information, and impressionistic notions are to be given significance and how that significance is to be expressed in thought and action cannot be avoided.

2. Practical Implications and Suggestions. Assuming the pastor is confronted with a common human situation of individual, family, or parish community life that demands pastoral interpretation and response, the following set of questions provides the rough outline of a procedure of hermeneutical inquiry that pastors may find useful:

(1) What has happened or is happening? What is going on here? Responding to these questions involves the pastor immediately in a choice of language paradigms; more specifically, it requires some designation of descriptive words and association of images from the interpreter's past experience. Some preunderstanding of what is or has happened is immediately brought to bear on this happening, designating it as perhaps in some ways like and perhaps in other ways unlike what the interpreter has seen happen before. Evaluative as well as descriptive imagery from prior experience shape this preunderstanding, especially descriptive languages and imagery found useful in previous experience.

(2) Why did it happen or why is this going on? Here the interpreter's preimaged notions of causation shape a way of seeing the sequential state of affairs or human predilections that may have brought about the situation at hand. Causal imagery may be influenced by popular psychological notions of causation, most of which tend to be either simplistically reductionistic or in subtle ways moralistically blame-placing. Mature pastoral interpretations will more often recognize the complexity of any human situation and call upon prior experience with use of a variety of psychological, social, and perhaps theological or ethical paradigms to make tentative, heuristic judgments about the possible antecedent causes of present situations. Interpretive judgments concerning causation will have a strong influence over judgments concerning appropriate pastoral response. Thus the richer and more varied the interpretive understanding of causation, the richer and more highly nuanced the response.

(3) What does it mean that this has happened or is happening? Here lies a question of significance that is at once a factual question, concerning the meaning being assigned to the situation by its participants, and a moral and theological or religious question. It is important that the pastor seek to understand the significance of whatever has occurred for those who are involved and have a stake in its outcome. But it is also important that the pastor place the situation in some larger theological and ethical context—a context of ultimate meaning. The pastor's interpretive judgments will largely shape the moral and religious climate within which the pastor approaches the situation and, insofar as he or she exercises symbolic power there, will also shape the participants' understanding of it.

(4) Within the narrative structure of meaning that shapes the collective self-understanding of the group or community of persons affected by what has hap-

pened or is happening, what is now the outcome or direction most desirable or normatively most appropriate or fitting? Here the pastor's interpretive judgment takes a teleological turn. Appropriate pastoral response is determined not only by understandings of causation and meaning, it is also influenced by the ends being sought. For example, pastoral response with the intention of reconciliation and movement of life toward wholeness will be substantively different from pastoral response with intention of political change designed to shift power alliances in the group or community.

(5) Given all of the above considerations, each of which involves interpretation by the employment of one or more hermeneutical keys, what is the appropriate pastoral response in the present time and situation? The purpose and direction of pastoral interpretation is almost always practical. Pastoral interpretations are therefore most often "action" interpretations or working hypotheses that provide a sufficient framework of understanding or explanation to undergird the next step or sequencing of pastoral response. Thus, pastoral interpretation is more appropriately seen as a hermeneutical process of testing and reconsidering tentative interpretations that suggest particular courses of action and response than as prescriptive, definitive diagnosis. The pastoral hermeneutical effort is consistently directed toward bringing the unintelligible elements of a situation or event into a degree of understanding so that a fitting response may be made and then tested in the crucible of ongoing ministry in the situation.

Bibliography. For an introduction to hermeneutics see Z. Bauman, *Hermeneutics and Social Science* (1978); R. E. Palmer, *Hermeneutics* (1969). For pastoral/practical hermeneutics see C. V. Gerkin, *The Living Human Document* (1984) and *Widening the Horizons* (1987); J. Whitehead and E. Whitehead, *Method in Ministry* (1980); C. Winquist, *Practical Hermeneutics* (1980).

C. V. GERKIN

PASTORAL THEOLOGICAL METHODOLOGY. The critical evaluation of the procedures for arriving at theological judgments, proposals, or assertions. Thus it is derived from theology, which has the task of explicating and critically appropriating the language of faith. The "language of faith" includes all of a community's religious phrases, gestures, narratives, or rituals. The focus of this article, however, is on the special task and context of pastoral theological reflection—the process of theological reflection or "theologizing" in the pastoral context or from a pastoral perspective.

We may employ the following distinctions. *First-order religious language* will designate the collection of phrases (e.g., God loves me, God is punishing me), narratives (e.g., remembered biblical stories), and liturgies (prayers, hymns, gestures) that are employed to give expression to the way in which a person or community's life is related to God.

Second-order religious language (theology) is the explication and critical evaluation or appropriation of their basic meaning, with the more or less provisional result yielding a theological judgment or proposal. When an entire community of faith attains or accepts the same judgment, the result is a doctrine.

Theological method, including pastoral theology, is a *third-order reflection* upon the way in which such judgments are made and a critical evaluation of the appropriateness of such procedures. Thus theological method is concerned with an evaluation of the sources, norms, and procedures of theological judgments.

1. Pastoral Care Itself as Theological Reflection. *a. Explicating religious meanings.* A frequently neglected dimension of pastoral care and counseling is that of assisting the person who comes for help to explicate and critically evaluate assumptions concerning the meaning of faith and the life of faith. Yet this is certainly a crucial aspect of pastoral counseling. Much of the work of counseling involves assisting persons to formulate explicitly what may have been only tacitly or subconsciously assumed, such as evaluations and expectations of self and of others, in order that they may be consciously elaborated, explained, evaluated, and possibly altered. If one supposes that a person's tacitly held religious assumptions are of comparable significance, then pastoral care must include assisting the person to expose, elaborate, and so to give some account of these assumptions.

Of course, this must be distinguished from simply encouraging persons to employ (first order) religious language and from employing it oneself in the counseling situation. For theology is not the uncritical or superficial use of a particular (religious) vocabulary but an attempt to understand the meaning or truth of that language. Theological reflection may begin by drawing attention to the religious language, imagery, and gesture employed and by teasing out its connections to other religious and nonreligious articulations of experience. This process assembles the data of theological reflection, which may then inquire about the fundamental meaning or generalizable significance of such first-order discourse. It is only in this process that underlying or tacit assumptions are made explicit and can thus be formulated and examined.

b. Evaluating religious meanings. But theological reflection is not only the explication of religious language in terms of meaning and significance. It also entails the evaluation of such explicit meanings in terms of their truth. That is to say, theology is a normative endeavor. This may at first seem inappropriate in a counseling situation in which, to be sure, the task of attentive and sympathetic listening is of paramount importance. Yet pastoral care necessarily entails the facilitation and application of normative judgments. Where one engages in a process that seeks not merely to maintain a given situation or pattern of behavior but to transform it, then one is engaged in the application of normative or evaluative judgments—for example, is this conducive to growth or decline, to healing or injury, to freedom or bondage, to maturity or infantilization, to integrity or fragmentation? The case is much the same with respect to matters of faith and to the theological judgments that explicate the language of faith.

With respect to the question of the truthfulness of a theological judgment, several kinds of tests may be employed: (1) Is it coherent? That is, is it intelligible, understandable, or is it confused or self-contradictory? (2) Is it consistent with other aspects of one's faith? For example, does what I say about life after death seem compatible with what I say about the nature of God, or my body? (3) Does it correspond to what I or we actually experience? (4) How does it relate to formulations that I take to be especially reliable (e.g., the doctrine of my community, the Bible)? These tests do not provide an automatic checklist to determine truth or falsity but indicate possible directions of reflection.

The task of theological reflection within the pastoral situation must be prosecuted with great care and sensitivity. It is not a substitute for but an instrument of the attentive and compassionate regard for the other that is at the heart of pastoral care. Thus it cannot be the goal of such a reflection to impose upon the other a vocabulary or conceptuality that is alien or heteronomous. Instead, the goal is that persons be able to speak more accurately, truthfully, and responsibly of their own pilgrimage as persons of faith.

2. Theological Reflection upon Pastoral Care. The development of a genuinely pastoral theology (that is, a theology rooted in and tested by pastoral practice) is crucial for the development of pastoral care and counseling as an activity of the church and as a discipline in the school of theology. This task has been often hindered by a division between practitioners of academic theology and practitioners of pastoral care. An appropriate pastoral theology will be the result of a collaboration between these disciplines, which will explicate and test the pertinence of theological proposals for pastoral care and test the theological insights generated from pastoral practice by the general canons of adequacy of theological inquiry generally. The development of pastoral theology consists then of a two-way movement between (theological) theory and (pastoral) practice.

a. From practice to theology. Pastoral theology does not consist merely in the employment of a first-order religious discourse as an alternative vocabulary for psychological or experiential insight. While insights gained through pastoral practice may be initially couched in religious, psychological, or experiential terminology, their theological significance appears only through the transition to a critically reflected or second-order religious discourse. Thus the pastoral counselor may query a particular episode, insight, or counseling practice concerning its theological appropriateness.

The first step is that of explication: what are its implications for an understanding of human nature and transformation; for an understanding of priestly or ecclesial office and role; for an understanding of divine agency and purpose? Once their theological relevance is carefully explicated, it is possible to inquire whether these implications are consistent with aspects of the Judeo-Christian tradition to which one or one's community is committed. Normally, this entails careful attention to biblical, confessional, and other sources and norms of theological formulation. Again the emphasis is not upon these as first-order discourse, but upon the basic or fundamental meaning of this discourse.

As a consequence of this procedure one may discover a mutually illuminating and confirming relationship between practice and theology. On the other hand, one may find it necessary to relinquish or revise the initial interpretation or practice as incompatible with one's theological position. So, for example, some therapeutic practices may be avoided or modified because they appear to contradict a theologically appropriate emphasis upon human freedom and responsibility, or because they fail to take with adequate seriousness the forces and structures that diminish or corrupt responsible freedom. If one concludes that it is the theological tradition itself that must be revised in the light of pastoral practice, then the latter becomes a norm.

b. *From theology to practice.* Pastoral practice provides a norm as well as a source for theological reflection and formulation. Theological or doctrinal assertions regarding the structure and dynamics of human brokenness and bondage (e.g., formulations of original and actual sin), as well as those concerned with the basic process and goal of transformation and growth (e.g., justification, reconciliation, sanctification), must be tested in clinical or pastoral contexts. Only if they prove to be actually illuminating of such contexts do they retain the general interpretive power that is necessary for second-order discourse. Thus with respect to a particular proposal or doctrine it is appropriate to inquire whether it has implications for understanding of or intervention in situations of pastoral care and counseling.

Once these implications are understood, it is then appropriate to inquire whether the situation is in fact clarified or the indicated intervention commensurate with pastoral experience. Where it is not, then, the theological formulation may require revision or may be abandoned for an alternative formulation. It is important in the process to keep clear the distinction between first- and second-order religious discourse. It is quite possible that first-order language (e.g., talk of sin) may be employed in ways that conceal rather than clarify the situation, or hinder rather than assist transformation, without thereby entailing that the second-order (reflective-critical) use of such terminology is similarly impaired.

The development of a pastoral theology may be greatly enhanced by paying attention to the way many doctrines of the church have been generated from and tested by pastoral practice. Many formulations of the doctrine of sin, for example, serve to diagnose underlying structures that produce experiential and relational conflict, boundness, or brokenness. Thus an inability to trust (unbelief), inordinate self-preoccupation (pride, despair, the heart turned inward), and the compulsive acquisition of things, persons, and symbols of value (concupiscence) are often elaborated with rich pastoral detail. Similarly corresponding categories explanatory of healing or transforming processes (justification, sanctification, election, etc.) are also often developed in the theological tradition in ways that clearly demonstrate their basis in and testing by pastoral insight. Thus contemporary pastoral practice may serve as a powerful heuristic device for interpreting past doctrinal formulations and thus for enriching the domain of contemporary pastoral theology.

c. *Liturgical reflection.* Insofar as pastoral care and counseling is understood to be an exercise of priestly or ministerial office, a reflection upon pastoral care as a direct application of the ministry of word and sacrament (and thus of the liturgical structure and foundation of pastoral care) may be an especially fruitful approach to the development of a pastoral theology. Certainly, Catholic traditions have an advantage here in the application of the sacrament of penance as such a pattern, while a Protestant bias in favor of word (preaching and teaching) has inhibited the development of such a pastoral/liturgical theology. As is true of any theological inquiry today, pastoral theology must be ecumenical.

3. Theology and the Human Sciences. *a. The need for dialogue*. Pastoral care turns not only to theology for theoretical generalization and illumination but also to the human sciences. Indeed, many practitioners of pastoral counseling may find themselves more at home within the realm of psychological or psychotherapeutic theory than in the sphere of theology. In extreme cases psychological theory may be the only second-order conceptuality with which the practitioner has any familiarity. In such cases religious language may be regarded only as data to be explained or understood in some other (e.g., psychological) terms. The existence of such cases makes especially urgent a critical dialogue between theology and the human sciences.

Such a dialogue has a strong precedent in the more familiar history of a dialogue between theology and philosophy, a dialogue that has enriched both disciplines. Theology has appropriated philosophical categories and methods to develop trinitarian and christological doctrines in the early church and to develop understandings of the being and attributes of God, the relation of God to the world, and notions of freedom and responsibility in theological ethics. Philosophical discourse has likewise been enriched through the development of theories of transcendence, relations, and language.

***b. Conditions for fruitful dialogue*.** A dialogue between theology and the human sciences is likely to be fruitful where (1) both are regarded as second-order discourses, and (2) the discussion is focused upon the common subject matter of human nature and transformation.

One factor that blocks significant dialogue is the tendency to regard all religious language as first-order discourse for which it is the task of the human science to give some explanation. This tendency is reinforced by the observation of ways in which first-order religious discourse may be employed so as to prevent the person from obtaining a realistic or truthful perspective upon their actual situation, or in ways that are destructive to possibilities for creative or healing transformation. Thus, for example, people may use talk of God's will to deny grief or anger, or they may use talk of sin in ways that increase a sense of hopelessness and powerlessness. Of course, any vocabulary and conceptuality may be employed in the aid of sickness rather than health. As the jargon of psychology becomes more widespread, it too is often employed in such ways. For genuine dialogue to occur it is important that each discipline take seriously the other's claim to be not only a first-order discourse but also a theoretical, reflective, and thus second-order language, whose clarity and general applicability and power of illumination it is then possible to discuss.

If dialogue between theology and the human sciences is to be fruitful, it should also be directed toward a common subject matter. The subject matter common to both is not the existence or nature of God but the nature and possible transformation of human existence. Too often dialogue is blocked by excessive preoccupation with the categories of the theism-atheism debate. This preoccupation may prevent the discovery of important areas of shared interest and possibly fruitful discussion.

c. Further considerations. The range of dialogue between theology and the human sciences is inordinately restricted when it is limited to representatives of the human sciences who appear to have a positive regard for the religious life and its vocabulary (so Jung vs. Freud) or to theologians who have appropriated some of the conceptuality of the human sciences (e.g., Tillich vs. Barth). But this overlap of vocabulary and conceptuality is by no means a prerequisite to dialogue and may even prevent dialogue by the reduction of both sides of the discussion to areas of explicit agreement. Thus one side is but the echo (or translation) of the other.

A useful test of the seriousness and fruitfulness of such a dialogue is whether the conceptuality and vocabulary of both sides is altered and enriched through the process. The reduction of different discourses to a table of equivalences (neurosis = sin, wholeness = salvation, acceptance = justification, etc.) is certainly not an enrichment of insight but the reduction of one discourse to another or of both to a lowest common denominator. The sign of a mature, responsible, and fruitful dialogue is that both sides come to require revision in light of the discussion. Thus we should expect that theological discourse, especially as it seeks to illumine the human predicament, will be transformed by such a dialogue. Indeed, the theological vocabulary has been formed in just this way—as a result of dialogue with other disciplines and discourses. But if pastoral theologians do their work properly, they will also succeed in enriching and correcting the conceptuality of the human sciences. Again, this does not mean that the human sciences will adopt a theistic or religious paradigm, but rather will understand ordinary human existence, its predicaments, and possibilities, more clearly, incisively, and accurately.

Bibliography. J. Cobb, *Theology and Pastoral Care* (1977). G. Ebeling, *Introduction to a Theological Theory of Language* (1973); *The Study of Theology* (1978). W. W. Everett and T. J. Bachmeyer, *Disciplines in Transformation: A Guide to Theology and the Behavioral Sciences* (1979). E. Farley, *Ecclesial Man* (1975). D. Gelpi, *Experiencing God* (1978). L. Gilkey, *Message and Existence* (1979). S. Hiltner, *Preface to Pastoral Theology* (1958). T. W. Jennings, *Introduction to Theology* (1976). G. Kaufman, *An Essay on Theological Method* (1975). B. Lonergan, *Method in Theology* (1972). A. C. McGill, *Suffering: A Test of Theological Method* (1982 [1968]). J. Metz, *Faith in History and Society* (1980). L. Monden, *Faith: Can Man Still Believe?* (1970). A. Nygren, *Meaning and Method* (1972). W. Pannenberg, *Theology and the Philosophy of Science* (1976). J. Patton, *From Ministry to Theology* (1990). K. Rahner, *Foundations of Christian Faith* (1978). F. Schleiermacher, *Brief Outline on the Study of Theology* (1970 [1830]). D. Tracy, *The Analogical Imagination* (1981).

T. W. JENNINGS JR.

RITUAL AND PASTORAL CARE. *Rituals* are repeated, normative, symbolic, and functional behaviors often associated with religious expression. The technical and popular uses of related words are imprecise. *Rites* are formal, institutionally sanctioned religious rituals, while *customs* are informal rituals associated with secular social experience. *Rites of passage* are informal but culturally recognized patterns through which the individual moves during stages of the life cycle. *Ritualizations* may be defined as informal rituals associated with secular individual experience.

Contemporary interest in ritual and pastoral care focuses on three fundamental questions: (1) How do ritual and pastoral care together participate in the larger dynamics of human society and religion? More specifically, how do ritual and pastoral care together contribute to cultural stability and change? (2) What is the relationship between ritual practices and modern, psychologically rational pastoral counseling? (3) What is the relation of ritual and pastoral care in promoting the health or pathology of individual experience?

1. The Relation of Ritual and Rational Methods of Care. Underlying the contemporary experience of tension between ritual and psychotherapeutic care—for example, between congregational or individual worship and therapeutic self-understanding—lie divergent social processes, the classic formulations of which were given by sociologists Max Weber and Émile Durkheim.

Durkheim (1915) describes how the rituals of primitive culture produce cohesion in the community, creating a moral order. He identifies the two distinguishing features of religion as rites and belief. Religious rites aim at helping individuals move from the profane to the sacred world. This movement is achieved by negative and positive "ritual attitudes." Negative rituals restrain ordinary activities such as physical contact, looks, words, and sexual activity, and prepare a person for the rite of initiation into the cult. Positive rituals, on the other hand, are the foundation of the great religious institutions of civilization. Positive rituals primarily center around a sacrificial meal, which signifies abundant food production. Rather than being an act of renunciation, the common sacrificial meal reinforces kinship among human beings and renews the natural kinship between humans and their god. The cycle of ritual feasts creates interdependence between the individual, society, and their god and provides the rhythm of social life.

In addition to rituals of sacrifice, "rites of imitation" solidify the community by creating identity between the members of the tribe and their god or totem animal. Rites of imitation impose an "invisible action over the mind." They become a source of social authority as they regulate social conformity. "Commemorative rites" create community by recollecting the past and making it present by dramatic representation. Commemoration "awakens certain ideas and sentiments which attach the present to the past or the individual to the group." "Piacular rites" are organized around sorrow. Rather than being focused on individual, spontaneous acts of mourning, piacular rites impose a moral duty on the community to mourn together, through which collective sentiments are renewed (Durkheim, 1915).

In some contrast to Durkheim, Weber (1922) noted an evolutionary process in the understanding of the ritual sacrifice. Beginning as a magical attempt to coerce the gods or to absorb their potencies, ritual sacrifice gradually evolved into the communion of humanity with gods. The development of the moral order in religion depended not on ritual per se but on beliefs about ritual and on the rejection of ritual by the ethical prophets. Primitive rituals gave rise to an ever-broadening thinking about the god concept and about the relationship of the human and the divine.

According to Weber, the initial meanings of ritual receded in light of this rationalization, giving way to a negation of ritual by the ethical prophets: the God of the Israelite prophets required not burnt offerings but obedience to the commandments. Thus an ethical type of congregational religion arose that created a moral power through preaching and rational pastoral care. Pastoral care, rather than priestly ritual, became the priests' real instrument of power. Priestly ritual reified social structure, but pastoral care as exercised by the ethical prophets enabled the restructuring of society. Thus, Durkheim and Weber demonstrate a clash between the power of ritual to create moral order in community and the power of pastoral care to create change.

In contemporary cultural anthropology Victor Turner (1969) offers an example of how ritual and pastoral care need not clash but stand in creative tension with each other. Ritual, Turner says, creates change within the community through "liminality" and "communitas," intense experiences of social intimacy that temporarily reverse social status and roles, reminding the exalted person of his or her bondedness to common humanity when he or she assumes the power of a higher status, for instance.

E. Norbeck (1961), like M. Gluckman (1962), identifies a relationship between social stability and change through "rites of rebellion." Rites of rebellion offer a contained, socially sanctioned opportunity for aggressive or hostile behavior. By providing a safe space for unacceptable behavior, they stabilize those social orders that are unquestioned. In a social order such as ours that is questioned, however, no such rites exist. Rather, alternative, unsanctioned rituals arise and challenge the existing order, with the capacity to create social and cultural change.

2. Ritual, Health, and Illness. Does ritual express or contribute to pathology, or does it foster health, for example, by creating stability and identity throughout the life cycle? Sigmund Freud was perhaps the original advocate of the view that ritual acts express psychic processes that are either identical with or very close to pathological conflict. Connecting cultural and social experience to the family and the individual, Freud (1907, 1909, 1913) understood the religious ritual of sacrifice to be derived from the incest taboo and the Oedipus complex, the source of psychopathology for Freud. Their origins, he believed, lay in a violent family feud in which the patriarch of the primal horde was killed by his jealous sons so that they could have access to the horde's females. After killing the patriarch they ate him in order to absorb his powers, and protected themselves from being similarly killed by limiting sexual relations to those women outside the immediate family. In order to commemorate the "awful deed," ritual sacrifice arose as the foundation of religious ritual. Freud also noted that some individuals express the pathology of their personality through private ritualizations that are expressions of unresolved conflicts, principally obsessive-compulsive personality disorders. Ultimately, Freud believed that religion and ritual were expressions of cultural and individual pathology for which psychoanalysis sought to become the cure.

V. Gay's (1979) interpretation of Freud's 1907 essay on ritual provides a bridge from Freud to later psychoanalysts who suggest that religious ritual is ego enhancing. Gay claims that Freud misinterpreted his own metapsychology when he disdained all religious ritual. Rather, Freud's 1907 essay implied that religious rituals are rounded on the non-pathological defense of "suppression" rather than the frequently pathogenic defense of "repression," thus aiding intrapsychic balance by assisting the ego to suppress dangerous id impulses and further the cause of adaptation.

E. Erikson (1972) has emphasized the healthy aspects of ritual and ritualization, pointing to the relationship between ritual and play. Ritualization becomes "creative formalization which helps to avoid both impulsive excess and compulsive self-restriction, both social anomie and moralistic coercion." Ritualization helps the ego orient itself within the worldviews that compete within a culture. In psychopathology, ritualizations have fallen apart, leaving the individual isolated. Ego-enhancing ritualizations allow for a mutuality of recognition, the overcoming of ambivalence, the transcendence of separateness, and the affirmation of distinctiveness. The ritualizations of the individual correlate with the rituals of religious institutions by providing the individual and the community with "faith in a cosmic order, a sense of justice, a hierarchy of ideal and evil rules, the fundamentals of technology, and ideological perspectives" (Erikson, 1972). Erikson recognizes the pathological distortion of ritual that Freud discovered, but he emphasizes the connection between the healthy structuring of the individual and of culture through rituals and ritualizations, which Freud negated.

3. Religious Ritual and Contemporary Pastoral Care. The clinical pastoral care and counseling movement of the later twentieth century arose out of the critique of mass culture (Holifield, 1983). As interest in pastoral care and counseling proliferated, and as countercultural criticism yielded to the disdain of social institutions of the 1960s, many churches became skeptical of traditional ritual practices.

The countercultural critics of the 1960s rejected hierarchy and formalism and emphasized equality and inclusiveness. These changes brought new trends in ceremony and ritual. Feminists challenged the hierarchy and formalism of patriarchy and popularized gender- and image-inclusive language. Their concern for inclusive language in worship resounds with Durkheim's assumption that ritual exercises invisible action over the mind. Laity demanded that their ministry be valued equally with the ministry of the clergy. Just as Luther's protest against the Vatican's abuses of ritual power initiated the modern meshing of the sacred and profane realms, the present emphasis on the ministry of the laity further obscures those neat distinctions, creating renewed discussion of the meaning and practices of baptism, Eucharist, and ordination. Blacks reclaimed African rituals and brought the music of slavery and oppression into liturgical renewal. After Vatican II Roman Catholicism introduced the vernacular Mass and communion in two kinds, significant signs of the permanent modernization of religious ritual. The movement from deconstructing some values through the denial of ritual to the restructuring of culture by incorporating new values into ritual life recalls Weber's observation that a prophetic message must be "routinized," or incorporated into the orthodox life of the church, for permanent change to occur.

Alternative rituals that have rarely been routinized by religious institutions, for example, the merger of African naming rituals with Christian baptism, covenant ceremonies for homosexual couples, or overt politicizing of ritual in base Christian communities, are forms of "rituals of rebellion." Such rituals function simultaneously as expressions of aggression against the ruling social order, and/or as transformations of aggression into identity and integrity within a marginalized space at the edge of the social order, and/or as a syncretic merger of cultural and religious rituals through which one claims plural identities.

Substantial changes in family structure have created renewed debate over the rituals of the life cycle, particularly the rituals that solidify adult commitments like marriage in a changing culture—adult commitments that were once considered permanent but now, at least in practice, are no longer irrevocable. Turner helps us understand how rituals have moved persons from a status the community has accepted as lower to one the community deems higher. Attempts to incorporate in ritual the reversal of that process, for example, releasing persons from marriage or religious vows, have floundered. Instead, the reversal of that process most often involves formal or informal shunning, banning, or exiling, as in the case of laicized priests or divorced pastors. The successful reentry into the community by persons formerly married or formerly ordained occurs most often through the process of rational (i.e., psychological) pastoral care and counseling.

At best, psychological pastoral care and counseling and ritual practices remain in creative tension with each other, holding together mind and body, word and action, logic and drama. E. Ramshaw (1987) suggests that both attend to the intrapsychic need for holding together ambivalent emotions. Together they provide nurture and significification for the passage through the stages of the life cycle, and locate people in social institutions and in culture.

In terms of pastoral practice, this means that ritual will continue to have a significant pastoral role to play in individual pastoral care, especially at the crisis and transition points of life like illness, accident, death, marriage, and birth. And rituals, formal and informal, will continue to be essential components in the life of communities of faith where they both express and form common vision, uniting individual and community, and nourishing individuals through their common life. The wise and caring pastor therefore is one who can discern when creative ritualizing is pastorally appropriate for individuals and for communities, when more rationally oriented forms of care are indicated, and how the two can be most artfully and gracefully combined.

Bibliography. W. Clebsch and C. Jaekle, *Pastoral Care in Historical Perspective* (1964). R. Duffy, *On Becoming A Catholic: The Challenge of Christian Initiation* (1984). E. Durkheim, *The Elementary Forms of the Religious Life* (1915). E. Erikson, *Toys and Reasons: Stages in the Ritualization of Experience* (1972). R. Fenn, "Recent Studies of Church Decline: The Eclipse of Ritual," *Religious Studies Review* 8 (1982), 124–28. S. Freud, "Notes upon a Case of Obsessional Neurosis," *SE* 10 (1909); "Obsessive Actions and Religious Practices," *SE* 9 (1907); *Totem and Taboo* (1913). V. Gay, *Freud on Ritual: Reconstruction and Critique* (1979). M. Gluckman, *Essays on the Ritual of Social Relations* (1962). E. B. Holifield, *A History of Pastoral Care in America* (1983). K. R. Mitchell, "Ritual in Pastoral Care," *J. of Pastoral Care* 43 (1989), 68–77. E. Norbeck, *Religion in Primitive Society* (1961). E. Ramshaw, *Ritual and*

Pastoral Care (1987). R. R. Ruether, *Women-Church* (1985). V. Turner, *The Ritual Process* (1969). R. L. Underwood, *Pastoral Care and the Means of Grace* (1993). United Methodist Church, *Ritual in a New Day* (1976). M. Weber, *Sociology of Religion* (1922).

P. COUTURE